Learning as Transformation

Jack Mezirow and Associates

Learning as Transformation

Critical Perspectives on a Theory in Progress

JOSSEY-BASS
A Wiley Company
www.josseybass.com

Published by

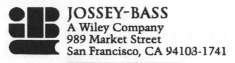

JOSSEY-BASS
A Wiley Company
989 Market Street
San Francisco, CA 94103-1741

www.josseybass.com

Jossey-Bass books and products are available through most bookstores. To contact Jossey-Bass directly, call (888) 378-2537, fax to (800) 605-2665, or visit our website at www.josseybass.com.

Substantial discounts on bulk quantities of Jossey-Bass books are available to corporations, professional associations, and other organizations. For details and discount information, contact the special sales department at Jossey-Bass.

We at Jossey-Bass strive to use the most environmentally sensitive paper stocks available to us. Our publications are printed on acid-free recycled stock whenever possible, and our paper always meets or exceeds minimum GPO and EPA requirements.

Library of Congress Cataloging-in-Publication Data

Mezirow, Jack, 1923–
    Learning as transformation: critical perspectives on a theory
in progress/JackMezirow and Associates.—1st ed.
      p. cm.—(The Jossey-Bass higher and adult education series)
    Includes bibliographical references and index.
    ISBN 0-7879-4845-4 (alk. paper)
    1. Transfer of training. 2. Adult learning. I. Title. II. Series.
LB1059 .M49 2000
370.15'23—dc21

                                  00-009158

FIRST EDITION
HB Printing 10 9 8 7 6 5

The Jossey-Bass
Higher and Adult Education Series

Contents

Preface

This book grew out of the First National Conference on Transformative Learning held at Teachers College, Columbia University, in April 1998. That conference marked the twenty-year development by adult educators of the concept of transformative learning as a learning theory.

This modest movement has produced several books, well over fifty doctoral dissertations, dozens of conference presentations and articles, and a continuing spirited discourse in the journal *Adult Education Quarterly* (see Taylor, 1998). The movement was initiated in 1978 by the publication of an ambitious study of women returning to community college after an extended hiatus (Mezirow, 1978). This research involved a grounded theory field study of 12 diversified "reentry" programs in community colleges, on-site analytical descriptions of an additional 24 programs, and responses to a mail inquiry by another 314. These new programs were created in the context of the women's movement in the United States in the 1970s that led to many women entering or returning to higher education. The women's movement pioneered transformative learning through its powerful innovation, consciousness raising.

The major theoretical finding of the study was the identification of *perspective transformation* as the central learning process occurring in the personal development of women participating in these college programs. By becoming critically aware of the context—biographical, historical, cultural—of their beliefs and feelings about themselves and their role in society, the women could effect a change in the way they had tacitly structured their assumptions and expectations. This change constituted a learned transformation; the process resulting from it was designated transformative learning.

Findings suggested a generic development in which maturity in childhood is understood as a *formative* process that includes assimilation of beliefs concerning oneself and the world, including socialization and learning adult roles. Adulthood was perceived as a *transformative* process—"involving alienation from those roles, reframing new perspectives, and reengaging life with a greater degree of self-determination." The process was characterized as "a praxis, a dialectic in which understanding and action interact to produce an altered state of being."

Transformations were often found to follow a learning cycle initiated by a disorienting dilemma and resulting in a reintegration into society on the basis of conditions dictated by the new perspective (see p. 22). Findings suggested that one does not return to an old perspective once a transformation has occurred, but there is seldom consistent forward movement. A learner can get stalled—temporarily or permanently—at any phase; typically, difficult negotiation and compromise, backsliding, and self-deception occur. This was found especially true at the beginning of transformative learning with its threat to a long-established sense of order, and later when awareness and insight call for a commitment to action that may seriously threaten important relationships.

The study found that solidarity, empathy, and trust are requisite to the learners' commitment to a transformative learning group, but such involvement must not become one of unconditional identification when this deters further transformative learning in new contexts and toward still broader perspectives.

Early Influences

Although the context and terminology were different, our understanding of transformative learning was influenced by the concept of *paradigm*, made popular as a factor in the development of scientific thought by Thomas Kuhn (1962), and that of *conscientization*, described by Paulo Freire in his influential *Pedagogy of the Oppressed* (1970). Freire never developed this idea as a significant mode of learning but turned his subsequent attention to education. The work of psychiatrist Roger Gould (1978) was also an influence in the development of Transformation Theory.

Another influence was the development of Critical Theory by the Frankfurt School of German philosophers and social critics that saw critical reflection as the means of unmasking hegemonic ideology (see Chapter Five). Later, the work of Jurgen Habermas (1984) was a major influence on Transformation Theory. His contribution is both an extension of Critical Theory and a significant alternative to it. Habermas builds on to the Kantian sense of "critique," in which reflection refers to reason's reflection on its own principles and categories, by adding the concept of reflection as a form of self-formation that emancipates as it releases one from the constraint of dysfunctional beliefs. In particular, Habermas's delineation of the concepts of communicative competence and instrumental learning as the major domains of learning; the recognition of the central role of discourse in validating beliefs; and the idea of reflection as a form of self-formation that emancipates as it dissolves the constraining spell of unexamined beliefs—all became building blocks for Transformation Theory (Mezirow, 1991).

As scholars from different disciplines tend to construe constructs from different frames of reference and with different vocabularies, the reader should understand that Transformation Theory, as summarized in Chapter One, has a "range of convenience" that is constrained by the fact that it has been formulated for adult educators by adult educators. Concepts have come from and have been elaborated and modified by the experience of practicing professionals (see Cranton, 1997; Taylor, 1998).

This theory is derived from culturally specific conditions associated with democratic societies and with the development of adult education as a vocation in Western Europe and North America, a liberal tradition that depends ultimately on faith in informed, free human choice and social justice. Rationality, self-awareness, and empathy are assumed values. Transformation Theory shares the normative goals of the Enlightenment of self-emancipation through self-understanding, the overcoming of systematically distorted communication, and the strengthening of the capacity for self-determination thorough rational discourse.

We can agree that human beings have a generic capacity to learn and to learn from each other with an inherent potential for action that they deem rational. Learning, including transformative learning, and action may or may not involve deliberate thought or critical reflection. Some cultures encourage the realization of this capacity for criticality and discourse; others discourage its development.

Transformation Theory suggests a model describing a generic adult learning capacity with significant implications for educators. It describes the process by which we acquire a greater degree of insight and agency as adult learners by highlighting the understandings, skills, and dispositions involved and the conditions under which transformative learning is facilitated or precipitated.

Content

Although the first chapter is intended as a point of departure for the others, each chapter may be read independently. Chapter One reviews the core propositions of Transformation Theory as they have evolved. The theory attempts to identify and make accessible the underlying principles of how adults learn to change their frames of reference. The gravamen of the chapter is that transformative learning is at the heart of significant adult learning and central to adult education. An adult's capacity to learn is not defined by cultural interests alone; human capabilities may be more fully realized through conditions that foster transformative learning.

The first part of this book reviews and analyzes the developing concept of transformative learning. In Chapter Two Robert Kegan presents an elaboration with illustrative narratives of a "constructive-developmental" perspective that places transformative learning in the context of adults acquiring successively complex and comprehensive rational epistemologies by which they constitute their reality. Development involves a qualitative evolution toward a self-authoring mind—a capacity to judge expectations and claims made on an individual—but also toward the capacity for us to distance ourselves from our transformed frame of reference so that we are open to learning from other meaning perspectives as well.

Mary Belenky and Ann Stanton emphasize the importance of asymmetrical relationships as a major problem in fostering transformative learning in Chapter Three. They review findings of feminist psychologists and writers who have exposed the effect of old dualistic categories and assumptions to help us understand how women learn. They differentiate types of knowledge and knowers and draw on the experience of educational programs and community organizations that have created new opportunities for marginalized people to find their voices. This chapter also includes a valuable description of the work of "midwife" teachers and community leaders that provides many leads for adult educators.

Chapter Four, by Laurent Daloz, describes the transformation of Nelson Mandela and draws on his remarkable experience to examine the meaning of transformative learning for social responsibility. This chapter discusses the formation of commitment and the dynamics of the transformation involved and conditions that contribute to transformation for the common good. Daloz identifies and discusses key conditions of transformation and analyzes the issue of how an adult educator should educate for social change.

In Chapter Five Stephen Brookfield presents a critique of Transformation Theory from a viewpoint compatible with current interpretations of Critical Theory. Brookfield argues that critical
reflection and transformation be exclusively understood as a challenge to hegemonic ideology. He understands critical reflection as
the process of uncovering power dynamics and relationships and
their hegemonic assumptions—uncritically accepted commonsense
assumptions that serve the interests of those who oppress us. For
Brookfield, power and influence permeate the very constitution of
knowledge.

Brookfield identifies differences in this orientation to Transformation Theory, which posits critical reflection and transformation
as a developmental learning process that recognizes the importance
of assessing ideological assumptions but includes a more generic
range of assumptions in psychological, epistemic, moral and ethical,
philosophical, aesthetic, and instrumental frames of reference as well.

The second part of the book is devoted to the practice of transformative learning, including educational concerns (also see Mezirow
and Associates, 1990; Cranton, 1994, 1997).

In Chapter Six, Kathleen Taylor examines similarities in the previous work of Kegan and Mezirow, identifies the relevant literature
dealing with related concepts, and suggests specific instructional
methods adult educators may use to teach with developmental intentions. Taylor identifies dimensions of development from the learner's
perspective and analyzes the process of facilitating adult development through transformative learning.

Patricia Cranton draws upon Jung's theory of psychological types
in Chapter Seven to discuss how differences in learners' and educators' psychological predispositions, or habits of mind, may influence transformative learning. She also explores the central process
of discernment and how educators may use these insights to foster
transformative learning.

In a perceptive study of transformative learning in a residential
adult learning community in Chapter Eight, Judith Cohen and Deb-

orah Piper analyze critical components: the setting, the breakdown of roles, the element of time, and curricular paradoxes. Through a case study of a mature learner, they illustrate "the process of weaving a personal narrative into a course of study."

Chapter Nine is devoted to an exploration by Elizabeth Kasl and Dean Elias of how a system may be re-created through group transformation. They summarize relevant concepts from the literature, illustrate the significance of cohort groups in adult education, and show how such groups have dealt with such difficult issues as interracial understanding. Kasl and Elias present a case history of how a group of former faculty members in a discontinued graduate program dedicated to transformative learning transformed itself into an independent learning group to become the Transformative Learning Collaborative. The Collaborative, without institutional support, sponsored a highly successful Second National Conference on Transformative Learning in San Rafael, California, in August 1999. One hundred educators attended.

Lyle Yorks and Victoria Marsick explore the concept of a collective transformation in their study of organizational learning in Chapter Ten. They argue that groups learn as discrete entities in ways that transcend individual learning within the group. These authors examine the relevance of Transformation Theory to the model of a learning organization through two learning strategies: action learning and collaborative inquiry.

Because the evolution and validation of Transformation Theory depends on continuing research and discourse by informed adult educators and others, the final section of the book deals with findings and issues.

Chapter Eleven is a review of emergent themes in present research and their implications for Transformation Theory. Edward Taylor surveys findings of forty-six doctoral studies of transformative learning, including seven not previously reported. Topics include the adult focus of the theory, the concept of perspective transformation, frame of reference, triggering transformative learning, affective learning, rational discourse, difference and context in adult learning, and fostering transformative learning.

In Chapter Twelve Colleen Aalsburg Weissner reports on ideas, issues, and findings emerging from the First National Conference on Transformative Learning, and Jack Mezirow reflects on issues and insights, including issues raised by contributors to this volume.

JACK MEZIROW

July 2000

References

Cranton, P. *Understanding and Promoting Transformative Learning*. San Francisco: Jossey-Bass, 1994.

Cranton, P. *Transformative Learning in Action: Insights from Practice*. New Directions for Adult and Continuing Education, no. 79. San Francisco: Jossey-Bass, 1997.

Freire, P. *Pedagogy of the Oppressed*. New York: Herter and Herter, 1970.

Gould, R. *Transformation: Growth and Change in Adult Life*. New York: Simon & Schuster, 1978.

Habermas, J. *The Theory of Communicative Action*. Vol. 1: *Reason and the Rationalization of Society*. (T. McCarthy, trans.). Boston: Beacon Press, 1984.

Kuhn, T. *The Structure of Scientific Revolutions*. Chicago: University of Chicago Press, 1962.

Mezirow, J. *Education for Perspective Transformation: Women Re-entry Programs in Community College*. New York: Center for Adult Education, Teachers College, Columbia University, 1978.

Mezirow, J. *Transformative Dimensions of Adult Learning*. San Francisco: Jossey-Bass, 1991.

Mezirow, J., and Associates. *Fostering Critical Reflection in Adulthood*. San Francisco: Jossey-Bass, 1990.

Taylor, E. *The Theory and Practice of Transformative Learning: A Critical Review*. Information Series, no. 374. Columbus, Ohio: ERIC Clearinghouse on Adult, Career, & Vocational Education, Center on Education and Training for Employment, College of Education, Ohio State University, 1998.

Acknowledgment

We want to acknowledge the leadership role that our publisher, Jossey-Bass, has played in advancing the concept of transformative learning in adult education.

JACK MEZIROW

This book is dedicated to our colleagues who have assessed, contested, confirmed, extended, or applied the concept of transformative learning over the past two decades.

The Editor

JACK MEZIROW is Emeritus Professor of adult and continuing education, Teachers College at Columbia University, and was chairman of the Department of Higher and Adult Education. Formerly he served as associate dean for statewide programs, University of California Extension, and director of the Division of Human Resource Development, Latin American Bureau, AID. He has been a consultant in community development, literacy, and adult education in Latin America, Asia, and Africa for several international agencies.

Mezirow's research interests are adult learning theory and education for social change. He initiated the transformative learning movement in adult education and has made presentations and led seminars on this subject at many universities in the United States and in fifteen other countries. His books include *Transformative Dimensions of Adult Learning* (1991) and *Fostering Critical Reflection in Adulthood* (with Associates, 1990); the latter received the Frandson Award for Outstanding Publication in Continuing Education. Both books have been translated into other languages. His *Last Gamble on Education* (with Darkenwald and Knox, 1975) won the Imogene E. Okes Award for Outstanding Research in Adult Education. He is author of other books, chapters, research reports, and numerous articles.

Mezirow holds a doctorate in adult education from UCLA and B.A. and M.A. degrees in social sciences and education from the University of Minnesota.

The Authors

MARY FIELD BELENKY is an educator and researcher who works with a variety of educational and community organizations interested in the empowerment process. She is research associate professor in the department of psychology of the University of Vermont. She studied at Antioch College and received an M.A. from the Committee of Human Development (1958) and an Ed.D. in developmental psychology from the Harvard Graduate School of Education (1978). Belenky's research has focused on women's intellectual and ethical development. She coauthored *Women's Ways of Knowing: The Development of Self, Voice and Mind* (second edition, 1997) and coedited *Knowledge, Difference and Power: Essays Inspired by Women's Ways of Knowing* (1997) with Blythe Clinchy, Nancy Goldberger, and Jill Tarule. More recently she coauthored *A Tradition That Has No Name: Nurturing the Development of People, Families and Communities* (1997) with Lynne Bond and Jackie Weinstock.

STEPHEN D. BROOKFIELD is distinguished professor at the University of St. Thomas in Minneapolis. He is also senior consultant to the doctoral program in adult education at National Louis University in Chicago. Prior to moving to Minnesota he spent ten years as professor in the Department of Higher and Adult Education at Teachers College, Columbia University, where he is still adjunct professor. He received his B.A. (1970) from Coverty University in modern studies, his M.A. (1974) from the University of Reading in sociology, and his Ph.D. (1980) from the University of Leicester in adult education. He also holds a postgraduate diploma (1971) from the University of London, Chelsea College, in modern social and cultural studies and a graduate diploma (1977) from the University of Nottingham in adult education. In 1991 he was awarded an honorary doctor of letters from the University System of New Hampshire for his contributions to understanding adult learning.

Brookfield's main research activities have been in the area of adult learning, teaching, and critical thinking. He currently serves on the editorial and advisory boards of *Adult Education Quarterly*, *Studies in Continuing Education* (Australia), *Studies in the Education of Adults* (United Kingdom), *Canadian Journal for the Study of Adult Education*, and *International Journal of University Continuing Education*. He is a three-time winner of the Cyril O. Houle World Award for Literature in Adult Education: in 1986 for his book *Understanding and Facilitating Adult Learning* (1986), in 1989 for *Developing Critical Thinkers* (1987), and in 1996 for *Becoming a Critically Reflective Teacher* (1995). *Understanding and Facilitating Adult Learning* also won the 1986 Imogene E. Okes Award for Outstanding Research in Adult Education.

His other books include *Adult Learners, Adult Education and the Community* (1984), *Self-Directed Learning: From Theory to Practice* (1985), *Learning Democracy: Eduard Lindeman on Adult Education and Social Change* (1987), *Training Educators of Adults: The Theory and Practice of Graduate Adult Education* (1988), *The Skillful Teacher: On Technique, Trust and Responsiveness in the Classroom* (1990), *Becoming a Critically Reflective Teacher* (1995), and (with Stephen Preskill) *Discussion as a Way of Teaching: Tools and Techniques for Democratic Classrooms* (1999).

JUDITH BETH COHEN is associate professor in the Adult Baccalaureate College of Lesley College in Cambridge, Massachusetts. She earned her B.A. (1965) in English literature at the University of Michigan, Ann Arbor, and her M.A. in educational psychology

(1966). Her Ph.D. in literature and creative writing (1993) is from the Union Institute in Cincinnati, Ohio. Cohen has been teaching in innovative programs for adults for over twenty years. Before coming to Lesley College, she taught at Goddard College in Plainfield, Vermont, a pioneer developer of adult programs. She was a senior preceptor in the Expositor Writing Program at Harvard College and also taught writing at the Harvard Business School and the Bard College Institute of Narrative and Life History (now called Narrative Inquiry). She is author of a novel, *Seasons* (Permanent Press, 1984), and numerous short stories. Her articles have appeared in *English Leadership Quarterly, Women's Review of Books, Boston Review,* and the *Christian Science Monitor.* She is currently collaborating with Deborah Piper on a book on adult residential learning.

PATRICIA CRANTON is an adjunct faculty member of the University of New Brunswick and director of the Institute for Personal and Professional Empowerment. She earned her B.Ed. (1971) and M.Sc. (1973) at the University of Calgary and her Ph.D. (1976) at the University of Toronto. From 1976 to 1986 Cranton was at McGill University in the Centre for Teaching and Learning and the Department of Educational Psychology and Counseling. From 1986 to 1996 she was professor of adult education and director of instructional development at Brock University.

Cranton's main research interests have been in transformative learning, self-directed learning, and instructional development. She was selected as Distinguished Ontario Scholar in 1991 in recognition of her research and writing. She received the Ontario Confederation of University Faculty Association's Teaching Award in 1993 and the Lieutenant Governor's Laurel Award in 1994 for an outstanding contribution to university teaching. Cranton's previous books include *Planning Instruction for Adult Learners* (1989; second edition, 1999), *Working with Adult Learners* (1992; published in Japanese, 1998), *Understanding and Promoting Transformative Learning* (1994; published in Chinese, 1997), *Professional Development as Transformative Learn-*

ing (1996), *Transformative Learning in Action* (1997), *No One Way: Teaching and Learning in Higher Education* (1998), *Personal Empowerment Through Type* (1998), and *Becoming an Authentic Teacher* (1999).

LAURENT A. PARKS DALOZ is the father of Kate and Todd, the husband of Sharon Daloz Parks, and associate director and faculty member of the Whidbey Institute in Clinton, Washington. He holds a B.A. in American history and literature from Williams College and an M.A.T. in English from Harvard. After a stint in Nepal with the Peace Corps he earned his doctoral degree in education planning at Harvard based on two years of research in New Guinea. Cofounder and first academic dean of the Community College of Vermont, he subsequently served as a faculty mentor with Vermont College and the Vermont State Colleges. For ten years on the faculty of Lesley College, he has also taught as adjunct professor at the Harvard Graduate School of Education and Teachers College, Columbia University. He is author of the award-winning book *Effective Teaching and Mentoring* (second edition entitled *Mentor: Guiding the Journey of Adult Learners*) and coauthor, with Sharon Daloz Parks and Cheruyl and Jim Keen, of *Common Fire: Lives of Commitment in a Complex World* (Beacon Press, 1996), a study of how people come to care for the common good. He has published widely in adult education.

DEAN ELIAS is a founding member of the Transformative Learning Collaborative, a praxis collective of twelve devoted to exploring transformative learning in human systems; dean of extended education at St. Mary's College, Moraga, California; and an adjunct professor at the California Institute of Integral Studies. His professional work has focused on the interaction between transformation and change within individuals and within institutions and communities. His teaching and scholarship focus on holistic education, design in human systems, transformative learning, and transformative leadership. He is currently exploring how archetypal psychology can illuminate experiences of conflict and experiences of synergy within individuals and small groups.

ELIZABETH KASL is a founding member of the Group for Collaborative Inquiry, a group of six scholar-practitioners from around the country who work to develop new forms of collaboration in the academic workplace, and of the Transformative Learning Collaborative, a praxis collective. She is currently a professor in the transformative learning program at the California Institute of Integral Studies (CIIS). Before coming to CIIS Kasl taught in the Adult Education Guided Independent Studies program at Teachers College, Columbia University. As a teacher and scholar, Kasl focuses on small-group learning, transformative learning, collaborative learning, and pedagogical practices that support these types of learning. She is engaged in developing academic discourse about rigor in emerging research strategies and paradigms, particularly participatory methodologies. Of European descent, she seeks also to foster her own and others' understanding of how a learning community is created amidst diversity, particularly race and ethnic diversity. Kasl earned a B.A. (1961) in English at Northwestern University and an M.A. (1972) and Ph.D. (1977) in adult and continuing education at Teachers College, Columbia University.

ROBERT KEGAN is professor of education and academic chair of the Institute for the Management of Lifelong Education at the Harvard Graduate School of Education. He earned his B.A. (1968) summa cum laude from Dartmouth College and his Ph.D. (1976) from Harvard University, where he has been a member of the faculty for more than twenty-five years.

A life span developmental psychologist with a particular interest in adult learning and professional development, Kegan is author of *The Sweeter Welcome* (1976), *The Evolving Self* (1982), and *In Over*

Our Heads (1994); and coauthor (with Lahey, Souvaine, Goodman, and Felix) of *The Subject-Object Interview: A Guide to Its Administration and Assessment* (1988) and (with Lahey) *Minds at Work: Personal Learning and Professional Development* (forthcoming). He is the recipient of many awards and honors including honorary doctorates of humane letters from the University of New Hampshire and the State University of New York, and recognition awards for his scholarly and professional work from the Association for Continuing Higher Education and the National University Continuing Education Association.

VICTORIA J. MARSICK is a professor of adult education and organizational learning in the Department of Organization and Leadership at Teachers College, Columbia University. She codirects the J. M. Huber Institute on Learning in Organizations at Teachers College and directs both a masters and doctoral program in adult education. Marsick holds a Ph.D. in adult education from the University of California at Berkeley and an M.P.A. in international public administration from Syracuse University. She is a founding member of Partners for the Learning Organization and of Leadership in International Management.

She currently consults with both the private and public sectors through these groups on the design of learning organizations and on action reflection learning for organizational change. Her clients have included AT&T, Coca-Cola, Imperial Oil/EXXON companies, CIBA-GEIGY, Travelers Companies, Public Service Electric & Gas, Canadian Imperial Bank of Commerce, UNICEF, the City of New York, and the Government of the People's Republic of China.

She codeveloped a diagnostic instrument (Dimensions of the Learning Organization) with Karen Watkins. She and Watkins have coauthored or coedited other books and articles on this topic, such as *In Action: Creating the Learning Organization* (1996), *Sculpting the*

Learning Organization (1993), *Informal and Incidental Learning in the Workplace* (1990), and *Learning in the Workplace* (1987). Marsick has researched team learning with Elizabeth Kasl and Kathleen Dechant and has codeveloped a team learning assessment instrument based on this research with Dechant.

She is director of ARL Inquiry, a group that is researching the impact of action learning programs in organizations. Until recently she chaired the Research Committee of the American Society for Training and Development and has been a member of the board of the Academy for Human Resource Development. Marsick lived and worked for many years in Asia and in Latin America prior to joining Teachers College. She was a training director at the United Nations Children's Fund and a resident program manager for World Education.

DEBORAH PIPER is a clinical psychologist in private practice and an adjunct professor at Lesley College. She earned her B.A. in adult training and development at the University of Massachusetts, Boston, in 1981. Her M.A. in counseling psychology is from Lesley College (1983). Her doctorate in psychology is from Antioch College. Piper's research has focused on class transition and illuminates the importance of collaborative learning models that embrace the life stories of adult students. Her article "Psychology's Class Blindness" appeared in *This Fine Place So Far from Home: Voices of Academics from the Working Class* (1995).

ANN V. STANTON is professor of liberal studies in the adult degree program at Vermont College of Norwich University, Montpelier, Vermont. She earned a B.A. in sociology from Pitzer College in 1970 after serving two years in El Salvador in the Peace Corps, working in community education. Her Ph.D. in human development and family studies is from Cornell University (1978). Stanton's interest in education as empowerment stems from her years in the Peace Corps, additional work in Peru and Mexico, teaching young women at Wells College in Aurora, New York, and her current work with adult women students.

EDWARD W. TAYLOR is an associate professor of adult education at Penn State Capitol College in Harrisburg, Pennsylvania. Before getting his doctorate in adult education from the University of Georgia, Taylor taught in elementary school and worked as a counselor and training supervisor for Eckerd Family Youth Alternatives, Inc., one of the largest long-term wilderness residential therapeutic programs for youth in the United States. He recently left Antioch University in Seattle, where he spent six years teaching adult education courses in the Graduate Program for Experienced Educators. Taylor is a recipient of the Cyril Houle Scholars Award in Adult Education, which provides two years of funding for his research on teaching beliefs of adult educators. He is a member of the Adult Education Quarterly Editorial Board and of the steering committee for the Adult Education Research Conference for 1999–2000, and he recently published a monograph entitled *Transformative Learning: A Critical Review*. Areas of interest include adult cognition and learning, critical pedagogy, multicultural/intercultural studies, and outdoor/adventure-based education.

KATHLEEN TAYLOR is associate professor and chair of the Department of Portfolio Development in the School of Extended Education at Saint Mary's College of California. She earned a Ph.D. in adult higher education from Union Graduate School (1991). Before returning to school in her late thirties as an adult undergraduate, Taylor was a consumer activist, author, and host of a television show on nutrition and healthful cooking. As an outgrowth of her adult learning–related development, Taylor's main research is on the intersections between adult learning and adult development. She has published articles and presented workshops at national and international conferences on learning that encourage developmental growth in adults. Among the teaching and learning strategies that she has highlighted are self-assessment, prior learning assessment, and learning based in experience, reflection, and meaning-making.

She coedited, with Catherine Marienau, a 1995 edition of New Directions for Adult and Continuing Education entitled *Learning Environment for Women's Adult Development: Bridges Toward Growth.* She has been an executive board member of the Adult Higher Education Alliance and is a lively workshop presenter and keynoter. Her forthcoming book (coedited with Catherine Marienau and Morris Fiddler), *Developing Adult Learners: Strategies for Teachers and Trainers,* is slated for publication by Jossey-Bass in fall 2000.

COLLEEN AALSBURG WIESSNER has been an educational consultant and writer since 1976, working in school, community, and religious organizations. Her work focuses on staff and leadership development and training and on program and curriculum planning and development. She also works as a peer learning coach for masters and doctoral level students. Wiessner earned her B.A. (1976) in sociology at Kalamazoo College. Her M.P.S. (1980) in humanistic education was earned at the State University of New York at New Paltz and her M.A. (1998) in education through the Department of Organization and Leadership was completed at Teachers College, Columbia University. She is a doctoral candidate in adult education at Teachers College. She has taught as an adjunct instructor at Ramapo College and Mid-Michigan Community College and as a teaching assistant at Teachers College and Western Theological Seminary. Wiessner has also studied at Rutgers University School of Graduate Education and at New Brunswick and Western Theological Seminaries.

In addition to transformative learning, Wiessner's research is focused on the use of narrative in emancipatory and popular adult education. Classroom practices that are inclusive, cooperative, experiential, and arts-oriented have also been an important focus of her research and practice. She has taught these methods to educators through presentations, curriculum materials, and training resources aimed at practitioners and is the author of many hands-on resources for educators. She has also published several stories for children.

Wiessner coauthored two articles on the use of narrative in transformative learning, one of which was presented by her coauthor at a conference on early school leavers in Chennal, India. The other was accepted for presentation at the Sixth International Conference on Adult Education and the Arts. She will continue her research in transformative learning as the manager of the Transformative Learning Conference, scheduled for fall 2000 at Teachers College. Weissner was the recipient of an American Association of University Women Career Development Grant while at Teachers College and was awarded the Ethics Prize for her work at Western Theological Seminary.

LYLE YORKS joined the faculty of Teachers College, Columbia University as an associate professor of adult education in January 1999, where he was an adjunct faculty member in the doctoral program in adult education. Yorks holds a B.A. from Tusculum College, M.A.'s from Vanderbilt and Columbia Universities, and a doctoral degree from Columbia University. He was formerly chair of the Department of Business Administration and professor of management at Eastern Connecticut State University (ECSU), where he helped establish and coordinates the Master of Science in Organizational Management Program. He is also a member of the executive development faculties at Louisiana State University and serves as a visiting professor in the Executive M.B.A. program at the University of Tennessee, Knoxville.

Yorks regularly serves as a consultant for private companies and organizations worldwide. Before coming to ECSU he was a senior vice president of Drake Beam and Associates in New York City. Before that he worked in the corporate management systems department at the Travelers Insurance Companies. He is the author of nine books and his articles have been published in *Academy of Manage-*

ment Review, California Management Review, Human Resource Development Quarterly, Performance Improvement Quarterly, Sloan Management Review, and many other professional journals and books. He recently edited (with Judy O'Neil and Victoria Marsick) a monograph on action learning in *Advances in Developing Human Resources,* sponsored by the Academy of Human Resource Development. Yorks's current research, consulting, and writing center around the effectiveness of action learning and participatory research strategies for fostering adult learning and organizational change.

Learning as Transformation

I

Developing Concepts
of Transformative Learning

1

Learning to Think Like an Adult

Core Concepts of Transformation Theory

Jack Mezirow

A defining condition of being human is our urgent need to understand and order the meaning of our experience, to integrate it with what we know to avoid the threat of chaos. If we are unable to understand, we often turn to tradition, thoughtlessly seize explanations by authority figures, or resort to various psychological mechanisms, such as projection and rationalization, to create imaginary meanings.

Making Meaning as a Learning Process

As there are no fixed truths or totally definitive knowledge, and because circumstances change, the human condition may be best understood as a continuous effort to negotiate contested meanings. Milan Kundera, in *The Book of Laughter and Forgetting*, wisely suggests that if there were too much incontestable meaning in the world we would succumb under its weight.

That is why it is so important that adult learning emphasize contextual understanding, critical reflection on assumptions, and validating meaning by assessing reasons. The justification for much of what we know and believe, our values and our feelings, depends on the context—biographical, historical, cultural—in which they are embedded. We make meaning with different dimensions of awareness and understanding; in adulthood we may more clearly understand our experience when we know under what conditions an expressed idea is true or justified. In the absence of fixed truths and confronted with often rapid change in circumstances, we cannot fully trust what we know or believe. Interpretations and opinions that may have worked for us as children often do not as adults.

Our understandings and beliefs are more dependable when they produce interpretations and opinions that are more justifiable or true than would be those predicated upon other understandings or beliefs. Formulating more dependable beliefs about our experience, assessing their contexts, seeking informed agreement on their meaning and justification, and making decisions on the resulting insights are central to the adult learning process. Transformation Theory attempts to explain this process and to examine its implications for action-oriented adult educators.

Bruner (1996) identifies four modes of making meaning: (1) establishing, shaping, and maintaining intersubjectivity; (2) relating events, utterances, and behavior to the action taken; (3) construing of particulars in a normative context—deals with meaning relative to obligations, standards, conformities, and deviations; (4) making propositions—application of rules of the symbolic, syntactic, and conceptual systems used to achieve decontexualized meanings, including rules of inference and logic and such distinctions as whole-part, object-attribute, and identity-otherness.

Bruner's list is incomplete. Transformation Theory adds a fifth and crucial mode of making meaning: becoming critically aware of one's own tacit assumptions and expectations and those of others and assessing their relevance for making an interpretation.

Kitchener (1983, p. 230) has suggested that there are three levels of cognitive processing:

> At the first level, individuals compute, memorize, read and comprehend. At the second level [metacognition], they monitor their own progress and products as they are engaged in first-order cognitive tasks. . . . The third level

. . . [the] epistemic cognition, must be introduced to explain how humans monitor their problem solving when engaged in ill-structured problems, i.e. those which do not have an absolutely correct solution. Epistemic cognition has to do with reflection on the limits of knowledge, the certainty of knowledge, and the criteria for knowing. . . . [E]pistemic cognition emerges in late adolescence, although its form may change in the adult years.

In this formulation, transformative learning pertains to epistemic cognition.

Learning is understood as the process of using a prior interpretation to construe a new or revised interpretation of the meaning of one's experience as a guide to future action. We appropriate symbolic models, composed of images and conditioned affective reactions acquired earlier through the culture or the idiosyncrasies of parents or caretakers—a highly individualistic "frame of reference"—and make analogies to interpret the meaning of our new sensory experience (Rosenfield, 1988). Learning may be intentional, the result of deliberate inquiry; incidental, a by-product of another activity involving intentional learning; or mindlessly assimilative. Aspects of both intentional and incidental learning take place outside learner awareness.

Construal in intentional or incidental learning involves the use of language to articulate our experience to ourselves or to others. A third type of construal Heron (1988) describes as presentational. In presentational construal we do not require words to make meaning, as when we experience presence, motion, color, texture, directionality, aesthetic or kinesthetic experience, empathy, feelings, appreciation, inspiration, or transcendence. We use language here only when we experience a problem in understanding or want to share the experience.

Beliefs do not need to be encoded in words. They may be encoded in repetitive interactions and generalized. Weiss reminds us that a person's beliefs about himself or herself and his or her world are intimately bound up with his or her affects. He writes (1997, p. 428):

> Indeed, research into the unconscious acquisition of knowledge demonstrates that the human being has an enormous capacity nonconsciously to make inferences from complex data, to solve difficult puzzles, and to make broad generalizations from particular experiences. . . . [T]he nonconscious capacity of people to acquire information is much more sophisticated and rapid than their conscious capacity to do this. Also human beings have no conscious access to the nonconscious process that they use to acquire information. People cannot describe them; they are conscious only of the *results* of their nonconscious mental activities.

Art, music, and dance are alternative languages. Intuition, imagination, and dreams are other ways of making meaning. Inspiration, empathy, and transcendence are central to self-knowledge and to drawing attention to the affective quality and poetry of human experience. Dirkx (1997, p. 85) writes of "learning through soul" involving "a focus on the interface where the socioemotional and the intellectual world meet, where the inner and outer worlds converge." Psychotherapists use *transference* to facilitate the making of meaning by their patients. *Modeling* a way of learning by an educator, such as becoming critically reflective of one's assumptions, may also influence the way a learner makes meaning.

Cognition has strong affective and conative dimensions; all the sensitivity and responsiveness of the person participates in the invention, discovery, interpretation, and transformation of meaning. Transformative learning, especially when it involves subjective reframing, is often an intensely threatening emotional experience in which we have to become aware of both the assumptions undergirding our ideas and those supporting our emotional responses to the need to change.

As language and culturally specific social practices are implicated in learning, understanding will be enabled and constrained by the historical knowledge-power networks in which it is embedded. The assumptions of these historical networks and their supporting ideologies need to be brought into awareness and critical reflection by the learner to make possible a greater degree of autonomous learning. We need to focus on who is doing the learning and under what circumstances to understand the transformative learning process.

The who, what, when, where, why, and how of learning may be only understood as situated in a specific cultural context. However, the content of a comprehensive learning theory cannot be dictated exclusively by cultural interests. What we have in common are human connectedness, the desire to understand, and spiritual incompleteness. Cultures enable or inhibit the realization of common human interests, ways of communicating and realizing learning capabilities.

Mindful learning is defined by Langer (1997, p. 4) as the continuous creation of new categories, openness to new information, and an implicit awareness of more than one perspective. Mindlessness involves relying on past forms of action or previously established distinctions and categories.

It should be understood that there are different degrees of comprehension and mindfulness regarding becoming aware of one's thoughts. In adulthood, knowing how you know involves awareness of the context—sources, nature, and consequences—of your interpretations and beliefs and those of others. In adulthood, informed decisions require not only awareness of the source and context of our knowledge, values, and feelings but also critical reflection on the validity of their assumptions or premises.

Transformative learning refers to the process by which we transform our taken-for-granted frames of reference (meaning perspectives, habits of mind, mind-sets) to make them more inclusive, discriminating, open, emotionally capable of change, and reflective so that they may generate beliefs and opinions that will prove more true or justified to guide action. Transformative learning involves participation in constructive discourse to use the experience of others to assess reasons justifying these assumptions, and making an action decision based on the resulting insight.

Transformation Theory's focus is on how we learn to negotiate and act on our own purposes, values, feelings, and meanings rather than those we have uncritically assimilated from others—to gain greater control over our lives as socially responsible, clear-thinking decision makers. As such, it has particular relevance for learning in contemporary societies that share democratic values. Because this theory particularly addresses the interests of adult education, as this vocation has evolved in the West, it assumes the perfectability of human beings when this refers to improving our understanding and the quality of our actions through meaningful learning.

Transformative learning has both individual and social dimensions and implications. It demands that we be aware of how we come to our knowledge and as aware as we can be about the values that lead us to our perspectives. Cultural canon, socioeconomic structures, ideologies and beliefs about ourselves, and the practices they support often conspire to foster conformity and impede development of a sense of responsible agency.

Domains of Learning

Habermas (1984) has helped us understand that there are two major domains of learning with different purposes, logics of inquiry, criteria of rationality, and modes of validating beliefs. One is *instrumental learning*—learning to control and manipulate the environment or other people, as in task-oriented problem solving to improve performance. The other is *communicative learning*—learning what others mean when they communicate with you. This often involves feelings, intentions, values, and moral issues.

Understanding in communicative learning requires that we assess the meanings behind the words; the coherence, truth, and appropriateness of what is being communicated; the truthfulness and qualifications of the speaker; and the authenticity of expressions of feeling. That is, we must become critically reflective of the *assumptions* of the person communicating. We need to know whether the person who gives us a diagnosis about our health is a trained medical worker, that one who gives us direction at work is authorized to do so, or whether a stranger who talks to us on a bus is just passing the time or trying to sell us something, proselytize, or pick us up. The meaning of the words the stranger uses depends on his or her assumptions.

Assumptions include intent, sometimes implied as a subtext; what is taken for granted, like conventional wisdom; a particular religious worldview; whether one means what is said and in what sense it is meant—literally or metaphorically, as a joke or caricature; the frame of reference; the character—liar, zealot, crook—and qualifications of the person communicating; and the relevance and timing of the communication and the context—biographical, historical, and cultural—within which what is being communicated makes sense. Communicative learning often involves a critical assessment of assumptions supporting the justification of norms.

Most learning involves elements of both domains. Hart (1990) pointed out that challenging premises involved in instrumental learning itself involves communicative learning. In instrumental learning, problem solving and inquiry follow a hypothetical-deductive logic (test a hypothesis; analyze its consequences). In communicative learning, inquiry assumes a metaphorical-abductive logic (make an analogy; let each step in understanding dictate the next one). Learning may involve a transformation in frame of reference in either domain.

We establish the validity of our problematic beliefs in instrumental learning by empirically testing to determine the truth of an assertion. In communicative learning, we determine the justification of a problematic belief or understanding through *rational discourse* to arrive at a tentative best judgment. The only alternatives to discourse for justifying a belief are to appeal to tradition, authority, or force.

Here rationality refers to assessing reasons supporting one's options as objectively as possible and choosing the most effective means available to achieve one's objectives. In instrumental learning, rationality is judged by whether we are able to achieve technical success in meeting our objectives (for example, use methods that result in improved performance). In communicative learning, rationality is judged by our success in coming to an understanding concerning the issues at hand.

In coping with the external world, instrumental competence involves attainment of improved task-oriented performance. But communicative competence refers to the ability of the learner to negotiate his or her own purposes, values, feelings, and meanings rather than to simply act on those of others (what I later refer to as autonomous thinking). We test our interpretations and beliefs instrumentally by hypothesis testing and empirical measurement when we can and justify them communicatively through reflective discourse when we cannot.

Although Habermas suggests a third learning domain, *emancipation*, Transformation Theory redefines this as the transformation process that pertains in both instrumental and communicative learning domains. Habermas also suggests two additional learning domains: *normative learning*—learning oriented to common values and an expectation of certain behavior reflecting those values—and *impressionistic learning*—learning to enhance one's impression on others.

Reflective Discourse

Discourse, in the context of Transformation Theory, is that specialized use of dialogue devoted to searching for a common understanding and assessment of the justification of an interpretation or belief. This involves assessing reasons advanced by weighing the supporting evidence and arguments and by examining alternative perspectives. Reflective discourse involves a critical assessment of assumptions. It leads toward a clearer understanding by tapping collective experience to arrive at a tentative best judgment. Discourse is the forum in which "finding one's voice" becomes a prerequisite for free full participation. Kegan (1994) writes that the two greatest yearnings in human experience are to be included and to have a sense of agency. Of course, agency is intimately dependent on others and on one's inclusion in discourse. Discourse always reflects wider patterns of relationship and power.

Effective participation in discourse and in transformative learning requires emotional maturity—awareness, empathy, and control— what Goleman (1998) calls "emotional intelligence"—knowing and managing one's emotions, motivating oneself, recognizing emotions in others and handling relationships—as well as clear thinking. Goleman elaborates emotional competencies for each of these dimensions of emotional intelligence. Major social competencies include empathy (understanding others and cultivating opportunity through diverse people and political awareness) and social skills (adeptness in getting desired responses from others). Self-regulation includes self-control and trustworthiness (maintaining standards of honesty and integrity). Based on his extensive qualitative research, Goleman claims that emotional intelligence accounts for 85 percent to 90 percent of success at work, more than I.Q. or expertise, a view that Warren Bennis (1998) shares.

Our culture conspires against collaborative thinking and the development of social competence by conditioning us to think adversarially in terms of winning or losing, of proving ourselves smart, worthy, or wise. Deborah Tannen (1998) writes of ours as an "argument culture," a cultural paradigm that conditions us to approach anything we need to accomplish together as a fight between opposing sides, like a debate or like settling differences by litigation. Political discourse becomes reduced to negative advertising.

In televised or radio talk shows public discourse becomes a process of finding spokespersons for different points of view who are the most extreme and polarized. We tend to believe that there are two sides to every issue and only two. We set out to win an argument rather than to understand different ways of thinking and different frames of reference, and to search for common ground, to resolve differences, and to get things done.

In an argument culture, the quality of information that we get is compromised: however bizarre and unwarranted a viewpoint may be, such as denial of the Holocaust, it becomes "the other side," as though everything has another side. Tannen's analysis of our argument culture is a valuable sourcebook for those who would facilitate transformative learning and have a priority in helping adults learn how to move from self-serving debate to empathic listening and informed constructive discourse.

Consensus building is an ongoing process, and a best collective judgment is always subject to review by a broader group of participants. A best (or more dependable) judgment is always tentative until additional evidence, argument, or a different perspective is presented that may change it. This is why it is essential to seek out and encourage viewpoints that challenge prevailing norms of the dominant culture in matters of class, race, gender, technology, and environmental protection. Agreement based on the unchallenged norms of a culture will be obviously less informed and dependable than those based on a wider range of experience.

Ideally, a best judgment is based on the broadest consensus possible, but consensus is not always feasible. In striving for consensus it is important not only to seek a wide range of views but to allow dissension. Discourse requires only that participants have the will and readiness to seek understanding and to reach some reasonable agreement. Feelings of trust, solidarity, security, and empathy are essential preconditions for free full participation in discourse. Discourse is not based on winning arguments; it centrally involves finding agreement, welcoming difference, "trying on" other points of view, identifying the common in the contradictory, tolerating the anxiety implicit in paradox, searching for synthesis, and reframing.

If one has a totally revolutionary way of expressing understanding, she may be unable to find support from others. It may take years to convince the world of the validity of a revolutionary idea, but for the concept to become validated, if it cannot be proven empirically, its justification must eventually be established through discourse.

Our option in the face of paradox is to bridge, through ongoing negotiations, the simultaneous existence of mutually exclusive internal, external, and relational realities. Bruner (1990, p. 30) defines open-mindedness as "a willingness to construe knowledge and values from multiple perspectives without loss of commitment to one's own values." Reflective discourse involves what the Greek Skeptics called *epoche*, a provisional suspension of judgment about the truth or falsity of, or the belief or disbelief in, ideas until a better determination can be made.

The generic role of discourse in human communication implies certain conditions for its full realization (and, by implication, a set of conditions for optimizing adult learning and education as well). To more freely and fully participate in discourse, participants must have the following:

- More accurate and complete information

- Freedom from coercion and distorting self-deception

- Openness to alternative points of view: empathy and concern about how others think and feel

- The ability to weigh evidence and assess arguments objectively

- Greater awareness of the context of ideas and, more critically, reflectiveness of assumptions, including their own

- An equal opportunity to participate in the various roles of discourse

- Willingness to seek understanding and agreement and
  to accept a resulting best judgment as a test of validity
  until new perspectives, evidence, or arguments are
  encountered and validated through discourse as yield-
  ing a better judgment

The claim is that if everyone could participate in discourse under these conditions there would be a consensus supporting them
as norms. These ideal conditions constitute a principle; they are
never fully realized in practice. They imply, in effect, what Bellah
and others (1985) refer to as "democratic habits of the heart": respect for others, self-respect, willingness to accept responsibility
for the common good, willingness to welcome diversity and to approach others with openness.

There is also a close relationship between the ideal conditions
of discourse and what Belenky and her colleagues (1986, pp. 143–
146) refer to as "really talking," in which emphasis is placed on
active listening, domination is absent, reciprocity and cooperation
are prominent, and judgment is withheld until one empathically
understands another's point of view: "Compared to other positions,
there is a capacity at the position of constructed knowledge to attend to another person and to feel related to that person in spite of
what may be enormous differences. . . . Empathy is a central feature
in the development of connected procedures for knowing . . . attentive caring is important in understanding not only people but also
the written word, ideas, even impersonal objects."

Discourse is the process in which we have an active dialogue
with others to better understand the meaning of an experience. It
may include interaction within a group or between two persons, including a reader and an author or a viewer and an artist.

Fostering discourse, with a determined effort to free participation from distortions by power and influence, is a long-established
priority of adult educators. The generally accepted model of adult
education involves a transfer of authority from the educator to the

learners; the successful educator works herself out of her job as educator and becomes a collaborative learner.

Although not necessarily a good example of connected knowing, the ideal of a graduate seminar may serve in some respects as a model of group discourse. In a model seminar, there are a set of commonly accepted norms that support the ideal conditions of discourse—there is no outside coercion (other than that internalized as a result of prior experience or of being expected to come to the seminar informed on the concepts and issues to be discussed), everyone has an equal opportunity to contribute, participants are informed on the topic to be discussed, and there are norms of courtesy, active listening, studying issues in advance, and taking turns to talk. Academic freedom permits anyone to be critically reflective of established cultural norms or viewpoints.

To assess and fully understand the way others interpret experience requires discourse, and to understand and assess the reasons for their beliefs and understandings requires the ability to become critically reflective of their assumptions and our own. Culture, history, and biography determine the manner and degree to which these human faculties for intersubjectivity, reflective discourse, and mindful learning become realized in time and place.

Values like freedom, equality, tolerance, social justice, and rationality provide essential norms for free full participation in discourse, that is, for fully understanding our experience. Cultures and societies differ in the degree to which critical reflection and discourse are encouraged. In a democracy, like all such norms that influence educational, political, and moral decisions, they are, at least in theory, dependent for their validity on an informed consensus by those effected. This is a consensus arrived at through discourse free from domination, ideally under the conditions specified earlier.

Preconditions for realizing these values and finding one's voice for free full participation in discourse include elements of maturity, education, safety, health, economic security, and emotional intelligence. Hungry, homeless, desperate, threatened, sick, or frightened adults are less likely to be able to participate effectively in discourse to help us better understand the meaning of our own experiences. This is one reason why adult educators are dedicated to social justice.

Full development of the human potential for transformative learning depends on values such as freedom, equality, tolerance, social justice, civic responsibility, and education. It assumes that these values are basic to our human need to constructively use the experience of others to understand, or make more dependable, the meaning of our experience. One might argue that their claim as human rights and their political significance are predicated on this foundation. To borrow a phrase from Camus, without these values "even a transformed world would not be worth living in, and man, even if 'new,' would not deserve to be respected" (quoted in Fulghum, 1997, p. 77).

Meaning Structures

A *frame of reference* is a "meaning perspective," the structure of assumptions and expectations through which we filter sense impressions. It involves cognitive, affective, and conative dimensions. It selectively shapes and delimits perception, cognition, feelings, and disposition by predisposing our intentions, expectations, and purposes. It provides the context for making meaning within which we choose what and how a sensory experience is to be construed and/or appropriated.

Frames of reference are the results of ways of interpreting experience. They may be either within or outside of our awareness. Many of our most guarded beliefs about ourselves and our world—that we are smart or dumb, good or bad, winners or losers—are inferred from repetitive affective experience outside of awareness. Because of such affectively encoded experience each person can be said to live in a different reality.

Our frames of reference often represent cultural paradigms (collectively held frames of reference)—learning that is unintentionally assimilated from the culture—or personal perspectives derived from the idiosyncrasies of primary caregivers. We tend to embrace frames of reference that complement each other. Particularly comprehensive and dominant paradigms or systems of belief that unite the particular with the universal become "worldviews," like the concept of *logos* in ancient Greece, Christian belief in the Middle Ages and Reformation, and science and technology in the twentieth century. One's frame of reference may include intentionally or incidentally learned philosophical, economic, sociological, and psychological orientations or theories as well.

A frame of reference is composed of two dimensions, a habit of mind and resulting points of view. A *habit of mind* is a set of assumptions—broad, generalized, orienting predispositions that act as a filter for interpreting the meaning of experience. Some varieties of habits of mind are the following:

- Sociolinguistic (cultural canon, ideologies, social norms, customs, "language games," secondary socialization)

- Moral-ethical (conscience, moral norms)

- Epistemic (learning styles, sensory preferences, focus on wholes or parts or on the concrete or abstract)

- Philosophical (religious doctrine, philosophy, transcendental world view)

- Psychological (self-concept, personality traits or types, repressed parental prohibitions that continue to dictate ways of feeling and acting in adulthood, emotional response patterns, images, fantasies, dreams; for a Freudian interpretation see Gould 1978, for a Jungian interpretation see Boyd 1991)

- Aesthetic (values, tastes, attitudes, standards, and judgments about beauty and the insight and authenticity of aesthetic expressions, such as the sublime, the ugly, the tragic, the humorous, the "drab", and others)

Habits of mind include conservative or liberal orientation; tendency to move toward or away from people; approaching the unknown fearful or confident; preference to work alone or with others; ethnocentricity (seeing people different from your group negatively or as inferior); tendency to respect or challenge authority; thinking like a scientist, soldier, lawyer, or adult educator; intepreting behavior as a Freudian or a Jungian; approaching a problem analytically or intuitively; focusing on a problem from whole to parts or vice versa; introversion or extroversion; patterns of acting as a perfectionist, victim, or incompetent; fear of change; thinking conventionally about one's roles; occupational, disciplinary, religious, educational, capitalist, Marxist, or postmodernist; and many other orientations and worldviews.

A habit of mind becomes expressed as a *point of view*. A point of view comprises clusters of meaning schemes—sets of immediate specific expectations, beliefs, feelings, attitudes, and judgments—that tacitly direct and shape a specific interpretation and determine how we judge, typify objects, and attribute causality. Meaning schemes commonly operate outside of awareness. They arbitrarily determine what we see and how we see it—cause-effect relationships, scenarios of sequences of events, what others will be like, and our idealized self-image. They suggest a line of action that we tend to follow automatically unless brought into critical reflection.

Our values and sense of self are anchored in our frames of reference. They provide us with a sense of stability, coherence, community, and identity. Consequently they are often emotionally charged and strongly defended. Other points of view are judged against the standards set by our points of view. Viewpoints that call our frames of reference into question may be dismissed as distorting, deceptive, ill intentioned, or crazy.

Who we are and what we value are closely associated. So questions raised regarding one's values are apt to be viewed as a personal attack. Learning tends to become narrowly defined as efforts to add compatible ideas to elaborate our fixed frames of reference. However, this disposition may be changed through transformative learning.

A frame of reference that is more dependable, as we have seen, produces interpretations and opinions that are more likely to be justified (through discursive assessment) or true (through empirical assessment) than those predicated on a less dependable frame of reference. A more dependable frame of reference is one that is more inclusive, differentiating, permeable (open to other viewpoints), critically reflective of assumptions, emotionally capable of change, and integrative of experience. Insofar as experience and circumstance permit, we move toward more dependable frames of reference to better understand our experience.

Transformations

Learning occurs in one of four ways: by elaborating existing frames of reference, by learning new frames of reference, by transforming points of view, or by transforming habits of mind.

Transformation refers to a movement through time of reformulating reified structures of meaning by reconstructing dominant narratives. The process may itself become a frame of reference, a dispositional orientation. As mentioned earlier, we transform frames of reference—our own and those of others—by becoming critically reflective of their assumptions and aware of their context—the source, nature, and consequences of taken-for-granted beliefs. Assumptions on which habits of mind and related points of view are predicated may be epistemological, logical, ethical, psychological, ideological, social, cultural, economic, political, ecological, scientific, or spiritual, or may pertain to other aspects of experience.

Brookfield (1995) emphasizes the importance of three common assumptions for critical reflection: paradigmatic assumptions that structure the world into fundamental categories (the most difficult to identify in oneself), prescriptive assumptions about what we think ought to be happening in a specific situation, and causal assumptions about how the world works and how it may be changed (the easiest to identify).

Transformative learning refers to transforming a problematic frame of reference to make it more dependable in our adult life by generating opinions and interpretations that are more justified. We become critically reflective of those beliefs that become problematic. Beliefs are often inferential, based on repetitive emotional interactions and established outside of our awareness. Frames of reference may be highly individualistic or shared as paradigms. Transformative learning is a way of problem solving by defining a problem or by redefining or reframing the problem. We often become critically reflective of our assumptions or those of others and arrive at a transformative insight, but we need to justify our new perspective through discourse.

Imagination is central to understanding the unknown; it is the way we examine alternative interpretations of our experience by "trying on" another's point of view. The more reflective and open we are to the perspectives of others, the richer our imagination of alternative contexts for understanding will be.

In instrumental learning we can transform our points of view by becoming critically reflective of assumptions supporting the *content* and/or *process* of problem solving. For example, in deciding how to assign grades to learners in a class we may become critically reflective of the content of the problem: How might one select and assign value to different indicators—standardized tests, written work, teacher-made tests, participation, group work, and others? We may also become critically reflective of the process of solving the problem: Do we have a sufficiently representative sample of student performance in the selected indicators to make a fair judgment? Critical analysis of content or process in instrumental learning can lead to significantly improved performance by the educator.

We may transform our habit of mind by becoming critically reflective of our *premises* in defining the problem, such as by questioning the validity of our assumptions supporting the concept of competitive grading in the first place rather than focusing assessment on individual learner gains, and perhaps we take action on our reflective insight by turning to another form of evaluation, such as portfolio assessment.

Becoming critically reflective of assumptions underlying content, process, or premise is common in both instrumental and communicative learning. Reflectivity involves reasoning and/ or intuition. Both are significantly influenced by conditioned emotional responses. Many beliefs are generalized from repetitive interactions outside of consciousness. Transformations may be focused and mindful, involving critical reflection, the result of repetitive affective interaction or of mindless assimilation—as in moving to a different culture and uncritically assimilating its canon, norms, and ways of thinking.

Transformations in habit of mind may be *epochal*, a sudden, dramatic, reorienting insight, or *incremental*, involving a progressive series of transformations in related points of view that culminate in a transformation in habit of mind. For example, a traditionally oriented woman takes a late-afternoon adult education class. She may come to wonder why the other women in the class stick around to discuss interesting issues when she has to rush home to make dinner for her husband. She may engage in transformative learning by becoming critically reflective of her point of view on this topic. If she experiences a related progression of such critically reflective questions about her assumptions in several different situations, this can lead to a transformation in her habit of mind regarding her role as a woman.

Cohen (1997) describes how an educator can help adult students with negative experiences in school to feel more secure as learners in doing classwork. Over time, a series of these transformations in point of view about oneself as a learner ("I *can* understand these ideas") may cumulatively lead to a transformation in self-concept ("I am a smart, competent person")—a habit of mind.

We change our point of view by trying on another's point of view. We are unable to do this with a habit of mind. The most personally significant and emotionally exacting transformations involve a critique of previously unexamined premises regarding one's self ("a woman's place is in the home, so I must deny myself a career that I would love").

Transformations often follow some variation of the following phases of meaning becoming clarified (see Chapter Eleven):

1. A disorienting dilemma

2. Self-examination with feelings of fear, anger, guilt, or shame

3. A critical assessment of assumptions

4. Recognition that one's discontent and the process of transformation are shared

5. Exploration of options for new roles, relationships, and actions

6. Planning a course of action

7. Acquiring knowledge and skills for implementing one's plans

8. Provisional trying of new roles

9. Building competence and self-confidence in new roles and relationships

10. A reintegration into one's life on the basis of conditions dictated by one's new perspective

Clark (1993) found that an earlier stage of exploration may be followed by encountering a "missing piece" that provides the integration necessary for a transformative experience.

Frosty (1998, p. 72) observes, "From women's and black consciousness movements come insights that psychic transformations involve a revisioning of self in the eyes and responses of similar others and/or a beneficial cycle of desire, identification and re-apportion of a stronger subjectivity through relations with those who themselves successfully transcend oppression."

Boyd (1991, p. 198) has identified two fundamental steps toward a personal transformation: "making public, primarily for ourselves, the historical dimensions of our dilemma" and "confronting it as a difficulty to be worked through."

Transformative learning may occur through objective or subjective reframing. *Objective reframing* involves critical reflection on the assumptions of others encountered in a narrative or in task-oriented problem solving, as in "action learning" (Revans, 1982). *Subjective reframing* involves critical self-reflection of one's own assumptions about the following:

- A narrative—applying a reflective insight from someone else's narrative to one's own experience

- A system—economic, cultural, political, educational, communal, or other—as in Freire's (1970) *conscientization*, consciousness raising in the womens' movement and the civil rights movement

- An organization or workplace—as in Argyris's (1982) "double loop learning"

- Feelings and interpersonal relations—as in psychological counseling or psychotherapy

- The ways one learns, including one's own frames of reference, per se, in some adult education programs—as in Isaacs' (1993) "triple loop learning"

Critical reflection in the context of psychotherapy focuses on assumptions regarding feelings pertaining to interpersonal relationships; in adult education its focus is on an infinitely wider range of concepts and their accompanying cognitive, affective, and conative dimensions. This distinction is important in differentiating between these two professional fields. Subjective reframing commonly involves an intensive and difficult emotional struggle as old perspectives become challenged and transformed.

A mindful transformative learning experience requires that the learner make an informed and reflective decision to act on his or her reflective insight. This decision may result in immediate action, delayed action, or reasoned reaffirmation of an existing pattern of action. Taking action on reflective insights often involves overcoming situational, emotional, and informational constraints that may require new learning experiences in order to move forward. As challenging one's cherished beliefs (a leap into the unknown) often invokes a threatening emotional experience, the qualities that constitute emotional intelligence (see p. 11) are essential conditions of transformative learning. Freedom involves not just the will and insight to change but also the power to act to attain one's purpose. As Novak claims: "Perspective transformation represents not only a total change in life perspective, but an actualization of that perspective. In other words life is not *seen* from a new perspective, it is *lived* from that perspective" (quoted in Paprock, 1992, p. 197).

Tennant (1998, p. 374) sees as a test of transformative learning "the extent to which it exposes the social and cultural embeddedness and taken-for-granted assumptions in which the self is located; explore[s] the interests served by the continuation of the self thus positioned; incite[s] a refusal to be positioned in this way when the interests served are those of domination and oppression; and encourage[s] alternative readings of the text of experience."

Critical reflection, discourse, and reflective action always exist in the real world in complex institutional, interpersonal, and historical settings, and these inevitably significantly influence the possibilities for transformative learning and shape its nature. The possibility for transformative learning must be understood in the context of cultural orientations embodied in our frames of reference, including institutions, customs, occupations, ideologies, and interests, which shape our preferences and limit our focus. We need to become critically reflective of their assumptions and consequences.

Adulthood

An adult is commonly defined as a person old enough to be held responsible for his or her acts. The assumption in democratic societies is that an adult is able to understand the issues, will make rational choices as a socially responsible, autonomous agent and, at least sometimes, is free to act on them. Even partial autonomy requires communicative competence and transformative learning.

A sense of agency implies that one can understand perceptively. Such understanding requires the ability and disposition to become critically reflective of one's own assumptions as well as those of others, engage fully and freely in discourse to validate one's beliefs, and effectively take reflective action to implement them.

But learning theory must recognize the crucial role of supportive relationships and a supportive environment in making possible a more confident, assured sense of personal efficacy, of having a self—or selves—more capable of becoming critically reflective of one's habitual and sometimes cherished assumptions, and of having the self-confidence to take action on reflective insights. The power to control and determine our actions in the context of our desires and intentions is a definition of will. Transformative learning includes this conative dimension. The development of these dispositions is intimately dependent on others and, by extension, on wider patterns of relationship and power. Maxine Greene observes: "It is actually through the process of effecting transformations that the human self is created and re-created" (1988, p. 21).

Although it is clear that our interests and priorities change in the different seasons of our lives, development in adulthood may be understood as a learning process—a phased and often transformative process of meaning becoming clarified through expanded awareness, critical reflection, validating discourse, and reflective action as one moves toward a fuller realization of agency. For Robert Kegan, "transforming our epistemologies, liberating ourselves from that in which we are embedded, making what was a subject into object so that we can 'have it' rather than to 'be had' by it—this is the most powerful way I know to conceptualize the growth of the mind" (1994, p. 34).

Döbert, Habermas, and Nunner-Winkler (1987, p. 296) comment: "Finally adolescents form the notions of *heteronomy* and *autonomy*; they recognize the difference between existing conventions and justifiable norms. The orientation guiding action becomes increasingly abstract, focusing first on concrete need, then duty and finally autonomous will."

Although adolescents may learn to become critically reflective of the assumptions of others, becoming critically reflective of one's own assumptions appears to be much more likely to occur in adults (see Chapter Two). King and Kitchener (1994) have found that it is well into adulthood that we develop reflective judgment, the process of participation in critical discourse to assess reasons and make tentative judgments regarding contested beliefs.

Toward a Philosophy of Adult Education

Adult education may be understood as an organized effort to assist learners who are old enough to be held responsible for their acts to acquire or enhance their understandings, skills, and dispositions. Central to this process is helping learners to critically reflect on, appropriately validate, and effectively act on their (and others') beliefs, interpretations, values, feelings, and ways of thinking. Our human need to understand our experience, the necessity that we do so through critical discourse, and the optimal conditions enabling us to do so freely and fully provide a foundation for a philosophy of adult education. Kegan (1994, p. 232) notes that learning that reflects on itself can only be accomplished through transformational education, "a 'leading out' from an established habit of mind," an order of mental complexity that enables self-direction, a qualitative change in *how* one knows.

Siegal (1990, p. 58) describes a liberated person as one "free from unwarranted and undesirable control of unjustified beliefs, unsupportable attitudes and paucity of ability which can prevent one from taking charge of her own life." Fostering these liberating conditions for making more autonomous and informed choices and developing a sense of self-empowerment is the cardinal goal of adult education.

Acquiring the ability to make more autonomous choices is a process never fully realized. An autonomous choice is one in which the individual is "free to act and judge independently of external constraints on the basis of her own reasoned appraisal" (p. 54).

This process has to do with assessing reasons supporting beliefs. To do so effectively, this involves becoming critically reflective of their assumptions, validating assertions through empirical test or discourse, and making a decision to act on one's critical insight. For Siegal and Transformation Theory, critical thinking is coextensive with rationality.

The process of self-empowerment, acquiring greater control of one's life as a liberated learner, is, of course, always limited by social, historical, and cultural conditions. Sociologists, feminists, and ecologists have helped us become aware that human beings are essentially relational. Our identity is formed in webs of affiliation within a shared life world. Human reality is intersubjective; our life histories and language are bound up with those of others. It is within the context of these relationships, governed by existing and changing cultural paradigms, that we become the persons we are. Transformative learning involves liberating ourselves from reified forms of thought that are no longer dependable.

Jansen and Wildemeersch (1998) point out that social conditions for acquiring a sense of autonomy in our society often implies *qualifications*—that only through a particular kind and quantity of education may one acquire the abilities to participate fully in social and economic life. This assumes social integration; marginalized groups are often excluded. The implication is that social identity and full-fledged social and economic participation require the proper qualifications and that we all have equal access to the necessary education and training to become qualified. Of course, this is a shibboleth. A further assumption is that there are always rewarding career opportunities out there for those who are qualified. Adult educators are committed to efforts to create a more equal set of enabling conditions in our society, to the ideal of social justice.

The postmodern emphasis that a person is constructed from sources outside oneself is a valuable insight. Rubenson (1998, p. 257) observes: "Lifelong learning for all is conditional on a working life organized in a way that promotes the use of literacy and a society where people are encouraged to think, act, and be engaged."

There are obvious inequities in the social structure reflecting asymmetrical power relationships and perpetuating inequalities that profoundly influence the way one understands experience. Learners need to become critically reflective of how these factors have shaped the ways they think and their beliefs so they may take collective action to ameliorate them.

There is a reciprocity between democratic theory and Transformation Theory. Warren (1992, p. 8) contends that democracies inherently create opportunities for self-transformation: "[W]ere individuals more broadly empowered, especially in the institutions that have most impact on their everyday lives (workplaces, schools, local governments, etc.), their experiences would have transformative effects: they would become more public spirited, more tolerant, more knowledgeable, more attentive to the interests of others, and more probing of their own interests."

Transformation Theory suggests that transformative learning inherently creates understandings for participatory democracy by developing capacities of critical reflection on taken-for-granted assumptions that support contested points of view and participation in discourse that reduces fractional threats to rights and pluralism, conflict, and the use of power, and foster autonomy, self-development, and self-governance—the values that rights and freedoms presumably are designed to protect.

Autonomous thinking may be understood as a competence acquired through transformative learning. Learning to become a more autonomous thinker clearly involves the interaction of personal and situational variables. We must ask: Who is granted the opportunity to achieve autonomous thinking? Who is excluded, cast as the Other to be excluded and, by implication, dominated? Tennant (1998, p. 370) challenges the postmodernist notion that autonomy implies an internalization of externally imposed disciplines of regulation, a way to produce cultural conformity.

Fostering greater autonomy in thinking is both a goal and a method for adult educators. (For a different view see Candy, 1991, p. 8.) As used here, achieving greater autonomy in thinking is a product of transformative learning—acquiring more of the understandings, skills, and dispositions required to become more aware of context of interpretations and beliefs, critically reflective of assumptions, able to participate freely and fully in rational discourse to find common meaning and validate beliefs, and effective in acting on the result of this reflective learning process.

Autonomy here does not represent a fixed goal to be achieved or an arbitrary norm, but movement in the process of transformative learning toward greater understanding of the assumptions supporting one's concepts, beliefs, and feelings and those of others. Emancipation in this context is no search for certainty and control through totalizing explanations and the elimination of difference. Nevertheless concepts such as autonomy, emancipation, rationality, education, and democracy are all contested meanings that require continuing critical reflection on their assumptions and practices, and validation through continuing discourse.

Learners may be helped to explore all aspects of a frame of reference: its genealogy, power allocation, internal logic, uses, affective and intuitive dimensions, advantages, and disadvantages. The frame may be understood as a coherent, meaningful way to organize events and feelings with costs and benefits that may be assessed. An intellectual and emotional grasp of a particular frame of reference opens space for the operation of others. The learner can look at the same experience from a variety of points of view and see that concepts and feelings depend on the perspective through which they occur. Kegan writes: "This kind of learning cannot be accomplished through *in*formational training, the acquisition of skills, but only through *trans*formational education, a 'leading out' from an established habit of mind" (1994, p. 232).

The broader purpose, the goal, of adult education is to help adults realize their potential for becoming more liberated, socially responsible, and autonomous learners—that is, to make more informed choices by becoming more critically reflective as "dialogic thinkers" (Basseches, 1984) in their engagement in a given social context. Adult educators actively strive to extend and equalize the opportunities for them to do so.

It is important to differentiate this goal of adult education from its objective—to help adult learners assess and achieve what it is they want to learn. Learning objectives may be personal, such as getting a better job or helping a child do homework, or may focus on social change (in the context of a social movement, some community development and literacy programs, or labor union education) or on organizational change. We need to recognize the difference between our goals as educators and the objectives of our learners that we want to help them achieve.

Transformative learners, with social or organizational change as objectives, seek out others who share their insights to form cells of resistance to unexamined cultural norms in organizations, communities, families, and political life; they become active agents of cultural change.

Adult educators are never neutral. They are cultural activists committed to support and extend those canon, social practices, institutions, and systems that foster fuller freer participation in reflective discourse, transformative learning, reflective action, and a greater realization of agency for all learners. Justification for the norms derived from these commitments is continually open to challenge through critical discourse.

Adult educators do not indoctrinate (for an alternative view, see Hart, 1990, p. 136); in our culture they create opportunities and foster norms supporting freer, fuller participation in discourse and in democratic social and political life. They make every effort to transfer their authority over the learning group to the group itself as soon as this is feasible, and they become collaborative learners. They model and share their commitment and act on their convictions by encouraging and assisting learners to critically assess the validity of norms from alternative perspectives, arrive at best tentative judgments through discourse, and effectively act on them. In social action contexts, such as social movements, labor and popular education, or community development programs, adult educators may choose to work with learners with whom they have a feeling of solidarity.

In fostering transformative learning efforts, what counts is what the individual learner wants to learn. This constitutes a starting point for a discourse leading to a critical examination of normative assumptions underpinning the learner's (and often the educator's) value judgments or normative expectations. (For methods of fostering critical reflection, see Mezirow and Associates, 1990; and Brookfield, 1995.)

Adult educators create protected learning environments in which the conditions of social democracy necessary for transformative learning are fostered. This involves blocking out power relationships engendered in the structure of communication, including those traditionally existing between teachers and learners. Central to the goal of adult education in democratic societies is the process of helping learners become more aware of the context of their problematic understandings and beliefs, more critically reflective on their assumptions and those of others, more fully and freely engaged in discourse, and more effective in taking action on their reflective judgments. Curricula, instructional methods, materials, assessment, and faculty and staff development should address both learner objectives and this goal of adult education.

References

Argyris, C. *Reasoning, Learning, and Action*. San Francisco: Jossey-Bass, 1982.

Basseches, M. *Dialectical Thinking and Adult Development*. Norwood, N.J.: Ablex, 1984.

Belenky, M., Clinchy, B., Goldberger, N., and Trule, J. *Women's Ways of Knowing*. New York: Basic Books, 1986.

Bellah, R., and others. *Habits of the Heart: Individualism and Commitment in American Life*. Berkeley: University of California Press, 1985.

Bennis, W. "It Ain't What You Know." *New York Times Book Review*, Oct. 25, 1998, p. 50.

Boyd, R. *Personal Transformations in Small Groups*. London: Routledge, 1991.

Brookfield, S. *Becoming a Critically Reflective Teacher*. San Francisco: Jossey-Bass, 1995.

Bruner, J. *Acts of Meaning*. Cambridge, Mass.: Harvard University Press, 1990.

Bruner, J. "Frames for Thinking: Ways of Making Meaning." In D. Olson and N. Torrance (eds.), *Modes of Thought*. New York: Cambridge University Press, 1996, pp. 93–105.

Candy, P. *Self-Direction for Lifelong Learning*. San Francisco: Jossey-Bass, 1991.

Clark, C. "Changing Course: Initiating the Transformational Learning Process." In *Proceedings* of the 34th Annual Adult Education Research Conference. State College: Pennsylvania State University, 1993, pp. 354–361.

Cohen, L. "I Ain't So Smart, and You Ain't So Dumb: Personal Reassessment in Transformative Learning." In Cranton, P. (ed.), *Transformative Learning in Action: Insights from Practice*. New Directions for Adult and Continuing Education, no. 74. San Francisco: Jossey-Bass, 1997.

Dirkx, J. "Nurturing Soul in Adult Learning." *Adult Education Quarterly*, 1997, 74, 79–87.

Döbert, R., Habermas, J., and Nunner-Winkler, G. "The Development of the Self." In J. Broughton (ed.), *Critical Theories of Psychological Development*. New York: Plenum, 1987, pp. 275–301.

Freire, P. *Pedagogy of the Oppressed*. (M. Ramos, trans.). New York: Herter and Herter, 1970.

Frosty, S. *Psychoanalysis and Psychology: Minding the Gap*. London: Macmillan, 1998.

Fulghum, R. *Words I Wish I Wrote*. New York: HarperCollins, 1997.

Goleman, D. *Working with Emotional Intelligence*. New York: Bantam Books, 1998.

Gould, R. *Transformations: Growth and Change in Adult Life*. New York: Simon & Schuster, 1978.

Greene, M. *The Dialectic of Freedom*. New York: Teachers College Press, 1988.

Habermas, J. *The Theory of Communicative Action*. Vol. 1: *Reason and the Rationalization of Society*. (T. McCarthy, trans.). Boston: Beacon Press, 1984.

Hart, M. "Critical Theory and Beyond: Further Perspectives on Emancipatory Education." *Adult Education Quarterly*, Spring 1990, 40, 125–138.

Heron, J. "Validity in Cooperative Inquiry." In Peter Reason (ed.), *Human Inquiry in Action*. London: Sage, 1988, pp. 40–59.

Isaacs, W. *Taking Flight: Dialogue, Collective Thinking and Organizational Learning*. Cambridge: Organizational Learning Center, Massachusetts Institute of Technology, 1993.

Jansen, T., and Wildemeersch, D. "Beyond the Myth of Self-Actualization: Reinventing the Community Perspective of Adult Education." *Adult Education Quarterly*, 1998, 48, 216–226.

Kegan, R. *In Over Our Heads: The Mental Demands of Modern Life*. Cambridge, Mass.: Harvard University Press, 1994.

King, P., and Kitchener, K. *Developing Reflective Judgment*. San Francisco: Jossey-Bass, 1994.

Kitchener, K. "Cognition, Metacognition and Epistemic Cognition." *Human Development*, 1983, 26, 222–223.

Kundera, M. *The Book of Laughter and Forgetting*. New York: Viking Penguin, 1981.

Langer, F. *The Power of Mindful Learning*. Reading, Mass.: Addison-Wesley, 1997, p. 4.

Mezirow, J., and Associates. *Fostering Critical Reflection in Adulthood*. San Francisco: Jossey-Bass, 1990.

Paprock, K. "Book Review." *Adult Education Quarterly*, 1992, 42, 195–197.

Revans, R. *The Origin and Growth of Action Learning*. Bickly, Kent, U.K.: Cartwell-Gratt, 1982.

Rosenfield, I. *The Invention of Memory*. New York: Basic Books, 1988.

Rubenson, K. "Adults' Readiness to Learn: Questioning Lifelong Learning for All." *Proceedings*, 39th Annual Adult Education Research Conference. San Antonio, Tex.: University of the Incarnate Word, 1998, pp. 257–262.

Siegal, H. *Educating Reason*. New York: Routledge, 1990.

Tannen, D. *The Argument Culture*. New York: Random House, 1998.

Tennant, M. "Adult Education and Technology of the Self." *International Journal of Lifelong Learning*, 1998, 16, 364–376.

Warren, M. "Democratic Theory and Self-Transformation." *American Political Science Review*, 1992, 86, 8–23.

Weiss, J. "The Role of Pathogenic Beliefs in Psychic Reality." *Psychoanalytic Psychology*, Summer 1997, 14(3), 427–434.

2

What "Form" Transforms?

A Constructive-Developmental Approach to Transformative Learning

Robert Kegan

Consider the case of Peter and Lynn as they tumble out of bed. "These days," each could say, "my work is too much with me." Different as their work is, they have noticed that in each of their jobs a similar circumstance has stirred them up.

Lynn has been at Highland Junior High School for twelve years, originally as an English teacher. Three years ago she became chair of the English department, and last year it was decided that chairpersons would become part of the principal's newly formed Leadership Council. The school had decided to adopt a site-based management philosophy in which the responsibility and authority for running the school would no longer be vested only in the principal, Carolyn Evans, but shared mainly among the principal and the faculty or its representatives.

Peter has worked at BestRest Incorporated for nineteen years. A bedding manufacturer with twelve regional factories, shipping to furniture and department stores, BestRest hired Peter during the summers while he was still in college. He caught the eye of Anderson Wright, then a plant manager, who became his mentor. As Anderson rose through the ranks he brought Peter along. Eventually, when he became a corporate vice president, he put Peter in charge of an independent product line. Peter enjoyed the continuing close association with Anderson, whom he consulted frequently and easily.

But life became more complicated for Peter when Wright decided to make the independent product line a separate company division and Peter its new head. "If you're game, Peter," said Wright, "and I think you're ready, I want you to think of the new line as a company on its own—SafeSleep Products—and I want you to run it. I want it to be your baby and I want you to think of me more as your banker. Plans, directions, and initiatives will come from you, not me. I'll review your plans like a banker would, evaluate their soundness, and extend credit or not. But if I do, it's still your project that's getting funded, not mine; it's your plan that's rising or falling, not mine. It'll be your responsibility to come through, make your payments, make a go of your business. Whaddaya think? You wanna be president of BestRest's SafeSleep division?" Peter could hear the excitement in Anderson's voice, his pleasure in offering Peter what Anderson clearly regarded as a wonderful present. He could feel how much Anderson loved the place to which he had just moved the relationship. So Peter, without hesitation or conscious deliberation and true to his deepest commitment where Anderson was concerned, moved himself to rejoin Anderson in this new place. "I love it," said Peter, like the spouse of a newly restationed military officer, happy to be reunited with one's partner but looking in sheer terror at the unfamiliar surroundings and wondering what life here could possibly be like.

Thus Lynn and Peter, the teacher and the business executive who seldom feel their work has anything in common, find themselves contending with a similar circumstance. One job is service oriented, the other product oriented; one is nonprofit, the other for profit; one involves a predominantly female environment, the other a male environment; one has an organizational culture distinguished by gentleness, safety, and nurture, the other a culture distinguished by competition, maneuvering, and results. Yet Lynn's and Peter's work lives are both out of equilibrium for the same reason: worker-participation initiatives have recast the issues of responsibility, ownership, and authority at work. One of the central aspirations of such initiatives is surely the revitalization and increased morale of the work-force. But no one would know that by looking at Lynn and Peter. Both are miserable and demoralized about the changes at work. Let's take a closer look to find out why.

"I can give you an example of why this thing is not working at Highland," Lynn says. "Probably every department chair and most of the faculty would agree that there are big flaws in the way we do faculty evaluations. First of all, except for the few first-year teach-ers, faculty evaluations are based on two class visits by the princi-pal. Two visits, that's it. And it's the principal who does them. They are announced visits, so teachers end up preparing for a perfor-mance, which they resent and which is a lousy basis for evaluation. The teachers don't feel that the principal gets a fair sample of their work. The kids know what's going on and act weird—they're on 'good behavior' too, and completely unspontaneous. The principal writes up a generally innocuous report, which the teacher then pours over like an old Kremlinologist trying to detect the hidden meaning in some routine public communiqué. Usually there is no hidden meaning. The principal is just discharging a duty that she finds as unpleasant and unrewarding as the teachers. Nobody is learning a thing, but at least the principal can tell the central office that 'everyone's been evaluated' and she has the paperwork, neatly typed in the files, to prove it.

"I went along with this like everyone else, but by the time I'd become the English department chair I'd begun to form some very different ideas about evaluation—about everything, really. I got the idea that the school should be a learning place for everyone, that we're supposed to be experts on learning, that we could evaluate everything we're doing on the basis of whether it's prolearning or not. I know at home my own kids are unbelievably aware of what Peter and I do; we teach them more by modeling than by explain-ing. I decided that if we want kids to be learning in school it would help them if we modeled learning ourselves. It was actually some version of this that got me excited about being on the Leadership

Council in the first place. I had some different ideas about faculty evaluation. I wanted to return the emphasis to learning, not file-filling. I wanted the teachers to identify what their learning agenda was and what they needed to fulfill it. And I wanted to use my chairmanship to advocate that the administrators be interested in supporting the teachers' learning. Especially, once the teacher was tenured, as most of our faculty is, I wanted the principal to get out of the evaluation business. I felt it was better handled within the departments. I thought Carolyn was a good administrator and that that was an honorable profession—after all, I'm married to one—but that it was different from being a schoolteacher. I felt that she was less effective when she crossed over from her profession into mine. My feeling is that a good hospital administrator runs the hospital well, but she doesn't tell the surgeon where to cut.

"So when Carolyn proposed sight-based management to our faculty I admired her for being willing to let some other voices come into the leadership of the school, but I wasn't thinking, 'Good, now we're going to take over.' I don't want to take over. I don't want to be the principal. But I don't want Carolyn being the department chair either, and I felt that we had a better chance of clearing these things up in group discussions, like we'd have on the council, than in one-on-one meetings in Carolyn's office.

"The whole thing started to fall apart for me this semester around just this issue of faculty evaluation, and it wasn't even my initiative. It's not as if we don't all know each other pretty well by now, but when Alan—he's the history chair—brought in his proposal, it was a complete surprise to me. It was not, as I think Carolyn was suggesting, some kind of conspiracy.

"Alan's proposal, basically, was that the history department be allowed to run a one-year experiment on evaluation. He wanted to get the performance-anxiety, test-taking dimension out of it. He wanted people to have the option of entering supervisory relationships with him or a few other senior members of the department that would really be more consultative than supervisory. No write-ups or evaluations of the teacher by the supervisor/consultant. The supervisor/consultant would, in effect, be 'hired' by the faculty member to advance the faculty member's learning goals. The teacher could 'fire' the consultant without consequences. No visits by the principal. If the teacher wanted the consultant to visit some classes for the teacher's purposes that could certainly be arranged, but not for the purpose of entering something in the faculty member's file. No file entries for one year. Try to get a sense of how the faculty used it and how much and what kind of learning was going on, but all anonymously, evaluating the experiment, not the teachers. That was basically it.

"I loved the idea, of course. I was envious that I hadn't thought of it myself. It seemed like a good way of putting into operation my idea that the faculty member should run his evaluation, that the evaluation should be aimed at learning, not putting on a show, that the chair could serve as a consultant and a resource to self-directed learning.

"We've now had three long discussions about this on the council, and we still haven't had the first word about the real merits of Alan's proposal. As I now realize I should have been more aware, the issue for Carolyn had less to do with promoting faculty learning than with the precedent it sets about accountability in general and accountability to her specifically. Stop visits by the principal? Let the faculty decide what they need to learn? No evaluations for the files by *anybody*? These didn't go down easily with Carolyn. Rather than take her usual stance of speaking last in a conversation in order to give everyone a chance to weigh in on the matter, she was the first to speak after Alan made his proposal, and what she had to say pretty much silenced the rest of us. She didn't identify any merits in the proposal. She didn't even acknowledge the implicit problems the proposal was at least trying to address. She didn't present her problems with the proposal as just her problems, which could still leave open for discussion whether these needed to determine the group's actual decision. She didn't invite anyone to help her with her problems with the proposal. She just said basically, 'This is something we can't do.'

"I'm not proud of the way I responded, but it was just such a unilateral and imperial stance for her to take, and I guess I got mad. What I said was, 'Why, Carolyn? Is it illegal what Alan is proposing?' and everyone else laughed and I could see that Carolyn was very angry. I hadn't meant it exactly the way it came out. I didn't mean she was out of line to object to the proposal. I was reacting to the way she framed it. I meant that Carolyn is the principal, and where the council strays into areas that may violate civil ordinances or the district charter, she has every right to take a unilateral position. But where the council is not straying into this kind of territory I didn't feel she had the right to just shut down the conversation. At the time I attributed my overreaction and sarcasm to the fact this was an especially important issue to me personally, and I resented how it was being dismissed. That didn't justify my sarcasm, but it did dignify it somehow.

"Anyhow, after that council session Carolyn asked to meet with me in her office, and she read me the riot act: How could I do that to her? Didn't I know how much she counted on my loyalty? Didn't I realize how powerful I was as a department chair, and that to take such a doubting view when she had clearly committed herself was terribly undermining? That she thought of us as partners, that we had worked so well together all these years, and how it was even more important with SBM that we read each other's signals well and be a good team. I had to say, 'Whoa, Carolyn, time out, I'm having too many reactions to all this.'

"We ended up having a good conversation, actually, one of our best in years, but it was really difficult. I had to tell her I thought it was unfair of her to trade on my loyalty to her, that that felt like a risky business. I told her I *did* respect her, and that we *were* friends, and I *was* grateful to her for her support to me professionally over the years, but that I was sure she was not interested in a friend who was a clone or in promoting a colleague because she was a yes-man.

I had to puzzle through all the different 'teams' we were on because I felt that I was still very much a team player even when I disagreed with her, although she seemed to feel I was abandoning the team if I disagreed. This got us into the whole SBM, Leadership Council thing, and whether that was itself a team, and what were the expectations about how we functioned as members of that council. Carolyn broke down and cried and said she was finding SBM terribly hard, that she had had no idea what she was getting into, that half the time she had nightmares that the school was going to fall apart because there was more chaos than leadership, and the other half of the time she had nightmares that the school was getting along too well without her running things and that she was slowly being relieved of her job, that SBM was about gradually making the principal irrelevant."

Were Peter to tell us what his new role as head of a division *really* felt like he might say something like this: "Honestly? It's definitely a different ball game! What game is it? Well, let's see. I guess you could say before I was president, I was playing a game of catch. Anderson would throw things at me and I'd catch them. I'd throw things back at him and he'd catch them. A good long game of catch. And now? Now I'd say I'm a juggler. There's not one ball, there are five, and then there are ten, and then there are fifteen! People keep tossing more in to me to add to those I'm juggling. But I'm not throwing to anyone. I'm just throwing them into the air. As soon as I get them I just toss them back into the air. And my job as the juggler is to keep them all going up there, not let any of them drop to the ground.

"You couldn't believe the number of things that come across my desk. 'Anderson says to take this to you now.' 'Anderson says he's not the guy on this anymore; you are.' I bet I heard that twenty times the first month we set up SafeSleep. If it wasn't one thing, it was another. You have to deal with a lot of people's feelings about this change. Everybody thought the company concept for SafeSleep was a hot idea when Anderson proposed it, but now that we're actually doing it, a lot of people aren't so sure. I told Lynn the other night I'm not even sure *Anderson's* so sure at this point. People keep asking me how I feel about the change, but the truth is, I don't have time to think about how I feel about it because I spend half my day dealing with how everybody *else* feels about it.

"Take Ted, for example. He's one of our salespeople. I've known Ted ten years in this business. His son and my Matthew are like brothers; they grew up in each other's homes. I probably see Ted's son as much as my own. Ted's putting a lot of pressure on me not to separate him from the SafeSleep line. Ted's a mattress salesman and a damn good one. He does excellent work for his customers. His customers are furniture stores and the mattress departments of two large chains of department stores. They love him and he loves them. The SafeSleep line got its start by accident, or what Anderson called 'entrepreneurial jujitsu,' turning a weakness into a strength. New government codes mandated that we manufacture flame-retardant mattresses and it cost millions of dollars to set up the capacity. Since we had the capacity, Anderson reasoned, why not use it for other things, too? Presto! The SafeSleep line. But originally these products were just an extra that the mattress salespeople offered their furniture stores. The store used them as 'sweeteners' to sell their customers our top-of-the-line mattresses. They'd throw in a king-size quilt along with the purchase of a king-size mattress and box spring. Stuff like that. Everybody was happy. The furniture store's customer liked the freebie; the store liked the mattress sale; our salespeople liked the increased mattress orders they got from the stores. And that's just the problem. Everybody was happy. 'So why are you ruining a nice thing?' Ted wants to know. 'Peter, I'm family,' he says to me. 'And Harold is not,' which is true. 'So why are you letting this guy take the bread off my table?' he says.

"I hired Harold soon after I became president of SafeSleep because Harold had sales experience in bedclothes. He was the first nonmattress salesperson in the place, and I thought we needed that for the new company. He's turned out to be a dynamo. The guy's got more ideas per square inch than I've ever seen, and most of them make sense. But they're also making some people, like Ted, mad. And I'm not so sure Anderson's very keen about him either.

"Harold's take was that BestRest was choking SafeSleep, that the best reason for setting up SafeSleep as a separate company was that its growth was stunted in the shadow of the mattress company. Furniture stores, he said, were not the place to be selling pajamas and not even the best place to sell quilts. He said our products were better than premium giveaways and should be promoted on their own merits. We should be placing them in the bed linen and pajama departments of our department stores, not the furniture and mattress departments. We should be making flame-retardants for grown-ups, not just kids. Grown-ups smoke in bed and are more likely to set themselves on fire than kids are. And on and on. It all made sense to me, but whenever you start talking about doing things differently people get worried about what it means for them. Harold said our real problem was that BestRest had a national sales force of mattress salespeople, not pajama salespeople. BestRest's customers were furniture stores, not pajama stores, and the conventions, shows, trade press, and brand recognition for BestRest are all oriented to the furniture trade, not bedclothes, white sales, or children's clothing. His view is that if SafeSleep is really going to be its own company, it needs its own *identity*, its own *purpose*, and its own *sales force* selling to its own *customers*. It has to get out of the hip pocket of BestRest.

"The problem with this is that as soon as you pull the SafeSleep line away from the mattress sales force, a guy like Ted, who has gotten a lot of mileage out of it, yells 'ouch.' I think Harold's basically right when he says that you can't establish the quality of a product by giving it away in one place and hoping to sell it somewhere else. But Ted's probably right, too, that his mattress orders will go down, at least for a while, if we pull the SafeSleep line from him, because that's what's already happened where we've begun to separate the line from the mattress business. Ted's not just worried about his volume, he's worried about his bonus benefits. He's doing one helluva job making me feel guilty, that it will be on my head to explain to both of our wives why he and Ada won't be along on this winter's 'customer cruise' since he'll be coming in under quota and won't qualify for the trip. Why doesn't he go make his *stores* feel guilty? It's their fault if they short-order him, not mine. But the truth is, Lynn and I had dinner with Ted and Ada last week and it was not a good time. You could feel the tension. By the end of the evening, I'd gone from feeling bad that I was making them both unhappy to being angry at them for making me so miserable. What right did they have making me feel guilty? I'm trying to run a business and they're upset about the Bahamas. Give me a break!

"I consider Ted and Anderson two of my best friends and if this new job ruins both of these friendships I won't be surprised. When Anderson offered me the presidency he said it was a way to move our relationship to a whole new level, that we were becoming true colleagues, that he couldn't wait to see what would come of it. It's a whole new level all right! I guess if you never want to see a guy again you should become true colleagues with him! But I know if you ask Anderson he'll say he's just as available, that it's *me*, that *I* don't call. And that's true. I just stay away from him these days and figure that when he needs to tell me something he will. I'd leave our meetings feeling as if we'd talked a lot but I had no clearer idea where I was when I left than when I'd come in. I'd run my sense of what was going on with SafeSleep or what needed to happen by him, and I'd have no idea where he stood on any of it. Half the time I felt he couldn't care less and had lost interest in the whole thing. Then he'd make some kind of comment like 'Nobody smokes anymore' when I'd bring up Harold's idea about an adult pajama line, and I'd spend a week trying to figure out which way the wind was blowing.

"It was very clear that he didn't want to be asked straight out what he thought we should do. It was very clear that he wanted me to have a plan. But it was also clear that he liked some plans better than others. He'd dump all over a lot of Harold's ideas. I'd leave his office and find myself down on Harold for the next three days. I'd feel that he was trying to warn me away from Harold but wouldn't come right out and say so. What I'd always liked about Anderson was that he was a straight shooter. He'd always tell you exactly what he wanted, and what he said he wanted turned out to be exactly what he really did want. You didn't have to decode him. I want Anderson to sign on to my plans and he keeps saying, 'If this is where *you* want to put *your* chips.' I feel that he's putting me out on a limb all by myself and saying he's down on the ground cheering for me. A fat lot of help that is! When I tell him it must be nice for him to be out of it he gets annoyed and says, 'Don't think for a minute I'm out of it! You're turning SafeSleep from a cute afterthought into a corporate factor, and if it goes down the tubes they'll be asking me what happened.' And then I feel even less reassured because now I'm responsible for *Anderson's* not getting hurt. That's a lot of what's different about being the president. I've got to worry about Ted. I've got to worry about Anderson. The balls keep dropping into my hands and I keep throwing them back up into the air and somehow it's all supposed to keep going and no one is supposed to fall to the ground. My arms are getting awfully tired, and I'm not exactly sure what I did to deserve this wonderful job."

———————

Peter and Lynn are dealing with what we might call the hidden curriculum of adult life as it expresses itself here in the world of work. If we were to look at the whole of contemporary culture in the West as a kind of school, and consider adult *roles* as the courses in which we are *enrolled*, most adults have a full and demanding schedule. The "courses" of parenting, partnering, working, and living in an increasingly diverse society are demanding ones, yet most adults are enrolled in all of them. What does it take to succeed in these courses? What is the nature of the change struggling students would have to undergo to become successful students?

These are the kinds of questions I posed in my book *In Over Our Heads* (1994), of which Peter and Lynn are the heroes. In the last several years since the book has been published, I have heard the thinking of a few thousand adult educators—faculty and administrators—about Peter and Lynn in various workshops, institutes, and summer conferences all over the United States. Most people see Lynn as more capable and handling better the new demands at work. Although people often want to claim that Peter has a number of external problems that Lynn does not—he has more at stake, they say; his organizational culture is less supportive, they say; he has a male boss, they say, who isn't as open to conversation as Lynn's boss—most people do not attribute Lynn's greater success to these external advantages alone.

Without using the terms, people find Lynn more capable in each of four familiar quadrants of the psychological self: *cognitive* ("Lynn seems to have more of a mind of her own"; "She has a Big Picture and an overall 'take' on things, but Peter seems lost and overwhelmed"), *affective* ("Lynn takes responsibility for how she feels, understands why she feels that way and can even step out of being controlled by her feelings"; "Peter seems swamped and overrun by his feelings"; "He blames other people for how he feels"), *interpersonal* ("Peter is like a victim"; "He's too dependent"; "Lynn is able to set clear boundaries in a complicated multidimensional relationship like the one she has with her boss and friend, but Peter is not, and seems run by his relationships to people at work who are his friends"), and *intrapersonal* ("Peter doesn't seem very self-reflective"; "He's thinking about what other people are thinking, and she's thinking about her own thinking").

What sort of transformation would it take for Peter to exercise the capabilities people see in Lynn? What capabilities does Peter *already* possess and what *prior* transformations in his learning might their presence imply? Why don't his present capabilities serve him in his new circumstances?

Transformational Learning and the Problem of Its Success

Some academic writing—that which is most frequently parodied and ridiculed—uses obscure language to hide the fact that nothing terribly original is being expressed. Some unappealingly obscure academic language is in the service of genuinely new ideas; the thinkers are just better at creating new thinking than at devising the language required to express it. And on occasion a richly heuristic set of novel ideas finds an appealing language for its expression and the field takes off. In psychology, Erikson's concepts of identity and identity crisis are examples. Gardner's multiple intelligence is a more recent one. And surely transformational learning is another. Jack Mezirow's genius and our good fortune derive from this double-header ability to provide accessible new language in service of valuable new ideas. But as Mezirow well knows, this kind of success spawns its own problems. As Brookfield notes in this volume, the language can become so appealing it begins to be used for myriad purposes; its meaning can be distorted, its distinct ideas lost. It can take on quasi-religious qualities, in this case of dramatic "conversion." Transformation begins to refer to any kind of change or process at all. Piaget (1954) distinguished between assmililative processes, in which new experience is shaped to conform to existing knowledge structures, and accomodative processes, in which the structures themselves change in response to new experience. Ironically, as the language of transformation is more widely assimilated it risks *losing* its genuinely transformative potential!

In this chapter I try to protect the genuinely landscape-altering potential in the concept of transformational learning by suggesting several of its distinct features that I believe need to be more explicit:

1. Transformational kinds of learning need to be more clearly distinguished from informational kinds of learning, and each

needs to be recognized as valuable in any learning activity, discipline, or field.

2. The *form* that is undergoing transformation needs to be better understood; if there is no form there is no transformation.

3. At the heart of a form is a way of knowing (what Mezirow calls a "frame of reference"); thus genuinely transformational learning is always to some extent an epistemological change rather than merely a change in behavioral repertoire or an increase in the quantity or fund of knowledge.

4. Even as the concept of transformational learning needs to be *narrowed* by focusing more explicitly on the epistemological, it needs to be *broadened* to include the whole life span; transformational learning is not the province of adulthood or adult education alone.

5. Adult educators with an interest in transformational learning may need a better understanding of their students' current epistemologies so as not to create learning designs that unwittingly presuppose the very capacities in the students their designs might seek to promote.

6. Adult educators may better discern the nature of learners' particular needs for transformational learning by better understanding not only their students' present epistemologies but the epistemological complexity of the present learning challenges they face in their lives.

The remainder of this chapter addresses each of these points in the context of the predicaments of Peter and Lynn.

Informational Learning and Transformational Learning

Learning aimed at increasing our fund of knowledge, at increasing our repertoire of skills, at extending already established cognitive capacities into new terrain serves the absolutely crucial purpose of deepening the resources available to an existing frame of reference. Such learning is literally in-*form*-ative because it seeks to bring valuable new contents into the existing form of our way of knowing.

No learning activity, discipline, or field is well nourished without continuous opportunities to engage in this kind of learning. A concrete thinker who has the capacity to hold in his mind a narrative episode in American history can also bring the same capacity to learning narratives of other peoples and continents. Certainly no passenger wants an airline pilot whose professional training was long on collaborative reflective dialogue leading to ever more complex apprehensions of the phenomena of flight but short on the technique of landing a plane in a crosswind; no patient wants a doctor well trained in such dialogue but unable to tell a benign lump from a cancerous tumor.

However, learning aimed at changes not only in *what* we know but changes in *how* we know has an almost opposite rhythm about it and comes closer to the etymological meaning of *education* ("leading out"). "Informative" learning involves a kind of leading in, or filling of the form (see Figure 2.1). Trans-*form*-ative learning puts the form itself at risk of change (and not just change but increased capacity). If one is bound by concrete thinking in the study of, say, history, then, yes, further learning of the informative sort might involve the mastery of more historical facts, events, characters, and outcomes. But further learning of a transformative sort might also involve the development of a capacity for abstract thinking so that one can ask more general, thematic questions *about* the facts, or consider the perspectives and biases of those who wrote the historical account *creating* the facts. Both kinds of learning are expansive and valuable, one within a preexisting frame of mind and the other reconstructing the very frame.

But only the latter would I call transformative or transformational. Transformation should not refer to just any kind of change, even to any kind of dramatic, consequential change. I know a ten-year-old who decided to read the entire encyclopedia, A through Z, for a summer project. His parents' friends asked him all summer

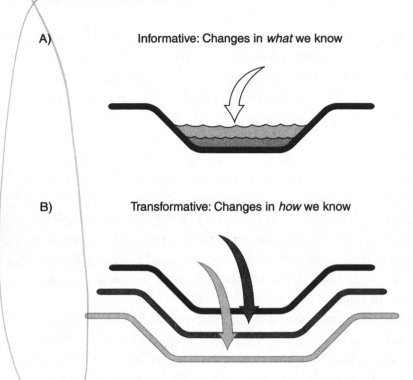

Figure 2.1. Two Kinds of Learning: Informative and Transformative.

long, in teasing admiration, "So what letter are you on now?" and listened with astonishment to his recall of facts about all things M, from magic to music. He was the talk of his neighborhood and dramatically increased his fund of content familiarities. His appetite and his recall were certainly impressive. His ability even to sustain his interest in a series of very short-term exposures was commendable. But I see nothing transformational about his learning.

Changes in one's fund of knowledge, one's confidence as a learner, one's self-perception as a learner, one's motives in learning, one's self-esteem—these are all potentially important kinds of changes, all desirable, all worthy of teachers' thinking about how to facilitate them. But it is possible for any or all of these changes to take place without any transformation because they could all occur within the existing form or frame of reference.

And much of the time there would be no problem whatever in this being exactly what occurs. Lynn, for example, already demonstrates the complex capacity to set boundaries, to keep separate her simultaneous relationship to Carolyn as friend and colleague so that the claims from one sphere are not inappropriately honored in another. She demonstrates the capacity to generate an internal vision that guides her purposes and allows her to sort through and make judgments about the choices, expectations, and proposals of others. Although it would certainly be possible for the underlying form of her way of knowing to undergo further transformation, it may not be necessary at the moment. She may be in greater need of learning additional skills at detecting more readily circumstances that are likely to risk such boundary violations, or how one more effectively gathers a consensus to bring to life the vision she is able intellectually to create. Such learnings could be extremely valuable, make her even more effective, increase her enjoyment of work and her circumstances—and none of that learning need be transformational.

Peter, on the other hand, would be ill-served by a kind of learning that was only informative. He is overreliant on the opinion of others, too dependent on signals from others to direct his own choices and behaviors. He could experience a kind of learning that might dramatically enhance his signal-detecting capabilities in twelve different ways. But dramatic as such changes might be I would not call them transformational because they do not give Peter the opportunity to reconstruct the very role of such signals in his life. Given his current work circumstances, if he cannot effect this change he is going to continue to have a difficult time.

Informational and transformational kinds of learning are each honorable, valuable, meritable, dignifiable activities. Each can be enhancing, necessary, and challenging for the teacher to facilitate. In given moments or contexts, a heavier weighting of one or the other may be called for.

What Form Transforms?
The Centrality of Epistemology

As the foregoing suggests, the saving specificity of a concept like transformational learning may lie in a more explicit understanding of the form we believe is undergoing some change. If there is no form there is no transformation. But what really constitutes a form?

Mezirow's term *frame of reference* is a useful way to engage this question. Its province is necessarily epistemological. Our frame of reference may be passionately clung to or casually held, so it clearly has an emotional or affective coloring. Our frame of reference may be an expression of our familial loyalties or tribal identifications, so it clearly has a social or interpersonal coloring. Our frame of reference may have an implicit or explicit ethical dimension, so it clearly has a moral coloring. But what is the phenomenon itself that takes on all these colorings? Mezirow, in this volume, says a frame of reference involves both a habit of mind and a point of view. Both of these suggest that, at its root, a frame of reference is a way of knowing.

"Epistemology" refers to precisely this: not *what* we know but our way of knowing. Attending to the epistemological inevitably involves attending to two kinds of processes, both at the heart of a concept like transformational learning. The first is what we might call *meaning-forming,* the activity by which we shape a coherent meaning out of the raw material of our outer and inner experiencing. Constructivism recognizes that reality does not happen preformed and waiting for us merely to copy a picture of it. Our perceiving is simultaneously an act of conceiving, of interpreting. "Percept without concept is blind," Kant said. "Our experience," Huxley said, "is less what happens to us, and more what we make of what happens to us."

The second process inherent in the epistemological is what we might call *reforming our meaning-forming.* This is a metaprocess that affects the very terms of our meaning-constructing. We do not only form meaning, and we do not only change our meanings; we change the very form by which we are making our meanings. We change our epistemologies.

These two processes inherent in epistemology are actually at the heart of two lines of social-scientific thought that should be in much closer conversations with each other: the educational line of thought is transformational learning; the psychological line of thought is constructive developmentalism. Constructive developmental psychology (Kegan, 1982, 1994; Piaget, 1954; Kohlberg, 1984; Belenky, Clinchy, Goldberger, and Tarule, 1986) attends to the natural evolution of the forms of our meaning-constructing (hence "constructive-developmental"). A more explicit rendering of transformational learning, I suggest, attends to the deliberate efforts and designs that support changes in the learner's form of knowing. Adult educators with an interest in supporting transformational learning can look to constructive-developmental theory as a source of ideas about (1) the dynamic architecture of "that form which transforms," that is, a form of knowing; and (2) the dynamic architecture of "reforming our forms of knowing," that is, the psychological process of transformations in our knowing.

Constructive-developmental theory invites those with an interest in transformational learning to consider that a form of knowing always consists of a relationship or temporary equilibrium between the subject and the object in one's knowing. The subject-object relationship forms the cognate or core of an epistemology. That which is "object" we can look at, take responsibility for, reflect upon, exercise control over, integrate with some other way of knowing. That which is "subject" we are run by, identified with, fused with, at the effect of. We cannot be responsible for that to which we are subject. What is "object" in our knowing describes the thoughts and feelings we say we have; what is "subject" describes the thinking and feeling that has us. We "have" object; we "are" subject.

Constructive-developmental theory looks at the process it calls development as the gradual process by which what was "subject" in our knowing becomes "object." When a way of knowing moves from a place where we are "had by it" (captive of it) to a place where we "have it," and can be in relationship to it, the form of our knowing has become more complex, more expansive. This somewhat formal, explicitly epistemological rendering of development comes closest, in my view, to the real meaning of transformation in transformational learning theory.

Let's consider a famous literary example of transformation in just these terms: Nora's speech to her husband Torvald in the closing scene of Ibsen's play "A Doll's House."

NORA: I mean, then I passed from Papa's hands into yours. You arranged everything the way you wanted it, so that I simply took over your taste in everything—or pretended I did—I don't really know. I think it was a little of both—first one and then the other. Now I look back on it, it's as if I've been living here like a pauper, from hand to mouth. I performed tricks for you, and you gave me food and drink. But that was how you wanted it. You and Papa have done me a great wrong. It's your fault that I have done nothing in my life.

TORVALD: Nora, how can you be so unreasonable and ungrateful? Haven't you been happy here?

NORA: No; never. I used to think I was; but I haven't ever been happy.

TORVALD: Not—not happy?

NORA: No. I've just had fun. You've always been very kind to me. But our home has never been anything but a playroom. I've been your doll-wife just as I used to be Papa's doll-child. And the children have been my dolls. I used to think it was fun when you came in and played with me, just as they think it's fun when I go in and play games with them. That's all our marriage has been, Torvald.

TORVALD: There might be a little truth in what you say, though you exaggerate and romanticize. But from now on it'll be different. Playtime is over. Now the time has come for education.

NORA: Whose education? Mine or the children's?

TORVALD: Both yours and the children's, my dearest Nora.

NORA: Oh, Torvald, you're not the man to educate me into being the right wife for you.

TORVALD: How can you say that?

NORA: And what about me? Am I fit to educate the children?

TORVALD: Nora!

NORA: Didn't you say yourself a few minutes ago that you dare not leave them in my charge?

TORVALD: In a moment of excitement. Surely you don't think I meant it seriously?

NORA: Yes. You were perfectly right. I'm not fit to educate them. There's something else I must do first. I must educate myself. And you can't help me with that. It's something I must do by myself. That's why I'm leaving you.

TORVALD [jumps up]: What did you say?

NORA: I must stand on my own feet if I am to find out the truth about myself and about life. So I can't go on living here with you any longer.

TORVALD: Nora, Nora!

NORA: I'm leaving you now, at once. Christine will put me up for tonight—

TORVALD: You're out of your mind! You can't do this! I forbid you!

NORA: It's no use your trying to forbid me any more. I shall take with me nothing but what is mine. I don't want anything from you, now or ever.

TORVALD: What kind of madness is this?

NORA: Tomorrow I shall go home—I mean, to where I was born. It'll be easiest for me to find some kind of a job there.

TORVALD: But you're blind! You have no experience of the world—

NORA: I must try to get some, Torvald.

TORVALD: But to leave your home, your husband, your children! Have you thought what people will say?

NORA: I can't help that. I only know I must do this.

TORVALD: But this is monstrous! Can you neglect your most sacred duties?

NORA: What do you call my most sacred duties?

TORVALD: Do I have to tell you? Your duties toward your husband, and your children.

NORA: I have another duty which is equally sacred.

TORVALD: You have not. What on earth could that be?

NORA: My duty towards myself.

TORVALD: First and foremost you are a wife and a mother.

NORA: I don't believe that any longer. I believe that I am first and foremost a human being, like you—or anyway, that I must try to become one. I know most people think as you do, Torvald, and I know there's something of the sort to be found in books. But I'm no longer prepared to accept what people say and what's written in books. I must think things out for myself, and try to find my own answer.

TORVALD: Do you need to ask where your duty lies in your home? Haven't you an infallible guide in such matters—your religion?

NORA: Oh, Torvald, I don't really know what religion means.

TORVALD: What are you saying?

NORA: I only know what Pastor Hansen told me when I went to confirmation. He explained that religion meant this and that. When I get away from all this and can think things out on my own, that's one of the questions I want to look into. I want to find out whether what Pastor Hansen said was right—or anyway, whether it is right for me.

TORVALD: But it's unheard of for so young a woman to behave like this! If religion cannot guide you, let me at least appeal to your conscience. I presume you have some moral feelings left? Or— perhaps you haven't? Well, answer me.

NORA: Oh, Torvald, that isn't an easy question to answer. I simply don't know. I don't know where I am in these matters. I only know that these things mean something quite different to me from what they do to you.

Note that Nora is not just coming to some new ideas, "changing her mind" in the sense that she is becoming less persuaded by formerly held ideas and more persuaded by some new set of emerging ideas. Rather, she is coming to a new set of ideas about her ideas, about where they even come from, about who authorizes them or makes them true. Her discovery is not just that she herself has some new ideas but that she has been uncritically, unawarely identified with ("subject to") external sources of ideas (her husband, her church, her culture). To be uncritically, unawarely identified with these external sources is to be unable to question or weigh the validity of these ideas because one is unable to see the sources, to take them "as object." One cannot see the sources (have them as object); rather one sees through them (is "had by" them as subject). Nora is not just rejecting the assumptions of her husband or church or culture;

she is rejecting her identification with these assumptions as truths. This process of rejection is a process of moving aspects of her knowing from subject to object. Her new "way of knowing" is not so much a matter of her new ideas, values, or beliefs (she hasn't yet figured out what these are), but that ideas, values, and beliefs are by their very nature assumptive. In fact, it is even possible that she could eventually come to the same beliefs as those held by these external sources. The beliefs she comes to endorse might be no different, and yet a transformation would still have occurred because the form of knowing that gives rise to these beliefs has been transformed (in this case, to internal authority instead of external identification); what was "subject" in her knowing has become "object."

This transformation, of which Nora gives us a glimpse through Ibsen's imagination at the end of the nineteenth century, may be no less relevant at the end of the twentieth if we think of Peter's predicament. He too is embedded in, overly defined by, and subject to external sources of value and reality definition. The implication of this line of argument is that the answer to our earlier question—What kind of transformation has to occur for Peter to understand his situation more like Lynn understands hers?—is that the form of Peter's knowing (the balance of subject and object) would need to undergo a transformation that moves what was subject in his knowing to what is object in his knowing.

Transformational Learning as a Lifelong Phenomenon

As all good teachers know, every student comes with a "learning past" that is an important part of his or her present and future learning. Important features of this past—for adult learners especially, and their teachers—include the history of their relationship to the subject at hand and the history of their personal disposition toward the enterprise of learning itself. But for the adult educator with an interest in supporting transformative learning, an important and often overlooked feature of their students' learning pasts is their history of prior transformations.

Although the more explicitly epistemological definition of transformative learning this chapter advances is intended to limit our definition of transformation (so that not every kind of change, even important change, constitutes transformation), it also expands our exploration of the phenomenon to the entire life span. Much of the literature on transformational learning really constitutes an exploration of what constructive-developmental theory and research identifies as but one of several gradual, epochal transformations in knowing of which persons are shown to be capable throughout life. This particular transformation, reflected in Nora's words and the contrast between Peter's and Lynn's constructions of their similar predicament at work, is empirically the most widespread gradual transformation we find in adulthood, so it is not surprising that adult educators have come to focus on it. But constructive-developmental theory suggests that (a) it is not the only transformation in the form of our knowing possible in adulthood; (b) even this transformation will be better understood and facilitated if its history is better honored and its future better appreciated; and (c) we will better discern the nature of learners' particular needs for transformational learning by better understanding not only their present epistemologies but the epistemological complexity of the present learning challenges they face in their lives.

The transformation reflected in Nora's words, or that Peter would undergo were he to construct experience more like Lynn, is a shift away from being "made up by" the values and expectations of one's "surround" (family, friends, community, culture) that get uncritically internalized and with which one becomes identified, toward developing an internal authority that makes choices about these external values and expectations according to one's own self-authored belief system. One goes from being psychologically "written by" the socializing press to "writing upon" it, a shift from a socialized to a self-authoring epistemology, in the lingo of constructive-developmental theory. (Or in the lingo of the theory of Belenky and colleagues in this volume, a shift from received learning to procedural knowing).

As pervasive and powerful as this gradual transformation may be, it is only one of several shifts in the deep underlying epistemology (the form that transforms) we use to organize meaning. Longitudinal and cross-sectional research, using a reliable interview instrument to discern what epistemologies an individual has access to (Lahey and others, 1988), identifies five distinctly different epistemologies (Kegan, 1994). As Figure 2.2 suggests, each of these can be described with respect to what is subject and what is object, and each shift entails the movement of what had been subject in the old epistemology to object in the new epistemology. Thus the basic principle of complexification of mind here is not the mere addition of new capacities (an aggregation model), nor the substitution of a new capacity for an old one (a replacement model), but the subordination of once-ruling capacities to the dominion of more complex capacities, an evolutionary model that again distinguishes transformation from other kinds of change.

An array of increasingly complex epistemologies, such as those described in Figure 2.2, works against the unhelpful tendency to see a person like Peter, who orders experience predominantly from the socialized epistemology, only in terms of what he cannot do, and to see a person like Lynn, who predominantly orders experience from the self-authoring epistemology, only in terms of what she can.

Surely any educator who wished to be helpful to Peter, especially one wishing to facilitate transformational learning, would do well to know and respect where Peter is coming from, not just where it may be valuable for him to go. A constructive-developmental perspective on transformational learning creates an image of this kind of learning over a lifetime as the gradual traversing of a succession of increasingly more elaborate bridges. Three injunctions follow from this image. First, we need to know which bridge we are on. Second, we need to know how far along the learner is in traversing that particular bridge. Third, we need to know that, if it is to be a bridge that is safe to walk across, it must be well anchored on both sides, not just the culminating side. We cannot overattend to where we want the student to be—the far side of the bridge—and ignore where the student is. If Peter is at the very beginning—the near side—of the bridge that traverses the socialized and the self-authoring epistemologies, it may be important to consider that this also means he is at the far side of a prior bridge. Only by respecting what he has already gained and what he would have to lose were he to venture forth is it likely we could help him continue his journey.

Although it is easy and tempting to define Peter by what he does not or cannot do (especially in comparison to Lynn), it is also true that his socialized epistemology permits him all the following capacities: he can think abstractly, construct values and ideals, introspect, subordinate his short-term interests to the welfare of a relationship, and orient to and identify with the expectations of those social groups and interpersonal relationships of which he wishes to feel himself a part.

From the vantage point of empirical research we know that it ordinarily takes the first two decades of living to develop these complex capacities and some people have not developed them even by then (Kegan, 1982, 1994). Many parents, for example, would be overjoyed were their teenagers to have these capacities. Consider as an example parents' wish that their children be trustworthy and hold up their end of family agreements, such as abiding by a curfew on Saturday night. What appears to be a call for a specific behavior ("Be home by midnight or phone us") or the acquisition of a specific knowledge ("Know that it is important to us that you do what you say you will") actually turns out to be something more epistemological. Parents do not simply want their kids to get themselves home by midnight on Saturday night; they want them to do it for a specific reason. If their kids abide by a curfew only because the parents have an effective enough monitoring system to detect if they do not and a sufficiently noxious set of consequences to impose when they do not, the parents would ultimately be disappointed

SUBJECT	OBJECT	UNDERLYING STRUCTURE
PERCEPTIONS *Fantasy* SOCIAL PERCEPTIONS/IMPULSES	Movement Sensation	Single point/immediate/atomistic
CONCRETE *Actuality* Data, cause-and-effect POINT OF VIEW Role-concept Simple reciprocity (tit-for-tat) ENDURING DISPOSITIONS Needs, preferences Self-concept	Perceptions Social perceptions Impulses	Durable category
ABSTRACTIONS *Ideality* Inference, generalization Hypothesis, proposition Ideals, values **MUTUALITY/INTERPERSONALISM** **Role consciousness** **Mutual reciprocity** INNER STATES *Subjectivity, self-consciousness*	Concrete Point of view Enduring dispositions Needs, preferences	Cross-categorical Trans-categorical

TRADITIONALISM

The Socialized Mind

Figure 2.2. Five Increasingly Complex Epistemologies.

MODERNISM — The Self-Authoring Mind

ABSTRACT SYSTEMS
Ideology
Formulation, authorization
Relations between abstractions

INSTITUTION
Relationship-regulating forms
Multiple-role consciousness

SELF-AUTHORSHIP
Self-regulation, self-formation
Identity, autonomy, individuation

POST-MODERNISM — The Self-Transforming Mind

DIALECTICAL
Trans-ideological/post-ideological
Testing formulation, paradox
Contradiction, oppositeness

INTER-INSTITUTIONAL
Relationship between forms
Interpenetration of self and other

SELF-TRANSFORMATION
Interpenetration of selves
Inter-individuation

Abstractions

Mutuality
Interpersonalism

Inner states
Subjectivity
Self-consciousness

Abstract system
ideology

Institution
relationship-
regulating forms

Self-authorship
Self-regulation
Self-formation

System/complex

Trans-system
Trans-complex

LINES OF DEVELOPMENT	
K	COGNITIVE
E	**INTERPERSONAL**
Y	*INTRAPERSONAL*

even though the kids are behaving correctly. Parents of teens want to resign from the role of "parent police." They want their kids to hold up their end of the agreement, not simply because they can frighten them into doing so but because the kids have begun to intrinsically prioritize the importance of being trustworthy. This is not first of all a claim on their kids' behavior; it is a claim on their minds. Nor will the mere acquisition of the knowledge content ("It is important to my parents that I do what I say I will") be sufficient to bring the child home by midnight. Many nonbehaving teens know precisely what their parents value. They just do not themselves hold these values! They hold them extrinsically, as land mines they need to take account of, to maneuver around so they do not explode.

What the parents are really hoping for from their teens is a transformation, a shift away from an epistemology oriented to self-interest, the short term, and others-as-supplies-to-the-self (the Instrumental Mind in Figure 2.2). This epistemology they ordinarily develop in late childhood. Rather they need to relativize or subordinate their own immediate interests on behalf of the interests of a social relationship, the continued participation in which they value more highly than the gratification of an immediate need. When they make this epistemological shift, sustaining a mutual bond of trust with their parents becomes more important than partying till dawn.

And when adolescents do make this shift (to the Socialized Mind in Figure 2.2), interestingly, we consider them to be responsible. For a teen the very capacity to be "written upon," to be "made up by," constitutes responsibility. It is Peter's misfortune that this perfectly dignifiable and complicated epistemology is a better match with the hidden curriculum of adolescence than that of modern adulthood, which makes demands on us to win some distance from the socializing press and actually regards people who uncritically internalize and identify with the values and expectations of others as insufficiently responsible! Parents who, for example, cannot set limits on their children, who cannot defy them, or who are susceptible to being "made up" by their wishes we regard as irresponsible. Nora's words suggest just this discovery of a whole different "responsibility curriculum." After years of responsibly meeting the expectations her father, husband, priest, and culture had for her as adolescent and adult woman, she has come to the challenges of a new course of study: the responsibility she has to herself. To master this new curriculum she needs, as Peter needs, a new epistemology. But this does not mean that she and Peter did not earlier undergo an important transformation (to the socialized epistemology), and it does not mean they did not learn well or did not learn enough. In fact, by all accounts they were both very successful learners. Their present difficulties arise because the complexity of the "life curriculum" they face has gotten qualitatively more challenging. In the words of Ronald Heifetz (1995), what they face are not technical challenges (the sort that can be addressed by what I call "informational learning"), but adaptive challenges, the kind that require not merely knowing more but knowing differently. For this reason they are in need of supports to transformational learning.

The particular epistemological transformation Nora is beginning and Peter needs help to begin—the transformation to a self-authoring frame of reference (to use Mezirow's term)—is the particular transformation we often find unwittingly privileged in writings on adult learning. In Chapter One, Mezirow talks about our need to pierce a taken-for-granted relationship to the assumptions that surround us. "We must become critically reflective of the assumptions of the person communicating" to us, he says. "We need to know whether the person who gives us a diagnosis about our health is a trained medical worker, or that one who gives us direction at work is authorized to do so." In essence, Mezirow says, we need to "take as object . . . what is taken for granted, like conventional wisdom; [or] a particular religious worldview," rather than being subject to it. This is not only a call for an epistemological shift, it is a call for a *particular* epistemological shift, the move from the socialized to the self-authoring mind. This is a call that makes nothing but good sense provided the adult learner is not too far from the entrance to this particular epistemological bridge (nor has already traversed it).

And even when it does make good curricular sense we must be careful not to create learning designs that get out too far ahead of the learner. For example, when Mezirow says transformational educators want to support the learner's ability "to negotiate his or her own purposes, values, feelings, and meanings rather than simply to act on those of others," he again sounds the call for the move toward self-authoring, and he quite understandably invokes a model of education that will support this shift: "The generally accepted model of adult education involves a transfer of authority from the educator to the learners." But even when this particular shift is the appropriate transformational bridge for our student, all of us, as adult educators, need help in discerning how rapidly or gradually this shift in authority should optimally take place for that student, which is a function of how far he or she is along this particular bridge.

The shift in authority to which Mezirow refers reflects the familiar call in the adult education literature for us to regard and respect all our adult students as self-directed learners, almost by virtue of their adult status alone. Gerald Grow (1991) defines self-directed learners as those who are able to "examine themselves, their culture and their milieu in order to understand how to separate what they feel from what they should feel, what they value from what they should value, and what they want from what they should want. They develop critical thinking, individual initiative, and a sense of themselves as co-creators of the culture that shapes them."

But when the adult education experts tell us they want students to "understand how to separate what they feel from what they should feel, what they value from what they should value, and what they want from what they should want," do they take seriously enough the possibility that when the socialized mind dominates our meaning-making, what we should feel is what we do feel, what we should value is what we do value, and what we should want is what we do want? Their goal therefore may not be a matter of getting students merely to identify and value a distinction between two parts that already exist, but of fostering a qualitative evolution of mind that actually creates the distinction. Their goal may involve something more than the cognitive act of "distinction," a bloodless word that fails to capture the human wrenching of the self from its cultural surround. Although this goal is perfectly suited to assisting adults in meeting the bigger culturewide "curriculum" of the modern world, educators may need a better understanding of how ambitious their aspiration is and how costly the project may seem to their students.

Adult students are not all automatically self-directing merely by virtue of being adults, or even easily trained to become so. Educators seeking self-direction from their adult students are not merely asking them to take on new skills, modify their learning style, or increase their self-confidence. They are asking many of them to change the whole way they understand themselves, their world, and the relationship between the two. They are asking many of them to put at risk the loyalties and devotions that have made up the very foundation of their lives. We acquire personal authority, after all, only by relativizing—that is, only by fundamentally altering—our relationship to public authority. This is a long, often painful voyage, and one that, much of the time, may feel more like mutiny than a merely exhilarating (and less self-conflicted) expedition to discover new lands.

Note how lost at sea Peter becomes when his long-time mentor unwittingly assumes his capacity for self-directed learning. Anderson no doubt sees himself as an emancipatory, empowering employer-as-adult-educator who scrupulously and consistently stands by his transfer of authority, taking care not to undermine Peter by taking on business that should properly be referred to him and refusing even Peter's veiled requests to step in and once again provide a map and a destination. What Anderson sees as his testimony to Peter's capacity for self-direction, Peter sees as a bewildering vacuum of externally supplied expectation and an indirect message from his boss that he no longer cares that much what happens to Peter. I have heard countless complaints about Anderson's ineffectiveness as a good leader, that he has asked too much of Peter all at once; and yet when we have the opportunity to examine our own leadership as adult educators few of us can escape the conclusion that we have ourselves—on many occasions with the most emancipatory of intentions—been Andersons in our own classrooms.

Finally, an array of epistemologies such as that depicted in Figure 2.2 reminds us that even as our designs can get too far ahead of where some of our students are, so they can also fall too far behind; even as we can fail to do Peter justice by seeing him only in terms of what he cannot do, we can fail to do justice to Lynn's learning opportunities by seeing her only in terms of those capacities she has already developed. The move toward the self-authoring mind—valorized though it may unwittingly be in the subtexts of our aspirations for transformational learning—is not the only fundamental epistemological shift in adulthood. Nor are the learning challenges that call for the self-authoring mind the only challenges adults of this new century will face.

The self-authoring mind is equipped, essentially, to meet the challenges of modernism. Unlike traditionalism, in which a fairly homogeneous set of definitions of how one should live is consistently promulgated by the cohesive arrangements, models, and codes of the community or tribe, modernism is characterized by ever-proliferating pluralism, multiplicity, and competition for our loyalty to a given way of living. Modernism requires that we be more than well socialized; we must also develop the internal authority to look at and make judgments about the expectations and claims that bombard us from all directions. Yet adult learners today and tomorrow encounter not only the challenges of modernism but of postmodernism as well. Postmodernism calls on us to win some distance even from our own internal authorities so that we are not completely captive of our own theories, so that we can recognize their incompleteness, so that we can even embrace contradictory systems simultaneously. These challenges—a whole different "curriculum"—show up in as private a context as our conflicted relationships, where we may or may not be able to hold the embattled sides internally rather than projecting one side onto our adversary; and in as public a context as higher education itself, where we may or may not be able to see that our intellectual disciplines are inevitably, to some extent, ideological procedures for creating and validating what counts as real knowledge. Lynn too, it seems, has further bridges to cross. She has her own particular needs for transformational learning, however different from Peter's these may be. She challenges educators to create yet another set of learning designs should they seek to support her own bigger becoming.

"The spirit," Hegel wrote in *The Phenomenology of Mind*, "is never at rest but always engaged in ever progressive motion, in giving itself a new form." How might we understand transformational learning differently—and our opportunities as educators—were we better to understand the restless, creative processes of development itself, in which all our students partake before, during, and after their participation in our classrooms?

References

Belenky, M. F., Clinchy, B. McV., Goldberger, N. R., and Tarule, J. M. *Women's Ways of Knowing*. New York: Basic Books, 1986.

Grow, G. "Teaching Learners to Be Self-Directed." *Adult Education Quarterly*, 1991, *41*, 125–149.

Heifetz, R. A. *Leadership Without Easy Answers*. Cambridge, Mass.: Harvard University Press, 1995.

Kegan, R. *The Evolving Self*. Cambridge, Mass.: Harvard University Press, 1982.

Kegan, R. *In Over Our Heads*. Cambridge, Mass.: Harvard University Press, 1994.

Kohlberg, L. *The Psychology of Moral Development*. New York: HarperCollins, 1984.

Lahey, L., and others. *A Guide to the Subject-Object Interview*. Cambridge, Mass.: Subject-Object Workshop, 1988.

Piaget, J. *The Construction of Reality in the Child*. New York: Basic Books, 1954.

3

Inequality, Development, and Connected Knowing

Mary Field Belenky, Ann V. Stanton

Mezirow grapples with a major question facing us at the century's beginning: How can we develop adequate and reliable knowledge in a world that is changing at an ever-accelerating rate? As the speed and modes of communication increase, people from vastly different cultures cross paths in ways unimaginable one hundred years ago. In this world there are no fixed truths. As people enter new arenas their mental maps no longer chart the terrain they are trying to explore. Revised maps become outdated before the ink is dry (see Kegan, 1994).

Mezirow provides us with a means of coping. We must, he says, develop the capacity to reflect critically on the lenses we use to filter, engage, and interpret the world. When our old ways of meaning-making no longer suffice, it behooves us to engage with others in reflective discourse, assessing the assumptions and premises that guide our ways of constructing knowledge and revising those deemed inadequate. Reflective discourse develops best when participants are well informed, free from coercion, listen actively, have equal opportunities to participate, and take a critical stance toward established cultural norms or viewpoints. He points to university seminars as a model of discourse devoted to assessing and improving the ways we justify interpretations and beliefs.

This collaborative process of assessing and reformulating one's basic assumptions about the knowledge-making process permits more inclusive, discriminating, permeable, and integrative ways of knowing the world. Reflective discourse and critical thinking thus provide the tools for continued intellectual and ethical development throughout adulthood, enabling participants to meet the challenges of a complex and changing society in creative ways. Transformative learning is an apt name for this highly evolved approach to knowledge making, as it enables continued growth and development. Mezirow's central insight is profound: we are all active constructors of knowledge who can become responsible for the procedures and assumptions that shape the way we make meaning out of our experiences.

Asymmetrical Relationships and Development

Although Mezirow's important theory provides an elegant, detailed description of one important endpoint of a long developmental process, it does not trace the many steps people take before they can "know what they know" in the highly elaborated form he describes. Imagining how the silenced and the young might be brought into full dialogue with others requires a detailed understanding of the growth over time of the meaning-making perspectives that shape the way people construct knowledge. A number of researchers have studied how these meaning-making structures evolve over the life span (Baxter Magolda, 1992; Belenky, Clinchy, Goldberger, and Tarule, 1996; Basseches, 1984; Kegan, 1982, 1994; King and Kitchener, 1994; Kuhn, 1996; Loevinger, 1976; Perry, 1970). Depicting a culminating meaning-making framework that has a good deal in common with Mezirow's, these researchers have also studied the many steps people take as they go about developing their capacities for reflective discourse.

Focusing narrowly on the endpoint of development as Mezirow does may be problematic for a theory that commands so much attention from adult educators. Unless it is understood that Mezirow's theory only depicts the culmination point, practitioners might overlook the reality of their students' lives. Most adults simply have not developed their capacities for articulating and criticizing the underlying assumptions of their own thinking, nor do they analyze the thinking of others in these ways. Furthermore, many have never had experience with the kinds of reflective discourse that Mezirow prescribes. This may be particularly true for adults returning to school relatively late in life. Many adult students delay their education because of traumatizing early school experiences. Many are the first in their family to seek further education. They often come from cultural communities that do not stress the kinds of values and activities associated with reflective discourse, especially its emphasis on developing and articulating ideas in a highly collaborative fashion. Many schools do not build such experiences into the curriculum.

Transformational theory also presumes relations of equality among participants in reflective discourse when, in actuality, most human relationships are asymmetrical. The university seminar, which Mezirow holds up as a model, is the result of a selection process that takes place over decades, leaving many by the wayside. Focusing on highly skilled mature thinkers, Mezirow does not concern himself with the problem of inequality. He writes in this volume: "Preconditions for realizing these values [of transformative learning] and finding one's voice for free full participation in discourse include elements of maturity, education, safety, health, economic security and emotional intelligence. Hungry, homeless, desperate, threatened, sick, frightened adults are less likely to be able to participate effectively in discourse to help us [sic] better understand the meaning of our own experiences."

Ignoring the problem of asymmetrical relationships has serious consequences. We fail to support many people in developing the full range of their potential. We do not struggle with injustice. We fail to harvest the knowledge that people (mostly women) have garnered while engaged in maternal practice in a democratic milieu: raising up the young in ways that will enable them to enter into positions of full and permanent equality with others in society (Greene,

1988, 1995; Martin, 1984; Noddings, 1984; Ruddick, 1995; Schweickart, 1996).

We argue that discourse communities can include the immature
and the marginalized. Participation in this kind of ongoing reflective dialogue would enable them (and us) better to understand the
meaning of their experiences as well as the nature of the society
they live in. Not only would participation and reflective dialogue
support their development as individuals, it could also support the
development of a more inclusive, just, and democratic society.

In this chapter we look closely at women's ways of knowing
(Belenky, Clinchy, Goldberger, and Tarule, 1986; Goldberger,
Tarule, Clinchy, and Belenky, 1996), a theory of development tracing the struggles of women to gain a voice and claim the powers of
mind. We also draw on experiences of educational programs (Stanton, 1996) and community organizations (Belenky, Bond, and Weinstock, 1997) that are well designed to grapple with the problem of
asymmetrical relationships. As a consequence, these programs have
been highly successful in drawing out the voices and minds of marginalized peoples, enabling them to participate in reflective discourse communities and become more fully integrated into the
social, economic, and political life of the whole society.

Dualistic Thinking and "Girl Stain"

When Enlightenment thinkers deemed all men to be created equal,
they too ignored the reality of inequality, as had the classical Greeks
before them (see, for instance, Martin, 1984; Noddings, 1984; and
Okin, 1989). This is also true of activists who have actually tried to
create deeply democratic communities. The kibbutz movement provides a striking example (Blasi, 1986). To realize their dream of living
together in a highly democratic fashion, the movement's founders
had to invent the form, as the highly stratified and hierarchical institutions of those times provided few models for guidance. The early
kibbutz members' commitment to equality was taken so seriously and
so literally that clothes were distributed to community members without any regard to body size!

The dilemma is a profound one. Equality should be proclaimed and ingrained. It should become the very bedrock of institutional life in any democracy. At the same time we must cultivate tools for dealing with the inequalities that exist and the new ones that are bound to rise.

Why do so many theorists take mature, independent thinkers as the subjects of their theories without any mention of how they got that way? Nel Noddings (1999), a feminist philosopher, argues that many people do not understand the processes involved in bringing people into maturity and relationships of equality. Lacking that knowledge, they assume that the process must be a dictatorial one. Thinkers who celebrate reason and disdain resorting to faith, tradition, and coercion ignore the problem of inequality because they reject authoritarian relationships.

We argue that people also find it difficult to think about asymmetrical relationships because the issue gets mired in dualistic thinking, that is, the persistent tendency of human beings to divide their experience into dichotomies or nonoverlapping categories of polar opposites (Belenky, Bond, and Weinstock, 1997). Male-female, thinking-feeling, and public-private are examples of interest here. Although polarities like public-private may seem complementary, they actually function as a hierarchy. One pole is prized; the other represents its opposite. One is sought; the other is avoided. In an "either/or" world the valued pole is regularly and profoundly identified with maleness. This pole sets the standard. It stands in opposition to its negative—the pole associated with femaleness. This hierarchy is communicated by the universal practice of uttering the value associated with maleness first. We say "male and female," not "female and male." The same is true of "mind and body," "thinking and feeling," "public and private," "productive and reproductive," "separate and connected," and "big and little" (see Bakan, 1966; Basseches, 1984; Haste, 1994; Keller, 1985; Labouvie-Vief, 1994; and Merchant, 1980).

In dichotomies the asymmetrical terms are either "unmarked" or "marked" (Bem, 1993). The positive pole remains unmarked. It can denote the scale as a whole, with the marked term used to indicate the negative end of the continuum. "Good" and "bad" provide an example. "How good is Chris?" is a question that uses the unmarked term. It implies nothing about Chris's goodness. But if someone asked, "How bad is Chris?" we would assume that Chris is quite bad. Qualities at the negative pole are flagged so that it is easy to avoid any association with the negative.

Philosopher Helen Haste (1994) says that "metaphors of pollution" abound whenever hierarchical models cast qualities in terms of polarity, antithesis, and negation. Barrie Thorne (1993) observed many pollution metaphors while studying children's play, calling the phenomenon "girl stain." Boys are easily "contaminated" by any association with girls or girls' things and see any peer contaminated with girl stain as a lesser person. Girls, however, often rise in stature when they join boys' games, wear boys' clothes, or play with boys' playthings.

Things associated with males are "unmarked." Because masculinity is highly valued, one need not be poised to avoid being polluted. Feminine things are always "marked" so one can be on guard. Although the ideal of mankind includes women, men would feel polluted if they were seen as part of womankind. Many men avoid asymmetrical relationships and caring work because of their association with women.

To avoid the issue of inequality, Western thinkers divide the world into two separate arenas—the public and the private (Greene, 1988; Noddings, 1984). In all of the early democracies men (with property) entered the public arena as rational, autonomous individuals endowed with citizenship and a series of inalienable rights. Women, children, servants, slaves, and serfs were confined to the private world of the family. Their rights were limited or nonexistent.

The task of caring for dependent members of the family and the broader community was assigned to the women. Even though women were themselves a subordinated class of people with few rights, they worked to raise others up so they might enter into relationships of full and permanent equality (Miller, 1976). In the process women garnered extensive knowledge about human development and the process of dissolving asymmetrical relationships. This knowledge has, however, remained largely ghettoized in the private world of the family. Many people do not even consider the kind of thinking that is useful for dealing with asymmetrical relationships to be either thought or knowledge. The same kind of polarized thinking that enabled the separation of the public from private life encourages people to conceptualize thinking and feeling as polar opposites (Haste, 1994). Any kind of practice that draws on one's emotional capacities, the subjective, and the particular—which good parenting always does—is simply not seen as involving thinking. Because women's capacity for thought was downplayed, it was assumed that women's caretaking was guided by maternal instincts, intuition, and mother's love but not by reflection and reason (Ruddick, 1995).

Articulating Women's Knowledge

Simplistic, black-and-white categories may continue to shape the thinking of people long after they have they have developed far more complex habits of mind. In every area of life, the old dualistic categories and assumptions must be reevaluated and replaced with more integrative ways of thinking before they will lose their staying power. Needless to say, feminist thinkers have led the reexamination of the kinds of dualistic categories that shape the ways we have conceptualized men and women, public and private, thinking and feeling, speaking and listening. The feminist project has been primarily concerned with reclaiming those aspects of our humanity that were shunted aside because of "girl stain." In essence, feminist thinkers keep asking, "What is lost when only men and men's experiences are used to define the human experience? What is important about women and women's experiences for the humanity of both men and women?"

Philosopher Sara Ruddick (1995) confronted these issues head-on when she reconsidered the work of mothering. She argued that maternal work is a discipline. Like all other disciplines, it is associated with a body of knowledge, a philosophy, and a set of practices. Maternal thinking establishes criteria for determining failure and success, sets priorities, and identifies the virtues required by the discipline. Maternal thinking is one kind of disciplined reflection among many, each with identifying questions, methods, and aims. It is, Ruddick says, "a revolutionary discourse" that has been silenced. Women have had to struggle to make their own viewpoint heard, even to themselves.

The Ethic of Care

Carol Gilligan (1982, 1993) uncovered a good deal of this discourse when interviewing women about a serious moral dilemma they were actually confronting. When Gilligan tried to place the women's reasoning on Lawrence Kohlberg's (1984) map of moral development, she found the map inadequate for characterizing women's experience. Kohlberg had constructed this important theory from extensive interviews with boys and men trying to resolve a series of hypothetical moral dilemmas. Like most researchers of his time, Kohlberg studied only men but generalized his findings to all humans.

To capture the considerations she had been hearing in the women's voice, Gilligan described what she called "the ethic of care" or "the response mode" to moral conflicts. In this mode conflicts are resolved through dialogue, as illustrated by this response to one of Kohlberg's hypothetical moral dilemmas: "Should Heinz steal some medicine to save the life of his dying wife? The druggist is charging an exorbitant price and won't let the husband defer payments." Should Heinz steal the drug for his wife? "I don't know. Maybe he could talk with the druggist. They might be able to work something out. Why is the druggist is charging such an outrageous amount? Maybe his wife is also dying. Heinz should also talk with his wife. What does she want? What is her condition? Maybe her life will be terribly impaired if she were to survive. Who would take care of their children if she died and he was in jail?"

In this mode, questioning, listening, and responding to everyone's concerns is seen as the way to bring about lasting and satisfying solutions to moral predicaments. Resolutions are reached through conversation, storytelling, and perspective sharing. One works especially hard to understand and present the perspective of those who are incapable of articulating their own thoughts well. This approach is questioning rather than assertive. Decisions are always changing because people and circumstances keep changing. All these themes will reappear when we discuss how educators and public leaders empower people to become articulate, reflective constructors of knowledge.

Gilligan compares the ethic of care with the notions of morality that Kohlberg found in the male voice. She calls the orientation he depicted "the ethic of justice" or "the rights mode." Here moral conflicts are resolved through the lone individual's impartial application of rules and principles whose hierarchy can be determined logically. An example: "Yes, it would be right for a man to steal [the outrageously priced medicine] if that was the only way he could save the life of his wife—or indeed, the life of anyone including a stranger. Logically the right to life must take precedence over property rights. Property can have no value unless human life is protected." In the rights mode everyone is to be treated equally and impartially. The central metaphor suggesting this approach is "Justice" standing blindfolded on a pedestal.

If everyone is really quite equal it is reasonable to formulate a body of principles based on commonalities. But in caring for those who are immature, impaired, or who have other vulnerabilities, one has to think and act on the level of the particular and the individual (Schweickart, 1996).

Needless to say, moral decisions made in the rights mode appear clear and certain whereas those in the response mode seem weak and indecisive. Although the rights mode provides principles for autonomous decision making, the responsibility mode outlines the methodology that draws everyone into the decision-making process. The rights mode emphasizes speaking; the response mode stresses listening. Nurturing the development of immature and subordinated peoples requires a profound openness to dialogue and connection rather than monologue, exhortation, and distance. Articulating what she heard in the women's voice, Gilligan was able to describe aspects of moral thought of great importance to both men and women. It was, however, thinking that had been muted and hard to hear in studies that looked only at men and men's experiences.

Women's Ways of Knowing

Another interview study, *Women's Ways of Knowing (WWK)*, revealed similar themes (Belenky, Clinchy, Goldberger, and Tarule, 1996). Following Gilligan's lead, *WWK* wondered if the inclusion of the women's voice might expand and elaborate another important developmental theory constructed out of data from males: William Perry's (1970) theory devised after interviewing college students each spring about how their thinking had changed during the past year. Perry's scheme showed students outgrowing the simplistic dualisms that once led them to see the world as sharply divided between "Authority/Right/We" and "Illegitimate/Wrong/Other." Perry's work seemed especially important to the *WWK* collective because black-and-white dualistic thinking undergirds authoritarianism and many other forms of prejudice besides sexism (see, for instance, Adorno, Frenkel-Brunswik, Levinson, and Sanford, 1950; Allport, 1958; Brown, 1965).

The collaborative conducted extensive interviews with 130 women from all walks of life. Each woman was asked to describe how she herself goes about getting knowledge and ideas. What had helped her gain a voice and develop the powers of mind? What had held her back? As the collaborative read and reread the verbatim interview transcriptions, they kept questions in the backs of their minds:

- How does this woman get her ideas? How does she think authorities get their ideas?

- Does this woman see truth and knowledge as something that can be discussed and passed from one person to another?

- Does she listen to her own inner voice, understanding that insight and truth can spring up from her own mind?

- Does she try to enter into another person's frame of mind, see the world as he or she sees it—even if the other person is coming from a very different place?

- Does she try to develop, test, and assess ideas? Can she follow a line of reasoning, looking for flaws of logic, looking for errors of omission? Does she take a critical stance with her own ideas? With those of peers? And those of authorities?

- Does she play "midwife," helping others give birth to new ideas? Does she ask good questions to draw out people's thinking? Does she try to understand what someone is thinking even when the person has not found the words needed to articulate the ideas well? Does she look for the strengths rather than the flaws in the lines of reasoning that others are developing? Does she document fledgling ideas so people can better see their creations in the making?

The research collaborative tried to place what the women said on Perry's map of development. Like Gilligan, they tried to be particularly aware when they had to push and shove to fit the women's thinking into the established scheme. Although Perry had described much of the women's experience quite beautifully, it became clear that the map did not cover the whole terrain. The collaborative began sketching in the missing details. The revised scheme grouped women's perspectives on knowing into five major epistemological categories or meaning-making frameworks. Although WWK looked only at women, it revealed aspects of thought that are of the utmost importance to all humanity, even if these qualities have been less prominent in the thinking of men.

We will lay the scheme out in some detail, as it describes the steps people must take before they can become full participants in the kind of discourse communities Mezirow advocates. In particular, the scheme depicts "connected knowing," an approach to Procedural Knowledge that provides tools for bringing even the very young and the silenced into voice so that they might develop their capacities for participating on an equal basis with others in society.

"Silenced"* describes an outlook that is unlike anything Perry saw among the college students he interviewed. Although Silenced women might see themselves learning from their own concrete actions, they do not believe themselves capable of learning from experiences mediated by language. Unable to give words to what they know, these women think of themselves as voiceless. They also find it difficult to acquire new understandings by listening to what others might have to say. Feeling incapable of both hearing and speaking, these women live profoundly isolated lives. A woman we call Susan provides an example (in the excerpts that follow, sentences in all-capital letters are the interviewer's prompts of the interviewees):

---

*In *Women's Ways of Knowing* this outlook was named "Silence." We have taken the liberty of changing the name to "Silenced." The added "d" helps distinguish this way of knowing from the approaches others have observed in some non-Western cultures (Goldberger, 1996; Schweickart, 1996). Here silence is associated with powerful modes of connecting with and apprehending the world that do not depend on language.

I felt kind of dumb, very, very. 'Cause for when I went to school, I was picked on for, [sigh] I don't know how long. . . . I felt dumb when I'd talk. You know, if I'd say something, it just didn't come out right. It just didn't sound right, and I felt like, oh, Susan, get out of here. . . . THINK ABOUT THE TIMES WHEN YOU ARE TRYING TO UNDERSTAND SOMETHING NEW. HOW DO YOU GO ABOUT IT? Well, I can cut hair but nobody's ever taught me. . . . I can knit, I can make slippers, and I don't even know how to do it. I couldn't even tell somebody how to do it because I don't even know how to do it myself. BUT YOU DO IT. Right. Well, um, I know how I do it but I couldn't tell you right now how to do it. You would have to watch me [Belenky, Bond, and Weinstock, 1997, pp. 141–142].

Invariably, Silenced women like Susan grew up in the midst of great violence. They were used to using words as weapons rather than as a means for passing meanings back and forth between people. The Silenced do not have the tools they need for participating in the kind of discourse community Mezirow describes. To bring them into an ongoing dialogue requires the creation of an extremely safe and caring community where people draw each other out and listen to one another with the greatest of care. That experience can be profoundly transformative (see Belenky, Bond, and Weinstock, 1997).

Received Knowers describes people who can and do understand things when they are explained. They learn by listening to those who know and remembering what they have to say. People who hold this outlook are not aware that they themselves can generate ideas of their own. Indeed, they do not even realize that the authorities *develop* knowledge. They simply assume that authorities *get* knowledge by listening to other authorities. Needless to say, these women are quite dependent on others for both knowledge and direction. Rachel explains how she gets ideas:

Well, I can understand things if somebody explains it to me. I know I can do good in school. . . . The work and stuff I always understood. . . . WOULD YOU COMMENT ON THIS STATEMENT MADE BY ANOTHER WOMAN: I LIKE TEACHERS WHO DRAW OUT YOUR IDEAS—TEACHERS WHO GET YOU ALL TOGETHER WORKING OUT YOUR PROBLEMS AND PROJECTS, FINDING YOUR OWN ANSWERS. I don't think that's right. No. The teacher should be teaching you how to—what to learn and stuff. How can you learn on your own? You have to have somebody teaching you. . . . The teachers have, you know, been to school and stuff—whereas they know how to teach it [Belenky, Bond, and Weinstock, 1997, p. 144].

Like Perry's Dualists, the categories that Received Knowers use for organizing their thinking about the world are cast in highly dichotomous terms. Things are either true or false, black or white. These women see truth spelled with a capital "T." Mezirow's idea of critically examining the assumptions used by authorities and others would baffle a Received Knower like Rachel. Who is she to question authority? Why would anyone think their ideas could be wrong? Many Received Knowers have even been taught that it is immoral to question authority.

Subjective Knowledge describes the outlook held by adults who are aware that they themselves can give birth to ideas of their own. They listen to their inner voice, articulate their own thoughts, and criticize their former dependence on authorities for knowledge and direction. Locating the source of knowledge, standards, and authority within the self is very liberating, often resulting in an explosion of energy. A woman we call Molly gives the flavor of this outlook:

HOW WOULD YOU DESCRIBE YOURSELF AS A KNOWER? My sister-in-law says I have a mind of my own. I might talk to her about my problems, just to talk about it, but I don't go looking for answers from anybody else, 'cause I have to get them from myself, in order for me to be happy. . . . WHEN YOU AND OTHERS DIS- AGREE, HOW DO YOU KNOW WHO IS RIGHT? Everyone is entitled to their own opinion. Who's to say one is better than another? CAN YOU SAY SOME AN- SWERS OR OPINIONS ARE *EVER* BETTER THAN OTHERS? Who's to say what's wrong and what's right anyway? It's what *you* believe and think. I mean, there are so many different kinds of people! [unpublished data].

Received Knowers think there is only one truth; Subjective Know- ers believe there are as many truths as there are people. They see their personal point of view as unique and precious. One's truth should not be compared or judged. It is the only truth that matters. Having previously been so susceptible to the standards and critiques promulgated by others, Subjective Knowers reject Mezirow's notion that one should take a critical, evaluating stance toward ideas.

Subjective Knowers also reject the notion, so central to Received Knowing, that truth can be embodied in words. To them ideas are so unique that it is not possible to capture their essence with words. Words diminish and distort insights and intuitions. This distrust of language, combined with their intense preoccupation with explor- ing their own inner world, makes it hard for Subjective Knowers to listen to others and see the world through their eyes. With such a jaundiced view of both authorities and language, students who hold this outlook may even see libraries as irrelevant.

Without special coaching, people who hold this outlook would also have a difficult time understanding the notion of reflective dis- course and critical thinking. Even though they are aware that they and others have ideas, insights, and intuition, they have not devel- oped the capacity to stand back and reflect on their ideas. Not engag- ing in meta-thinking, they "are" their ideas rather than people who "have" ideas (Kegan, 1994). To them, taking a critical stance toward ideas threatens an erasure of self.

Procedural Knowledge provides the essential tools people must have if they are to participate in a highly reflective dialogue. With this perspective it is understood that ideas can be communicated, analyzed, developed, and tested by making good use of procedures. Two markedly different modes were identified: the "separate" and "connected" approaches to Procedural Knowing (see also Clinchy, 1996, 1998).

"The believing game" and "doubting game" are metaphors that suggest the key differences between these two different modes (Elbow, 1973). Separate Knowers play the doubting game. They are always standing back, following a line of reasoning, looking for flaws in logic and errors of omission (Elbow, 1973; Clinchy, 1996; Moulton, 1983). A classic example: "I never take anything someone says for granted. I just tend to see the contrary. I like playing the devil's advocate, arguing the opposite of what somebody's saying, thinking of exceptions, or thinking of a different train of logic" (Belenky, Clinchy, Goldberger, and Tarule, 1996, p. 100).

An argument that survives this kind of scrutiny is thought to be better or more "defensible" than one that does not. Mezirow captures the spirit of Separate Knowing well in Chapter One when he describes Habermas's theory of communicative learning:

> Understanding in communicative learning requires that we assess the intentions behind the words; the coherence, truth, and appropriateness of what is being communicated; the truthfulness and qualifications of the speaker; and the authenticity of expressions of feeling. That is, we must become critically reflective of the assumptions of the person communicating. . . . In communicative learning, we determine the *justification* of a problematic belief or understanding through *rational discourse* to arrive at a tentative best judgment. The only

alternatives to discourse for justifying a belief is to appeal
to tradition, authority, or force.

The goal of communicative learning (or Separate Knowing), as
Mezirow makes very clear, is not winning an argument for argument's sake or proving that one is smart, worthy, or wise. The goal
is to achieve consensus about the best judgment the discourse community is capable of reaching with the information currently available. Mezirow places this kind of critical thinking at the heart of
transformative learning, as it provides the tools for analyzing the
weaknesses in current arguments and points the way toward more
adequate conceptualizations. As such, it provides many of the tools
one needs for continued development, but not all.

Connected Knowing provides another set of procedures for developing and testing ideas, but it takes a radically different stance.
People who take this approach play the believing game. They look
for strengths, not weaknesses, in another's argument. If a weakness is
perceived they struggle to understand why someone might think that
way. An example: "When I have an idea about something, and it differs from the way another person is thinking about it, I'll usually try
to look at it from that person's point of view, see how they could say
that, why they would think they are right, why it makes sense to
them" (Belenky, Clinchy, Goldberger, and Tarule, 1996, p. 100).

The more Connected Knowers disagree with another person the
harder they will try to understand how that person could imagine
such a thing, using empathy, imagination, and storytelling as tools
for entering into another's frame of mind. We call them Connected
Knowers because they actually try to enter into the other person's
perspective, adopting their frame of mind, trying to see the world
through their eyes. Striving to get the big picture, they try to see
things holistically, not analytically. As Noddings (1984, p. 30)
describes the process: "I set aside my temptation to analyze and to
plan. I do not project; I receive the other into myself, and I see and
feel with the other. I become a duality. I am not thus caused to see

or to feel . . . for I am committed to the receptivity that permits me to see and to feel in this way. The seeing and feeling are mine, but only partly and temporarily mine, as on loan to me."

Even though Connected Knowers might understand full well that a person's point of view is partial and inadequate, they suspend judgment when they are struggling to understand another person's point of view. They worry that marshaling counterarguments would impair their ability to understand what the other person is really trying to say. It is too difficult to embrace another's perspective fully while trying to dismantle their ideas. They also worry that counterarguments might freeze the minds of people who are trying hard to gather and develop their thoughts. Mezirow resonates with these concerns when he argues for withholding judgment while trying to understand a point of view that is very different from one's own. Once the other's point of view is understood and appreciated, however, Mezirow stresses the importance of analyzing the logic and determining which line of reasoning is the best. Needless to say, standing back and taking a critical stance to ideas can be proper and welcome; it can also be inappropriate and even, in some circumstances, destructive.

Connected Knowers have no qualms about playing the doubting game as long as it is played on a level playing field. Separate Knowing, with all of its doubting, can harm those who lack confidence in their abilities to develop and articulate ideas. When the germ of an idea is just beginning to develop, doubting can bring about stillbirths even for the most accomplished thinkers.

Groups that place Connected Knowing at the center of their practice can achieve an unusually high degree of creativity and solid intellectual work. The believing game encourages listening. People work hard to understand each other. They learn of each other's stories, visions, and goals. They help each other push pet projects along. In these highly collaborative, creative learning communities, unusual ideas are often explored and developed with zest and success. In competitive communities that overemphasize Separate Knowing, thinking can become quite stagnant. Too many new ideas are shot down before they have a chance to become airborne.

People often have a hard time recognizing Connected Knowing as a procedural approach to knowledge making. No doubt the dualistic categories that separate thought from feeling make it difficult for people to honor an approach to thinking that embraces personal experiences, feelings, and narrative over abstract conceptualizations. In a culture that perceives competition—not collaboration—as the great animator, it makes sense that taking a "critical stance" and determining "the very best" argument would become the procedure of choice.

That procedure, however, effectively shuts out immature or marginalized people. Critical discourse, the doubting game, can only be played well on a level playing field. The believing game, in contrast, is a game for everyone no matter how immature or silenced. Connected Knowing creates a level playing field where even very dissimilar people can meet as equals. Joyce provides a good example when she describes her relationship with her four-year-old son, Peter:

> Well you know, [Peter's] got such an active mind . . . . He is always trying to figure out how things tick. . . . If I ask him to do something . . . he's always asking, "Why?" He really wants to understand what's the goal—what's the purpose—how come? . . . He's real interested in figuring out how one thing leads to another. It's great, because sometimes he helps me realize that I haven't really thought through why I'm saying what I am. And so we do think it through. WHAT DO YOU MEAN? I mean, he gets me to think it through—*with* him, you know. He asks me "Why?" and I realize we got to think it through together, because I don't really know why I told him to do what I did. I mean, I have a feeling why, but I'm not really sure about it, so Peter and I talk about some reasons why he should or shouldn't do what I asked and we

think through what really makes sense. It's really useful sometimes, you know? [Belenky, Bond, and Weinstock, 1997, p. 130]

If Joyce had embraced Mezirow's procedures and regularly ranked her own and her young son's arguments to determine "the best tentative judgment," most certainly the child would be found wanting and become discouraged. It is likely that Joyce's very willingness to kneel down and place herself on Peter's level will make it easier in the long run for Peter to learn how to take a take a critical stance toward authorities and the status quo.

Constructed Knowledge is a perspective held by people, like Joyce, who see themselves and everyone else—even the smallest child—as active constructors of knowledge. Constructivists understand that knowledge is constructed by the mind and not by procedures, however useful procedures might be. Because they see the knower as such an integral part of the known, people who work out of this perspective do a lot of meta-thinking: they evaluate, choose, and integrate the wide range of procedures and processes they bring to the meaning-making process.

Constructivist Knowers actively cultivate the whole range of approaches. They learn from concrete experience as with the Silenced; they learn by listening to others as with Received Knowers; they learn from experience, intuition, feelings, and insights as with Subjective Knowers; and they learn from both the Separate and Connected approaches to Procedural Knowing. They stand back, question, take apart, and criticize points of views they see as partial, unfair, and/or destructive. They also move inward, see the whole, listen, understand, integrate, build up, and create.

Constructivists have thrown aside the dichotomies that privilege men over women, speaking over listening, thinking over feeling, doubting over believing, and public over private. The dethroning of dualism can also be seen by tracing the ways authorities are conceptualized by people with different ways of knowing. Received

Knowers think of an authority as a superior person while they themselves are inferior—that is, the master and the subservient. Here the inequality and distance between authorities and nonauthorities is vast and unbridgeable. Subjective Knowers stand the hierarchy on its head. By casting themselves as the only relevant authority, they place themselves above and beyond others—even those with great expertise. Procedural Knowing is the first position where the knowers see themselves and authorities carrying on a dialogue as equals. The Separate Knower stands back, looks for flaws in the authority's logic, and presents alternative arguments for consideration. The Connected Knower steps forward, enters into the authority's perspective, and tries to see the world through his or her eyes. Both procedures require the knower and the authority to situate themselves at the same level.

Many find it a pleasure to see the self on the same plane as an authority but find it exceedingly difficult to place the self on the level of someone who could be construed as lesser. Anyone who worries about "girl stain" might not want to lower himself or herself to meet a child, eye to eye, in the way Joyce encounters her son, Peter. With the achievement of both Separate and Connected Knowing, however, one has the ability to stand on a level playing field with everyone in society, from the newly born to the wisest of elders.

It is clear that transformative learning—that is, the capacity for reflective discourse, critical thinking, and evaluating one's basic assumptions and meaning-making frameworks, as described by Mezirow—places Separate Knowing in a central role in the construction of new knowledge and adult transformations. It seems equally clear that there are other processes that are equally vital but less well described in this body of work.

Midwife-Teachers

We turn now to practice, specifically in higher education. How can these concepts be put into play and with what results?

The WWK perspectives are ideal types—the equivalent of snapshots of an ongoing developmental process. They are a convenient way of conveying in general terms how the developing person is apprehending truth, herself as a knower, relationships, conflicts, and learning opportunities. They provide a road map that can help us see where people are coming from and where they might be trying to go—at least in a culture like ours. Having snapshots and a map is of great practical use for educators intent on nurturing students' development.

Also important is a conscious strategy for dealing with inequalities of power and epistemological development in the classroom. A large body of work critically analyzes the power relationships inherent in educational practice (for example, Freire, 1985; Giroux, 1992) with feminist thinkers in particular reminding us of the importance of attending to the particular, the personal, and the contextual (Collins, 1991; Maher and Tetreault, 1994; Mitchell, 1996; Weiler, 1991). *Women's Way of Knowing* coined the term "midwife-teacher" to describe educators who see their students as active constructors of knowledge and work hard to draw out their best thinking:

> Midwife-teachers do not administer anesthesia. They support their students' thinking, but they do not do the students' thinking for them or expect the students to think as they do. . . . The midwife-teacher's first concern is to preserve the student's fragile newborn thoughts, to see that they are born with their truth intact, that they do not turn into acceptable lies. . . . The cycle is one of confirmation-evocation-confirmation. Midwife-teachers help students deliver their words to the world, and they use their own knowledge to put the students into conversation with other voices—past and present—in the culture [Belenky, Clinchy, Goldberger, and Tarule, pp. 217–219].

Such teachers, of course, share a great deal in common with the ideal teacher described in the adult education literature, emphasizing the students' strengths, incorporating their experiences, deemphasizing competition and hierarchy in the classroom (for example, Mezirow, 1990; Brookfield, 1996). However, adult educators often do not attend to the epistemological assumptions that shape their students' meaning-making efforts. Seeking this kind of understanding encourages teachers to take a "believing" stance toward students who otherwise might be perceived as resistant, passive, intellectually lazy, or illogical. The task becomes one of discerning the students' basis for thinking as they do and finding ways to affirm what and how they know, as well as finding the means to challenge and stimulate them to develop more elaborate approaches to the construction of knowledge.

In recent years adult educators have worked hard to dethrone "the sage on the stage" in favor of "the guide on the side" (Daloz, 1999). We think the guides can profit from developmental maps emphasizing not only the ultimate destination but the landmarks along the way. Working from the WWK map, for example, and understanding the distinction between Subjective Knowing and Connected Knowing help a teacher to conduct a classroom discussion differently. A "Subjective" discussion would encourage students to air their opinions or relate their experiences in an atmosphere of nonjudgmentalness. While maintaining an aura of careful listening and acceptance, a "Connected" discussion would go beyond that, pointing out where opinions are different, helping participants uncover the sources of and reasons for the differences, exploring the implications of each position, and asking the class to reconcile different opinions. The Connected mode supports everyone to listen deeply and respectfully and models how to draw out others' ideas. Received Knowers are challenged to attend to classmates' ideas and to formulate and voice their own opinions. Subjective Knowers are challenged to stand back and look at their own ideas amidst an array of others and to subject all ideas to similar questioning. Procedural Knowers are challenged to integrate and synthesize ideas and to practice the use of both separate and connected modes. Attending to such a variety of perspectives requires teachers who are fast on their epistemological feet, observing, drawing out, summarizing, working many levels at once.

Sharing such "maps of development" with students enables teachers and students to discuss and arrive at common understandings about the process, not just the content, of learning. A map can help students see and track the growth of their capacities for reflective discourse. For example, psychologist Paul Hettich (1990) taught his students Bloom's (1956) taxonomy of educational objectives and Perry's theory of intellectual and ethical development. Student journals, originally assigned so that students could use personal experience to make theoretical topics more relevant to their lives, were stretched into exercises in meta-analysis. The students evaluated their own journal entries according to Bloom's or Perry's theoretical categories. They reported that these evaluation efforts made them aware of their own levels of thinking, stimulated more critical thinking, and helped them understand other course concepts.

Neither Bloom nor Perry included Connected Knowing in their schemes. Ann Stanton (1993) worked to create a learning community where students were encouraged to engage in Connected Knowing: developing skills, studying theories, and sharing their stories of finding a voice and feeling the power of their minds. Three minicourses taught WWK perspectives and Kolb Learning Styles, providing experience in their use through weekly small-group sessions over a period of five or six weeks. Active listening and engaging in dialogue were modeled and emphasized throughout. Pre- and posttests found that participants in the minicourses gained significantly more on WWK perspectives compared to those in control groups. A sophomore in college we call Amy responds to the question, How is the way you see yourself now different than the way you saw yourself a year or so ago? "I remember being in tears and saying, 'I can't seem to get a grip on what I'm trying to pull off here.' Now I see myself as much more confident, much more capable. I know more; I can articulate more. I feel like I'm balancing two ways of thinking—[I think more] creatively and analytically. I haven't mastered it but I'm close to mastering it. I clearly see these amazing spurts of growth" (Stanton, 1993, p. 38).

Connected Knowing and developmental theory come together most powerfully when the students are deeply understood and teachers can tailor questions and responses to push students' thinking forward. When the reflective dialogue takes place in writing, the whole process slows down. Ideas can be framed with great care, with the writer able to stand back and reflect on her own thinking. The reader can come back to the writing again and again to refresh and deepen understanding. A university student describes her experience in a large lecture course (about ninety students) on religion: "[The professor] is an enthralling lecturer, but even better she writes letters. Every two weeks or so she writes a letter to each student in the class, and we write back. She pushes me to ask deeper questions and to see things from many different perspectives. It's been the most powerful learning experience I've ever had" (Stanton, 1999).

Chemistry professor Michael Strauss (1995) places student letters at the center of everyone's learning. Students in a large class write him anonymous letters that contain questions, concerns, interpretations, and student breakthroughs: "Wow, I've got it, there are seven carbons in the longest chain!" Strauss makes these letters into transparencies and uses the next lecture hour to discuss and elaborate on the letters, noting, "Such writing expresses the students' own concerns about the chemistry, in their own language, about what they really *want* to know. And often the writing itself leads to insights for the writer, which I then share with all the students. . . . [They] can see this—the process, the insights, *and* the content" (p. 9). Strauss's pedagogy embodies such Connected Knowing concepts as meeting students where they are, drawing out their ideas, listening with care, and honoring process.

Careful attention to both process and content and centering education on what students want to know are key elements of undergraduate education at Vermont College's Adult Degree Program (Hathaway, 1999), whose design drew on the theories of John Dewey (1966) and such models of progressive education as Myles Horton's (1990) Highlander Center for Research and Education. Written reflective dialogue between student and faculty is its centerpiece. The program operates on a low-residency model where the larger educational community (students and faculty advisors) comes together for brief but intense residencies, followed by the students returning to their families and jobs and working at a distance on independent studies in collaboration with a faculty advisor. Their work together takes the form of critical book reviews, essays, and "vigorous dialogue" through long letters about the process and contents of the study. This format allows for intense intellectual relationships, where faculty can be attuned precisely to students' thinking and development (Stanton, 1999). Sarah Mitchell (1996) documents teachers' use of Connected Knowing—openness to dialogue and connection, drawing out students' thinking, documenting their strengths and fledgling ideas—in the written exchanges, leading to students experiencing profound transformations. As one student expressed this, "At first I was in a panic about the work and worried this panic would be insurmountable. It was such a miracle to me that I had someone out there who could hold the vision for me that I could do this work. I can hold that vision for myself now. I am beginning to know what I am capable of doing and being and many of the barriers have given way to trust in my intelligence and my voice."

Midwife-Leaders

Educational institutions are not the only social institutions that regularly sponsor the development of voice and mind among adults. A study of four community organizations with long histories of bringing people from the margins into voice revealed a group of community leaders who shared a vision of an inclusive, caring society and held a passionate belief in the capacity of people to lead themselves (Belenky, Bond, and Weinstock, 1997). As public leaders, these women had all reflected deeply on the issue of gender. After an extensive reexamination of traditional gender roles, they rejected some of the conventions and reinterpreted others. Each embraced, with renewed passion, those aspects of traditional gender roles that charge women with the responsibility of supporting the development of the most vulnerable members of society. In their minds, a proper leader "draws out" and "draws in" the missing voices. Like midwife-teachers, midwife-leaders valued, practiced, and taught the skills involved in Connected Knowing.

The root metaphor for describing what midwife-leaders actually do is "raising up" not "ruling over." Although conventionally oriented leaders stand at the helm, gathering followers and leading the way, these leaders stand in the background and push others to the fore. Their effectiveness at drawing out the potential of people earns them the right to be called midwife-leaders.

Sponsoring the development of the most vulnerable members of society, these women bring knowledge, values, and practices to public life that are usually associated with private life. These leaders draw on certain skills and values associated with women's traditional roles, and all would agree that this form of leadership—like midwife teaching—should be cultivated by men and women alike.

Even though these leaders and their organizations serve different cultural communities and social classes, they have much in common. A leisurely, highly reflective conversation is probably the most salient of the commonalities. Each organization has customs, rules, and rituals that allow these kinds of conversations to happen regularly. Whenever a voice is missing, someone notices and begins the drawing-out process.

All of these organizations have created a caring community where people feel deeply connected to one another. The depth of these connections is suggested by Lakoff and Johnson (1980). Again and again women would say, "We're like a family." When asked how ordinary neighborhood women can build so many complex programs in a deteriorating area of an inner city, one leader says, "We are like a family; we have made a lifelong commitment to each other. People who know they're going to be together over the long haul can take on something that might take ten years or more to accomplish" (Belenky, Bond, and Weinstock, 1997, pp. 259–260). These organizations have dissolved the barriers between public and private life so successfully we think of them as "public homeplaces."

Connected Knowing is widely practiced in all of these organizations. People work hard to understand one another. They look for and document one another's strengths. They hold up mirrors for one another that are specifically focused on dreams, accomplishments, critiques of old ways, struggles, and new plans. They focus on the "growing edge," or that which is struggling to be born. Seeing such reflections, everyone can articulate the goals more clearly, understand better the foundations already in place that they can build upon, and find companions who want to travel similar paths.

All of these organizations find ways of taking the dialogue into the broader community. Some put their reflections and stories into videos that can be shared and discussed with others. The African American cultural workers take the people's stories and weave them into new songs and dramas. The musical and theatrical productions become public events, bringing the voices of the excluded into public discourse. Others see themselves as historians, keeping track of women's contributions to the neighborhood. When the neighborhood women tried to claim they were not leaders, there were numerous and detailed histories of the leadership roles the women had actually undertaken. In these ways the women provided one another with mirrors that allowed them to see themselves in an astonishing new light. Realizing how the story of women's leadership was left out of the official history of the community, the women began fighting to get the whole story told. In the process of "doing" history, the women found themselves "making" history.

These organizations are like community think tanks that take a problem-solving approach and generate one action project after another. The women are always asking, What is the problem here? What should be changed? What are our dreams for this community? How can we move forward? They then develop plans and carry them out. After a project is launched, women step back and ask even more questions: What did we hope to do? What did we actually do? What did we accomplish? What were the strengths and the weaknesses in our analyses, plans, and processes? What needs to be done now? Before long they are back at the drawing board. People develop their skills for critical thinking and separate knowing in the context of action projects. Combining the practices of dialogue, building on strengths, a problem-solving approach, and a commitment to action unleashes the developmental processes that transform individuals and their communities.

Developing the capacity for critical thinking or Separate Knowing as well as the skills of Connected Knowing is of the utmost importance for people who have been excluded and silenced. The ability to question authorities, tradition, and basic assumptions is especially important to those who have been treated unjustly. Paulo Freire (1970) makes that abundantly clear. These capacities develop most fully in communities where every voice gets heard, where people's stories are listened to with great care, and where their visions, struggles, and strengths are well documented. This enables groups to take their critiques forward, forge common goals, and engage in action projects that have the potential of transforming whole communities as well as the people involved.

Even if his theory does not articulate elements we believe are central to the form, our experience of Mezirow's practice—attending the conference that gave birth to this volume—convinces us that he is a gifted midwife-teacher and leader who has helped give birth to a vibrant community of learners. Major emphasis was placed on participating, processing, and discussing the presentations. All conference attendees were welcomed around the table on an equal basis; all were encouraged to build on speakers' ideas. The collegial and collaborative nature of the discussions was different from anything we had experienced previously in conferences held in university settings. The evening event, a moving and emotional tribute to Paulo Freire, further illustrated how this learning community has broken through such dualisms as thought and action, theory and practice, thinking and emotion.

References

Adorno, T. W., Frenkel-Brunswik, E., Levinson, D. J., and Sanford, N. *The Authoritarian Personality*. New York: Harper, 1950.

Allport, G. *The Nature of Prejudice*. Garden City, N.Y.: Doubleday, 1958.

Bakan, D. *The Duality of Human Existence*. Chicago: Rand McNally, 1966.

Basseches, M. *Dialectical Thinking and Adult Development*. Norwood, N.J.: Ablex, 1984.

Baxter Magolda, M. *Knowing and Reasoning in College*. San Francisco: Jossey-Bass, 1992.

Belenky, M. F., Clinchy, B. McV., Goldberger, N. R., and Tarule, J. M. *Women's Ways of Knowing*. (2nd ed.). New York: Basic Books, 1996.

Belenky, M. F., Bond, L. A., and Weinstock, J. S. *A Tradition That Has No Name*. New York: Basic Books, 1997.

Bem, S. *The Lenses of Gender*. New Haven, Conn.: Yale University Press, 1993.

Blasi, J. *The Communal Experience of the Kibbutz*. New Brunswick, N.J.: Transaction Books, 1986.

Bloom, B. S. (ed.). *Taxonomy of Educational Objectives*. New York: Longmans, Green, 1956.

Brookfield, S. D. *Understanding and Facilitating Adult Learning*. San Francisco: Jossey-Bass, 1996.

Brown, R. *Social Psychology*. New York: Free Press, 1965.

Clinchy, B. McV. "Connected and Separate Knowing: Toward a Marriage of Two Minds." In N. Goldberger, J. Tarule, B. McV. Clinchy, and M. F. Belenky (eds.), *Knowledge, Difference, and Power*. New York: Basic Books, 1996.

Clinchy, B. McV. "A Plea for Epistemological Pluralism." In B. McV. Clinchy and J. K. Norem (eds.), *A Reader in Gender and Psychology*. New York: New York University Press, 1998.

Collins, P. H. *Black Feminist Thought: Knowledge, Consciousness, and the Politics of Empowerment*. New York: Routledge, 1991.

Daloz, L. *Mentor: Guiding the Journey of Adult Learners*. San Francisco: Jossey-Bass, 1999.

Dewey, J. *Democracy and Education*. New York: Free Press, 1966 [1916].

Elbow, P. *Writing Without Teachers*. New York: Oxford University Press, 1973.

Freire, P. *Pedagogy of the Oppressed*. (M. B. Ramos, trans.). New York: Herder and Herder, 1970.

Freire, P. *The Politics of Education*. New York: Seabury Press, 1985.

Gilligan, C. *In a Different Voice*. Cambridge, Mass.: Harvard University Press, 1982; 1993.

Giroux, H. *Border Crossings*. New York: Routledge, 1992.

Goldberger, N. "Cultural Imperatives and Diversity in Ways of Knowing." In N. Goldberger, J. M. Tarule, B. McV., Clinchy, and M. F. Belenky (eds.), *Knowledge, Difference, and Power*. New York: Basic Books, 1996.

Goldberger, N., Tarule, J. M., Clinchy, B. McV., and Belenky, M. F. (eds.). *Knowledge, Difference, and Power*. New York: Basic Books, 1996.

Greene, M. *The Dialectic of Freedom*. New York: Teachers College Press, 1988.

Greene, M. *Releasing the Imagination*. San Francisco: Jossey-Bass, 1995.

Haste, H. *The Sexual Metaphor*. Cambridge, Mass.: Harvard University Press, 1994.

Hathaway, R. "The Friendly Pioneer: An Informal History of the Adult Degree Program." In M. Blanchard (ed.), *Transformative Learning*. Northfield, Vt.: Norwich University Press, 1999.

Hettich, P. "Journal Writing: Old Fare or Nouvelle Cuisine?" *Teaching of Psychology*, 1990, *17*(1), 36–39.

Horton, M. *The Long Haul: An Autobiography*. (H. Kohl and J. Kohl, eds.). New York: Doubleday, 1990.

Kegan, R. *The Evolving Self*. Cambridge, Mass.: Harvard University Press, 1982.

Kegan, R. *In Over Our Heads*. Cambridge, Mass.: Harvard University Press, 1994.

Keller, E. F. *Reflections on Gender and Science*. New Haven, Conn.: Yale University Press, 1985.

King, P. M., and Kitchener, K. S. *Developing Reflective Judgment*. San Francisco: Jossey-Bass, 1994.

Kohlberg, L. *Essays on Moral Development*. San Francisco: HarperCollins, 1984.

Kuhn, D. "Is Good Thinking Scientific Thinking?" In D. Olson and N. Torrance (eds.), *Modes of Thought*. New York: Cambridge University Press, 1996, pp. 261–281.

Labouvie-Vief, G. *Psyche and Eros*. New York: Cambridge University Press, 1994.

Lakoff, G., and Johnson, M. *Metaphors We Live By*. Chicago: University of Chicago Press, 1980.

Loevinger, J. *Ego Development*. San Francisco: Jossey-Bass, 1976.

Maher, F. A., and Tetreault, M. K. *The Feminist Classroom*. New York: Basic Books, 1994.

Martin, J. R. *Reclaiming a Conversation*. New Haven, Conn.: Yale University Press, 1984.

Merchant, C. *The Death of Nature*. New York: HarperCollins, 1980.

Mezirow, J. (ed.). *Fostering Critical Reflection in Adulthood*. San Francisco: Jossey-Bass, 1990.

Mezirow, J. *Transforming Dimensions of Adult Learning*. San Francisco: Jossey-Bass, 1991.

Miller, J. B. *Towards a New Psychology of Women*. Boston: Beacon Press, 1976; 1987.

Mitchell, S. "Penelope's Daughters: Women Mentoring Women—The Value of Relational Dialogue in Adult Learning." Unpublished doctoral dissertation. Graduate School of the Union Institute, 1996.

Moulton, J. "A Paradigm of Philosophy: The Adversary Method." In S. Harding and M. Hintilla (eds.), *Discovering Reality*. Boston: D. Reidel, 1983.

Noddings, N. *Caring*. Berkeley: University of California Press, 1984.

Noddings, N. "Renewing Democracy in Schools." *Phi Delta Kappan*, Apr. 1999, *80*(8), 579.

Okin, S. M. *Justice, Gender, and the Family*. New York: Basic Books, 1989.

Perry, W. G. JR. *Forms of Intellectual and Ethical Development in the College Years*. New York: Holt, Rinehart and Winston, 1970.

Ruddick, S. *Maternal Thinking*. Boston: Beacon Press, 1995.

Schweickart, P. P. "Speech Is Silver, Silence Is Gold: The Asymmetrical Intersubjectivity of Communicative Action." In N. Goldberger, J. M. Tarule, B. McV. Clinchy, and M. F. Belenky (eds.), *Knowledge, Difference, and Power*. New York: Basic Books, 1996.

Stanton, A. V. *Integrating Student Services*. Final Report on Grant P116B91692–90, Dept. of Education (FIPSE), Washington, D.C., 1993.

Stanton, A. V. "Reconfiguring Teaching and Learning in the College Classroom." In N. Goldberger, J. M. Tarule, B. McV. Clinchy, and M. F. Belenky (eds.), *Knowledge, Difference, and Power*. New York: Basic Books, 1996.

Stanton, A. V. "The Role of Intimacy in Distance Education." In M. Blanchard (ed.), *Transformative Learning*. Northfield, Vt.: Norwich University Press, 1999.

Strauss, M. "Writing and Science." *Writing Teacher*, Mar. 1995, 6–9.

Thorne, B. *Gender Play*. New Brunswick, N.J.: Rutgers University Press, 1993.

Weiler, K. "Freire and a Feminist Pedagogy of Difference." *Harvard Educational Review*, 1991, *61*, 449–474.

4

Transformative Learning for the Common Good

Laurent A. Parks Daloz

Nelson Mandela was not born special. He grew up in a small village in a remote corner of South Africa surrounded by people of his own tribe. And yet he became leader of a fiercely divided nation, taking it through shoals of dramatic change almost without bloodshed, holding together angry constituencies who had sworn before the entire planet never to live together. Today he is among the most widely admired leaders on earth. Quite apart from his courage, his endurance through years of imprisonment, and his skillful leadership, however, one is struck in reading his autobiography (Mandela, 1994) by the man's extraordinary *consciousness*—his ability to recognize the essential humanity of others, no matter how different from himself. Again and again he has reached across the boundaries that separated himself and "his kind" from others and "their kind," often at mortal risk. Now, in the "Truth Commissions" of South Africa, he has helped to create a forum for reconciliation, a place of discourse across profound difference, that holds a promise for perhaps the most dramatic and hopeful foundation of any society in modern times. Although towering challenges remain, by almost any measure one would have to view Mandela's life and his nation as powerfully transformed.

In this chapter we explore the nature of the transformative learning that occurs as a person develops a sense of social responsibility. Beginning by clarifying the terms *transformative learning* and *social responsibility*, I then describe what appears to be the single most important factor in the formation of commitment to the larger good and draw on several different strands of research to explore the actual dynamic of that transformation more closely. Toward the end, we discuss four conditions for transformation that seem to contribute in significant measure to transformation for the common good, and several specific steps that adult educators might take are offered. Finally, I suggest a response to one of the gnawing ethical and educational questions that emerge from the work.

Transformation and Social Responsibility

When I use the term *transformative learning*, I am working from the definition generally used in this volume—a deep shift in frame of reference as Mezirow defines it. As a constructive developmentalist, I also assume that such changes toward "more dependable frames of reference" are probably developmentally related. That is, although Mezirow does not necessarily make that assumption, he would agree that what shifts in the transformative process is our very epistemology—the way in which we know and make meaning. In his latest work, Kegan (1994) refers to these meaning-making frameworks as "orders of consciousness," arguing forcefully that they are driven both intrinsically by developmental forces in the individual and extrinsically by conditions in the world, particularly by social complexity. That is, although the *capacity* to develop more adequate meaning-making frameworks is always there, transformative learning is by no means inevitable and depends strongly on the particular environmental and cultural forces at work in the individual's life. In effect, people have the potential to make the kinds of deep shift described here, but whether they will or not depends on the particular conditions in their lives. Clearly some conditions, such as an effective education and good friends, are more conducive to transformation than, say, growing up alone in a hostile world. From Piaget on, it has been forcefully argued that human development is interactive with the environment. This is an important point because who we become as moral beings, as actors in the world, is invariably affected by the quality of the world in which we are formed. Our social context matters enormously as we become enculturated first within our immediate families, then to the broader culture, and finally, if circumstances encourage it, through critical reflection on our own formation to a larger sense of self—one that identifies with all people and ultimately with all of life.

It is the growth toward this capacity to identify one's own sense of self with the well-being of all life that undergirds our use of the term *social responsibility*. In the *Common Fire* study of the lives of one hundred socially responsible people (Daloz, Keen, Keen, and Parks, 1996), my colleagues and I sought people who had demonstrated a long-term commitment to the common good rather than to primarily their own private welfare. This type of commitment is grounded in the metaphor of the commons, a place where the entire community comes together to do business, celebrate, and recognize their shared interdependence. By definition the commons belongs to no single entity, and although it has a marked shadow—slaves were sold and protesters hanged on the commons—in principle it is a place held in common, a place where the community comes together to work out its destiny over and over, each time imperfectly but on behalf of the good of all. Thus commitment to the common good is understood not as a final state but rather as a stance of openness to necessary and ongoing dialogue with those who differ or who may not yet be full participants on the commons. When justice is defined as a matter of who is included and who is excluded (Marstin, 1979), commitment to the common good means a commitment to justice. Yet it is an unending process; justice is never "done," and discourse is itself an essential part of vibrant democracy (Chambers, 1995).

Transformation is often understood as a lonely and rather sudden event—Saul falls off his horse and becomes transformed into Paul. This may be true in some cases (Everett, 1984; Lesy, 1991), but as Courtenay, Merriam, and Reeves (1998, p. 78) point out, the "catalytic events" that often precipitate transformation are not isolated but rather "emanate from a support system of family and friends, support groups, and/or spirituality." That is, transformation has a context that is historical and developmental as well as social. Mezirow refers to this as "incremental transformation," and Taylor's exhaustive survey of transformative learning practice (1998) further reinforces the point. Indeed it was very clear in the *Common Fire* study that although a single event may catalyze a shift or a particular story might dramatize a transformation, closer examination reveals that change or shift was long in coming and its possibility prepared for in myriad ways, generally across years. We found no instance of transformation as the result of an isolated, epochal event. Indeed, the idea that profound change can occur literally out of the blue flies in the face of everything we know about human development. (For related studies, see especially Oliner and Oliner, 1988; Colby and Damon, 1992; Glendon and Blankenhorn, 1995.) This is not to say, however, that there were none of what Mezirow calls "disorienting dilemmas." On the contrary, as Mandela's story demonstrates, there were many, and although they often went unremembered they exerted a steady, cumulative effect.

Nelson Mandela

Reflecting on his gradual conversion to the great work of his life, Nelson Mandela says, "I had no epiphany, no singular revelation, no moment of truth, but a steady accumulation of a thousand slights, a thousand indignities, a thousand unremembered moments produced in me an anger, a rebelliousness, a desire to fight the system that imprisoned my people. There was no particular day on which I said, From henceforth I will devote myself to the liberation of my people; instead, I simply found myself doing so, and could not do otherwise" (Mandela, 1994, p. 95).

At least in his own eyes Mandela's transformation was a gradual one. But was it the result only of painful experiences? Less well remembered than the thousand slights and indignities, but probably equally powerful, were the ten thousand positive events, relationships, and voices that taught him his interdependence with others, that gave him the trust to reach out to the wary and cynical, that granted him the will to risk his life over and over to empower others. And beneath this lies the story of a persistently widening sense of self, a self that matured into the man's extraordinary commitment to include all South Africans in a common future.

Mandela's early years in a small village gave him a lifelong core identity, and in this safe environment he learned early a sense of both trust and power. At the same time, the boundaries that held him there, even then, were permeable and were too soon breached when his father, an important local chief, died. Nine-year-old Nelson was taken in by the ruling family of the surrounding region and spent the next decade living both within and outside his family of origin, where he felt at once accepted and scorned as a "yokel." Although his secondary schooling placed him beside students from throughout South Africa, at the age of nineteen he was, in his own words, "still, at heart, a Thembu. . . . My horizons did not extend beyond Thembuland and I believed that to be a Thembu was the most enviable thing in the world" (p. 36).

But then he went to college, where he received an English-style liberal arts education. It was there that he made his first real friend from a different tribe. "I remember feeling quite bold," he remarks, "at having a friend who was not a Thembu" (note: the actual quotation reads "Xhosa," the name of the language spoken in the Thembu region; I have changed it to avoid confusion). And when he came to admire a teacher who had married a wife of a different tribe, he began to lose the grip of "the tribalism that still imprisoned me. I began to sense my identity as an African, not just a Thembu or even a Xhosa."

As he moved from there to a larger university college, his circle of friends widened yet further. He became active in student politics, learning the importance of building coalitions with students of differing loyalties. And he encountered faculty who infused him with a pride in pan-African culture, giving him a larger source of his identity. Later, having moved to Johannesburg, he served as a clerk in a liberal Jewish law firm. This young adult internship brought him into a mentoring environment where he experienced for the first time a sense of meaningful participation in the adult world. He and another black, Gaur Redebe, were the only two Africans in the firm. Gaur, ten years his senior, became Mandela's close associate and served as a significant model for him as he was drawn slowly into the urban resistance movement. It was at this time as well that he met Walter Sisulu, the man who was to become his primary mentor as he deepened his commitment to the liberation of South Africa. And, of equal importance, he found himself for the first time treated essentially as an equal with whites. It was then that he formed his first friendship with a white man, a fellow his own age who introduced him to Communist thought—an ideology that intrigued him but that he was unwilling to accept because of its explicit atheism. The experience of becoming part of a group of people "who did not seem to pay attention to color at all" was, for this young man, both frightening and exhilarating.

Clearly, these years saw a profound transformation in Mandela's consciousness as he moved from earlier, unexamined tribal "givens" through reflection on his identity to a new, critical awareness of his condition. Recalling a time when he was asked to return to his homeland and work there, he muses that "in my heart I knew I was moving toward a different commitment. Through my friendship with Gaur and Walter, I was beginning to see that my duty was to my people as a whole, not just a particular section or branch. I felt that all the currents of my life were taking me away from the Transkei and toward what seemed like the center, a place where regional and ethnic loyalties gave way before a common purpose" (p. 89).

Then, in the very next paragraph, we see Mandela's own critical reflection at work: "I was struck most forcefully by the discrepancy between my old assumptions and my actual experience. I had discarded my presumptions that graduates automatically became leaders and that my connection to the Thembu royal house guaranteed me respect. Having a successful career and a comfortable salary were no longer my ultimate goals. I found myself being drawn into the world of politics because I was not content with my old beliefs" (p. 89).

Quite explicitly Mandela tells us that his earlier assumptions have come into question, challenged by his direct experience, but we must add that those currents of his life also include a rich ecology of mentors, colleagues, adversaries, events, and critical discourse—a conversation that seeks to bring the givens and tacit assumptions into dialogue with perceived experience and alternative interpretations of cause, motivation, and reality itself.

Time and again over his subsequent lifetime, intensified by his twenty-seven years of imprisonment, Mandela describes engagements with others, initially with those who are different though sympathetic but increasingly with those who stand apparently unalterably opposed to him. At one point, after years of brutal incarceration, the "most callous and barbaric commanding officer" in the camp shakes his hand as he departs and warmly wishes him good luck. Jarred by the unexpected gesture, Mandela reflects that "all men, even the most seemingly cold-blooded, have a core of decency. . . . [U]ltimately Badenhorst was not evil; his inhumanity had been foisted on him by an inhuman system" (p. 462). Later, nearing release, one of his Afrikaner guards "became like a younger brother to me." Experiences like these, he speculates later, ultimately "reinforced my belief in the essential humanity even of those who had kept me behind bars" (p. 562). And it is this conviction of the essential humanity of the other that turns a former "us" and "them" into a shared "we," making possible work for the *common* good.

The Encounter with the Other

In our study of lives committed to the common good, we describe a number of key patterns in the formative years of the participants, including feeling recognized as a child, having at least one socially engaged parent, growing up in a diverse neighborhood, and being mentored. But the only experience common to all, what we have called *a constructive engagement with otherness*, came as a surprise. Everyone described at least one significant experience at some point during their formative years when they developed a strong attachment with someone previously viewed as "other" than themselves. Often there were childhood friendships with others from a different class or ethnic group; travel was a frequent catalyst. And although for many European-American males these experiences happened relatively late, for people of color who often were the "other" themselves the encounter took many forms across their early years. But regardless of the specifics, for the experience to be more than simply an encounter, for it to be a *constructive engagement*, there had to be some sense of empathic connection with people different from themselves. In some significant way the inner experience of the other was engaged, a bond was formed, and some deep lesson about connection across difference was learned.

For the meaning of the experience to mature, however, the differences as well as the similarities must be acknowledged. Sometimes that recognition precedes the experience of commonality, sometimes the reverse, but for the experience to ripen into mature power there must be an acknowledgment not simply of difference, nor simply of commonality, but of both and of the interplay between them. Perhaps the engagement with difference itself can be transformative.

This conviction undergirds the work of Yongming Tang (1997), a Chinese-American scholar with a commitment to personal and organizational transformation. For him, "the rhythmic dance of differentiating and integrating" is central to transformation. What he calls the "syngergic inquiry" process brings about transformation through a series of cycles of engagement with the other. Each cycle begins by differentiating self from other, then integrates the two in a larger frame by cultivating "the capacity to hold different consciousnesses as equals." This capacity itself is then reequilibrated as "a new synergic consciousness." Those who have achieved such a consciousness display the ability to hold a rich sense of legitimate difference without compromising their own cultural identities. In effect, they sound a lot like Cornel West's (1993) "race-transcending prophets"—those who never lose contact with their own particularity yet are not confined by it. In the ability to hold formerly discrete cultural frameworks along with one's own, this new consciousness bears a certain resemblance to Kegan's fifth "order of consciousness" as well as the culminating consciousness in William Perry's (1967) developmental scheme. And Tang's insight is consonant with a line of developmental theory from Riegel back through Piaget and Werner. But if this dance with difference is so powerful, how does it work? Does this new consciousness simply emerge full-blown after enough encounters with difference, or is there some sort of progression, some reiterative inching up on it?

Intrigued by Perry's developmental scheme, Milton Bennett (1986), a cross-cultural educator, examined how the transformations that Perry describes might inform the process through which adults come to terms with cultural difference. Building on Perry's stages of the adaptation to authority, Bennett constructed a sequence of six distinctly delineated phases of adaptation to otherness. Not everyone progresses through the entire sequence, of course, and some move more rapidly than others, but each step represents a qualitatively different response to the encounter with difference, each a small transformation in how we make meaning of the place of the other in our lives. The earliest response, he proposes, is simply to deny difference. A kind of cultural autism, this assumes that everyone else shares one's own beliefs and assumptions. Those who do not are ignored or dehumanized. When otherness can no longer be denied, one attempts first to defend against it, sometimes by placing it lower on some hierarchy and sometimes by minimizing the differences. If circumstances are right, however, we may move from our former ethnocentrism to ethnorelativism. We acknowledge that difference exists, we then adapt to and perhaps even celebrate the difference, and finally we integrate this deeper knowledge of the other with our own sense of personal and cultural identity. With this integration comes the ability to make contextual judgements (similar to Perry's contextual relativism), and a new kind of "constructive marginality."

In this time of emerging global culture that threatens to obliterate distinctive particularities, this series of transformations helps to counteract a kind of reaction formation in which we turn to narrow "tribal" identities in a quest for refuge, belonging, and a sense of participation. What, then, have we learned about the conditions under which these transformations are most likely to occur?

Four Conditions of Transformation

Given that the engagement with otherness plays a key role in transformation, that it does so through an incremental process of differentiation and integration, and that the process involves a series of identifiable steps, what are the conditions under which those steps might occur? In particular, what are the conditions under which engagement with otherness might lead to greater social responsibility?

Let's consider four particular conditions: the presence of the other, reflective discourse, a mentoring community, and opportunities for committed action. These are not the only conditions by any means, but they seem from our experience to be particularly salient ones.

The Presence of the Other

In his book *The Diversity of Life*, naturalist E. O. Wilson (1992) compellingly argues that it is the very rub of difference that makes life possible. Without diversity, evolution itself could not occur. At the same time, diversity must come in the right doses. Where there is too little the species may simply not evolve; where there is too much at once, however, the species can become overwhelmed and simply die out. How we engage with difference makes all the difference.

There was, in fact, very little diversity in the village where Mandela was born. He led his early years confident in the knowledge that he lived at the center of a secure universe. His discovery that there were others out there quite different from himself was gradual, and the recognition that some of those others considered him to be markedly inferior came only after he had grown relatively secure in his own identity. We often heard a similar tale from those we interviewed. Although a number had grown up in neighborhoods marked by ethnic or class diversity, for the most part the differences were equally valued and people were shielded in their early years from the worst depredations of oppression. Thus the exposure to difference was appropriately modulated, neither so slight that their uniqueness went unchallenged nor so strong that it was crushed. In our *Common Fire* study, a prominent women's educator who had grown up in an egalitarian home and been educated in an all-girls high school recalls her shock when a college date casually informed her that women couldn't do math, and a civil rights leader tells how he was able to hold his head high in the face of intense hatred because he had grown up the son of the local pastor in a small, segregated town and had been protected from direct contact with racist behavior. But the differences were not simply social or ethnic. Some had grown up with siblings who were physically or developmentally challenged, and others had experienced particularly powerful connections with animals and the natural environment. The exact nature and significance of the difference varied with each person but, whatever its form, the encounter crossed some earlier boundary between "us" and "them" and made available an alternative way of being, a different voice that challenged the earlier assumptions about how life is and made possible the construction of a new "we."

Reflective Discourse

As much of the current work on transformative learning makes apparent, however, for mature transformation to occur, at some point there must be conscious, critical reflection on our early assumptions about how life is. Developmentalists would argue that this capacity must await the flowering during the late adolescent years of full formal operations, the ability to think about one's own thought. Thus Nelson Mandela recalls the excitement of veiled political conversations with both black and white South Africans at the law firm where he first served as clerk, and later the more exuberant and challenging arguments at Walter Sisulu's home. A "Mecca for activists," it was a place of hospitality for many radical young Turks at the time, and it was there that Mandela engaged in rich discourse about white colonialism, black nationalism, and the imperative of revolution. It is this sort of participation in a "community of understanding that involves shared commitments" that political theorist Mark Warren (1992) argues can powerfully foster democratic "self-transformation."

For Mezirow, this sort of "reflective discourse" is the primary form through which transformative learning takes place. Noting in this volume that it is "the process in which we actively dialogue with others to better understand the meaning of an experience," he adds that it includes emotional and social as well as cognitive components. Because transformation involves the whole person, we should not be surprised at this. Moreover, the conditions "for its full realization" that he spells out in Chapter One find a resonance throughout much of the literature of personal change. They are characterized by the establishment of a climate of safety in which people feel free to speak their truth, where blaming and judging are minimal, where full participation is encouraged, where a premium is placed on mutual understanding, but also where evidence and arguments may be assessed objectively and assumptions surfaced openly.

Mezirow's work is further enriched by consideration of a contribution from the emerging field of conflict resolution known as "transformative mediation." In their book *The Promise of Mediation*, Robert Bush and Joseph Folger (1994) suggest that when participants meet across differences in accord with certain key principles, they emerge with a transformed capacity to hold their own uniqueness along with that of the other in a new, more adequate way. Central to the process is the idea that transformation requires mutual perspective taking and that true understanding must precede reliable agreement. The purpose is less to identify objective truth on which the parties may agree than to establish what Rothman (1996) calls an "intersubjective resonance" within which each can come to a shared understanding of "core narratives, meaning, and motives." This can then lead to "recognition" of the other—of their legitimate concerns, fears, and hopes. Essential elements of successful discourse include an emphasis on empowerment and self-determination of the participants, a participant-based agenda, validation of emotions as a part of the process, and a recognition that confusion is invariably involved and legitimate. Once again, if the process is successful participants are able "to articulate their own voices clearly *and to recognize each other's voices as valid*" (Rothman, p. 351, italics mine).

In these observations, these mediators complement the conditions that Mezirow has suggested, proposing from yet another angle that transformation proceeds from the progressive taking-in, digesting, and reconstructing of perspectives different from our own.

A Mentoring Community

"Our life histories and language are bound up with those of others," Mezirow reminds us, and it is clear that if we really want to understand transformative learning richly we need to recognize the extraordinary power of the webs of relationships in which we are invariably held. For from the very beginning, as developmentalist Fogel (1993) has shown us, we develop through relationships and our sense of "self" is best understood as a composite of many selves, each constructed out of the intercourse with our evolving worlds. The *Common Fire* study identified a number of "significant others" who contributed to the makeup of the participants. They included older adults, teachers, youth leaders, business people, and clergy in the neighborhood or community who saw something special in the young person and who encouraged a deeper sense of purpose. During the "critical years" (Parks, 1986) between roughly twenty and thirty, mentors played a particularly prominent role for many young adults, helping them to shape their budding commitments in public life, nurturing critical thought, dispensing advice, opening doors of opportunity, challenging and supporting them to take their place as committed adults, and demonstrating in their own lives the possibility of a life committed to the common good. Mentors appear in almost every field of human endeavor and their importance in human development is richly documented (Levinson and others, 1978; Murray, 1991; Wunsch, 1994; Cohen, 1995; Galbraith and Cohen, 1995; Daloz, 1999; Parks, 2000). But important as they are, we have found that people who are able to act on and sustain long-term commitment to a positive vision often describe in their past or current lives a "mentoring community"—an ecology of relationships with people who value diversity and transformative discourse (Parks, 1992).

This was certainly the case with Mandela, who describes an extraordinary network of mentors, helpers, colleagues, and friends who shaped his values, strengthened his resolve, and supported, challenged, and inspired his work. The Youth League of the African National Congress (ANC), which he helped to organize, brought him together with his lifelong friend, Oliver Tambo, his mentor, Walter Sisulu, and many others who subsequently became central to the independence movement. Under Sisulu's wise tutelage, the young attorney learned both a radical social vision and the capacity to keep his head under stress. "Sometimes one can judge an organization by the people who belong to it, and I knew that I would be proud to belong to any organization in which Walter was a member," he writes. Subsequently, the ANC became the primary mentoring community for Mandela. And it was his involvement with the ANC that provided him the fourth key element: an opportunity for committed action.

Opportunities for Committed Action

Although transformative discourse and the presence of a mentoring community are essential to the formation of durable commitment to the common good, the opportunity to act on one's evolving commitments, to test and ground one's growing convictions in action, is vital. Such extended experiential learning opportunities as internships, Peace Corps and VISTA, or other similar work are powerful formative factors shaping a mature commitment to the common good.

As he moved into the leadership of the Transvaal branch of the ANC, Mandela became increasingly involved with the workings of the organization, making decisions and taking adult responsibility for actions that affected people's lives. "I now came," he writes, "to identify myself with the congress as a whole, with its hopes and despairs, its successes and failures; I was now bound heart and soul" (p. 108). Such experiences with value-based, often socially marginal communities serve both to form and sustain long-term commitments. Virtually none of the people we studied were Lone Rangers, and although they might often enough feel alone, those who were able to sustain commitments over the long haul under difficult circumstances were inevitably linked to larger communities of "solidarity, resistance, and persistence" (Welch, 1990). Many of these communities were characterized by periods of profound reflection on their purposes and a commitment to a praxis methodology in which action and reflection were intimately related.

What We Can Do

What concrete steps emerge from our discussion thus far? What can adult educators do to lead students toward a greater commitment to the common good? Here are some beginning steps.

- Work to bring students and faculty together across differences—ethnic, economic class, physical differences, age.

- Encourage explicit recognition and creation of the sorts of settings that value mutual respect, safe disclosure, careful listening, and yet genuine willingness to look at difference.

- While recognizing differences, place equal emphasis on seeking areas of common ground, of shared experience and deep human connection.

- Encourage reflective discussion of the effects of social conditioning on our own understandings of "the way things are" while fostering an openness to change and a commitment to creating more adequate arrangements.

- Help students to recognize their own supportive communities and to seek out communities that share their emerging values and commitments in ways that combine both confirmation and challenge.

- Provide opportunities for socially committed groups and organizations to come together and reflect with one another or with those who differ about their deep hopes and aspirations for a world that works better.

- Create experiential learning opportunities—field experiences, practicums, internships—that engage learners with tough issues and dilemmas; encourage critical reflection on these issues and press for action steps.

- Provide at least some opportunities for students to come together to hold the ambiguity, to reflect on the mystery of their lives and commitments—to practice holding their lives and convictions against the backdrop of both radical doubt and unshakeable faith.

What We Must Learn

Yet if we take these steps, aren't we at risk of moving beyond the legitimate bounds of adult education into a kind of activism? That's a hoary and honorable question: As educators, should we direct our efforts toward specific social changes, even "defining the enemy" as Michael Newman (1994) suggests, or should we restrict ourselves to fostering general intellectual growth, as Mezirow maintains in this volume (and as I have argued elsewhere), assuming that such growth will lead to socially responsible choices?

There are pragmatic arguments and counterarguments on either side. If we take the former position, what is to keep the teacher in the next class with whom we vigorously disagree from doing the same thing until our field becomes one great ideological battleground? Moreover, to take that avenue is to risk alienating powerful forces in the society, possibly hindering our own effectiveness and very likely jeopardizing our personal security. And yet to take the conventional "liberal" stance on this issue—sticking to process and leaving the content up to the students—dodges the issue of the very real injustice and oppression that surrounds us and opens our practice to charges of pasty-faced dilettantism. Are we content merely to build the missiles, as Tom Lehrer used to say about Werner Von Braun, and never mind where the things will come down?

But beneath these arguments lies a deeper tension, one based on the question of rights. What *right* have we to impose our values, romantic, conventional, or radical, on our students? Don't they have a right to come to their own conclusions as rational individuals? And yet as Justice Holmes made clear, the right of communities to safety, social justice, or a healthy environment may, under certain circumstances, transcend the right of an individual to cry fire in a crowded theatre. So if we do care about a sustainable and just future for all the beings on the planet, how do we hold our own convictions while honoring our students' rights to theirs?

The debate lies at the core of democratic discourse and rapidly expands from the classroom to the legislative chambers. But, in the end, we are left with what Mary Ann Glendon (1991) has called "a dialogue of despair." We seem tangled in a Gordian knot of "rights talk" in which the competing rights of one group seem destined to be trumped by those of another. What we need, Glendon suggests, is not simply a new doctrine of group rights but rather "a fuller concept of human personhood and a more ecological way of thinking about social policy" (p. 137). In effect, we need to think more richly into the implications of our growing recognition that we human beings are radically socially constituted from the earliest moments of our lives. If we really take this truth seriously, then the issue of rights or even responsibilities takes its proper place in the context of our given interdependence. Whether we have a right as individuals or communities to impose our ideas on another remains an important question always, but it must now be understood in light of the recognition that *our very selves* are constituted out of a lifelong dialogue with the ideas, predispositions, fears, longings, attitudes, and assorted wisdoms of our surroundings.

What we must learn, finally and yet again, is that we are both apart from and a part of the world. Thus, "emancipatory learning" is not about *escape from* but rather about a deeper *immersion into* the rough-and-tumble of human relationship. An education that reveals and enhances our radical interdependence with all creation frees us from a "false consciousness" of our separateness into a richer understanding of our underlying relatedness. I believe that as we deepen our apprehension of this truth we will grow ever less vulnerable to the either-or thinking of "self versus other" and more able to recognize that we are always beings-in-relation (Buber, 1958). The real work of our adulthood is to grow ever more deeply in love with the world. And as this happens, the possibility of deliberately injuring another person will grow as unthinkable as deliberately injuring ourselves. Our responsibility as adult educators goes beyond merely teaching critical reflection, important as that is. Our responsibility is to work to bring about transformation at the individual and societal level that will enable us to realize our fundamental interdependence with one another and the world. One of the best treatments of this stance appears in Robert Kegan's *In Over Our Heads* (1994), in which he describes the "inter-institutional order of consciousness," an orientation strikingly similar to that of many interviewees in *Common Fire*.

Reflecting on his lifelong commitment to working on behalf of a just society, Nelson Mandela concludes, "I simply found myself doing so, and could not do otherwise" (p. 95). This sense of inevitability appears again and again in our interviews, often cropping up as a double negative: "I can't not act," "You can't not do it," "I couldn't do otherwise." Whether they worked for social justice, ethical business practice, environmental restoration, educational reform, community health, animal rights, or conflict resolution, people would describe their choice to do their work as if the choice were not entirely their own. Said an attorney with a history of work with social reform, "I really have no choice. It's become a part of me. It's what I feel I'm about . . . ." At the same time, note that he said, "It has become . . ." He is aware that he has undergone a journey of transformation and it is searingly clear from even a glance at the circumstances of his life, as among the others we studied, that his life was graced and nurtured by webs of relationships within which ongoing transformation occurred through rich dialogue with others. In a world that ruthlessly offers greater material incentives and a bombardment of encouragement to place one's own welfare before that of the larger community, to care for the larger good seems almost an act of civil disobedience. And yet the lessons are right before us. Deep change takes time, strategic care, patience, the conviction that we are not working alone, and the faith that there is something in the universe, as Robert Frost said, "that doesn't love a wall." It calls us as teachers and as citizens to seek out and encourage engagement with those different from ourselves, to foster critical reflection on the meaning of our differences, to create mentoring communities where socially responsible commitments can be formed and sustained, and to make available opportunities to practice these emerging and vital commitments. These are small steps, but each one makes another possible.

References

Bennett, M. "Towards Ethnorelativism: A Developmental Model of Intercultural Sensitivity." In M. Paige (ed.), Cross-Cultural Orientation. Lanham, Md.: University Press of America, 1986, 76–118.

Buber, M. *I and Thou*. New York: Scribner, 1958.

Bush, R., and Folger, J. *The Promise of Mediation: Responding to Conflict Through Empowerment and Recognition*. San Francisco: Jossey-Bass, 1994.

Chambers, S. "Discourse and Democratic Practices." In S. K. White (ed.), *The Cambridge Guide to Habermas*. Cambridge, U.K.: Cambridge University Press, 1995, 233–263.

Cohen, N. *Mentoring Adult Learners: A Guide for Educators and Trainers*. Malabar, Fla.: Krieger, 1995.

Colby, A., and Damon, W. *Some Do Care: Contemporary Lives of Moral Commitment*. New York: Free Press, 1992.

Courtenay, B., Merriam, S., and Reeves, P. "The Centrality of Meaning-Making in Transformational Learning: How HIV-Positive Adults Make Sense of Their Lives." *Adult Education Quarterly*, 1998, 48(2), 65–84.

Daloz, L. *Mentor: Guiding the Journey of Adult Learners*. San Francisco: Jossey-Bass, 1999.

Daloz, L., Keen, C., Keen, J., and Parks, S. *Common Fire: Leading Lives of Commitment in a Complex World*. Boston: Beacon Press, 1996.

Everett, M. *Breaking Ranks*. New York: Bantam, 1984.

Fogel, A. *Developing Through Relationships: Origins of Communication, Self, and Culture*. Chicago: University of Chicago Press, 1993.

Galbraith, M., and Cohen, N. *Mentoring: New Strategies and Challenges*. San Francisco: Jossey-Bass, 1995.

Glendon, M. *Rights Talk: The Impoverishment of Political Discourse*. New York: Free Press, 1991.

Glendon, M., and Blankenhorn, D. (eds.). *Seedbeds of Virtue: Sources of Competence, Character, and Citizenship in American Society*. Lanham, Md.: Madison Books, 1995.

Kegan, R. *In Over Our Heads: The Mental Demands of Modern Life*. Cambridge, Mass.: Harvard University Press, 1994.

Lesy, M. *Rescues: The Lives of Heroes*. New York: Farrar, Strauss & Giroux, 1991.

Levinson, D. J., and others. *The Seasons of a Man's Life*. New York: Knopf, 1978.

Mandela, N. *Long Walk to Freedom*. Boston: Little, Brown, 1994.

Marstin, R. *Beyond Our Tribal Gods*. Maryknoll, N.Y.: Orbis Press, 1979.

Murray, M. *Beyond the Myths and Magic of Mentoring*. San Francisco: Jossey-Bass, 1991.

Newman, M. *Defining the Enemy: Adult Education in Social Action*. Sydney, Australia: Stewart Victor, 1994.

Oliner, S., and Oliner, P. *The Altruistic Personality: Rescuers of Jews in Nazi Europe*. New York: Free Press, 1988.

Parks, S. *The Critical Years: The Young Adult Search for Faith, Meaning, and Commitment.* San Francisco: HarperCollins, 1986.

Parks, S. *The University as a Mentoring Environment.* Indianapolis: Indiana Office for Campus Ministries, 1992.

Parks, S. *Big Questions, Worthy Dreams: Mentoring the Young Adult Search for Meaning, Purpose, and Faith.* San Francisco: Jossey-Bass, 2000.

Perry, W. *Forms of Intellectual and Ethical Development in the College Years: A Scheme.* Austin, Tex.: Holt, Rinehart and Winston, 1967.

Rothman, J. "Reflexive Dialogue as Transformation." *Mediation Quarterly,* 1996, *13*(4), 345–352.

Tang, Y. "Fostering Transformation Through Differences: The Synergic Inquiry Framework." *Revision,* 1997, *20*(1), 15–19.

Taylor, E. *The Theory and Practice of Transformative Learning: A Critical Review.* Information Series No. 374, Eric Clearinghouse on Adult, Career, and Vocational Education. Columbus, Ohio: Center on Education and Training for Employment, College of Education, Ohio State University, 1998.

Warren, M. "Democratic Theory and Self-Transformation," *American Political Science Review,* 1992, *86*(1), 8–23.

Welch, S. *A Feminist Ethic of Risk.* Minneapolis: Fortress Press, 1990.

West, C. *Race Matters.* Boston: Beacon Press, 1993.

Wilson, E. O. *The Diversity of Life.* New York: Norton, 1992.

Wunsch, M. *Mentoring Revisited: Making an Impact on Individuals and Institutions.* San Francisco: Jossey-Bass, 1994.

5

Transformative Learning as Ideology Critique

Stephen D. Brookfield

Helping learners become more critically reflective of the assumptions they and others hold is argued by Mezirow to be a cardinal function of adult education and central to a transformational theory of adult learning. Although critical reflection is an ineradicable element of transformative learning, it is not a synonym for it. Adapting a distinction borrowed from the philosophy of science, critical reflection is a necessary but not sufficient condition of transformative learning. In other words, transformative learning cannot happen without critical reflection, but critical reflection can happen without an accompanying transformation in perspective or habit of mind. In this chapter I argue that examining power relationships and hegemonic assumptions must be integral to the definition of critical reflection, thus turning it into a political idea. I also problematize the idea of transformative learning, explore the relationship between critical reflection and transformative learning, and comment on the connection between transformative learning and social action.

Defining Critical Reflection

Reflection and reflective practice must be some of the most commonly invoked terms in the world of educational theorizing today. Complicating this situation is the frequent conflating of the terms *reflection* and *critical reflection,* as if adding "critical" somehow makes reflection deeper and more profound. The word *critical* is in real danger of losing any connection to one of the most important intellectual traditions from which it sprang: the Frankfurt School of Critical Social Theory and ideology critique. This chapter tries to recapture this tradition and locate critical reflection firmly within it.

In my view reflection is not, by definition, critical. It is quite possible for adult educators to work reflectively while focusing solely on technical decisions, on the nuts and bolts of classroom process. For example, we can reflect on the timing of coffee breaks, whether to use blackboards or flip charts, or the advantages of using a liquid crystal display panel over previously prepared overheads. All these decisions rest on assumptions that can be identified and questioned, and all of them can be looked at from different perspectives. But these are not in and of themselves examples of *critical* reflection. Of course, just because reflection is not critical does not mean it is unimportant or unnecessary. We cannot get through the day without making numerous technical decisions concerning timing and process. These decisions are made rapidly and often instinctively. They are also usually made without an awareness of how the apparently isolated and idiosyncratic world of the classroom embodies forces, contradictions, and structures of the wider society.

What is it, then, that makes reflection critical? Is critical reflection a deeper, more intense and probing form of reflection? Not necessarily. Critical reflection on experience certainly tends to lead to the uncovering of paradigmatic, structuring assumptions. But the depth of a reflective effort does not, in and of itself, make it critical. For me the word *critical* is sacred and I object to its being thrown around indiscriminately. For something to count as an example of critical learning, critical analysis, or critical reflection, I believe that the persons concerned must engage in some sort of power analysis of the situation or context in which the learning is happening. They must also try to identify assumptions they hold dear that are actually destroying their sense of well-being and serving the interests of others: that is, hegemonic assumptions.

I don't mean by this to suggest that critically reflective learning can only be about politics or economics. I think one can learn critically about chemistry, art, soccer, literature, spirituality, music, or sex (among many other things). These always have a political dimension in that they are all structured by and entail power relationships, dominant and contending discourses, and unequal access to resources. The critically reflective dimension to learning in these areas is evident when we learn to identify and challenge the criteria that define how good art, edifying literature, skillful sexual conduct, or beautiful music should be judged, or when we learn how certain socially valued protocols and expressions of appreciation came to constitute the standard or norm. Even things as apparently idiosyncratic as taste and style are social creations reflecting the battle between opposing worldviews that themselves often reflect factors of class and status (Hebidge, 1979).

Critical learning about the natural sciences would focus on understanding how the hypothetico-deductive method (which often assumes an unproblematized status as a universally valid mode of inquiry) was developed in a specific context and disseminated through certain already-established networks of communication. One could plausibly trace the genesis of this method to Bacon's *Novum Organon*—a book produced by a privileged individual in a particular time and place. This does not mean, by the way, that we automatically reject these criteria as inherently oppressive or exclusionary because they represent Eurocentric worldviews. But it does mean that we acknowledge that their position of preeminence has not been attained because they exhibit some sort of primal universal force or truth; rather, their acceptance is socially and politically created.

We can learn critically about the emotional dimension to our lives when we investigate the extent to which our instinctual feelings and automatic emotional responses to certain situations are socially learned. Sometimes we realize this is the result of deliberate engineering, of manufacturing outrage or hysteria. Sociologist Stanley Cohen (1972) observed how mass media regularly create moral panics in which various groups take turns to be demonized.

Large-scale patriotic fervor is a social phenomenon. Even an apparently spontaneous emotional eruption, such as the mass grieving for Princess Diana, can be analyzed as a social flow or momentum. We also learn moral revulsion and approbation by watching how authority figures (such as parents) or exemplary models (such as good friends or personal heroes) react in certain ways to certain situations and how they decree that a certain emotional response is appropriate.

The Centrality of Ideology Critique to Critical Reflection

I believe that the ideas of critical theory—particularly that of ideology critique—must be central to critical reflection and, by implication, to transformation. *Ideology critique* is a term associated with thinkers from the Frankfurt School of Critical Social Theory, particularly Adorno (1973), Horkheimer (1947), and Marcuse (1964). It describes the process by which people learn to recognize how uncritically accepted and unjust dominant ideologies are embedded in everyday situations and practices. Critical reflection as ideology critique focuses on helping people come to an awareness of how capitalism shapes belief systems and assumptions (ideologies) that justify and maintain economic and political inequiy. To the contemporary educational critic Henry Giroux (1983, pp. 154–155), "the ideological dimension that underlies all critical reflection is that it lays bare the historically and socially sedimented values at work in the construction of knowledge, social relations, and material practices. . . . [I]t situates critique within a radical notion of interest and social transformation." An important element in this tradition is the thought of Antonio Gramsci (1978), whose concept of hegemony explains the way in which people are convinced to embrace dominant ideologies as always being in their own best interests.

Ideology critique is close to what Mezirow (1998) calls "systemic" critical reflection and he deals extensively with it in the part of his transformative learning theory that focuses on probing sociocultural distortions (Mezirow, 1990). As well as including a theory of social analysis, ideology critique also contains within it the promise of social transformation and frames the work of influential activist adult educators such as Freire, Tawney, Williams, Horton, Coady, and Tomkins. At the basis of criticality in this tradition is the understanding and challenging of dominant ideologies. Understanding ideology means knowing how it's embedded in the inclinations, biases, hunches, and apparently intuitive ways of experiencing reality that we think are unique to us. To challenge ideology we need to be aware of how it lives within us and works against us by furthering the interests of others. Without this element of ideology critique, the process of clarifying and questioning assumptions is reflective but not necessarily critical.

Ideologies are sets of values, beliefs, myths, explanations, and justifications that appear self-evidently true and morally desirable. What we think are our personal interpretations and dispositions are, in Marcuse's terms (1964), ideologically sedimented. French social theorists Louis Althusser (1969) and Pierre Bourdieu (1977) argue that what seem to us to be natural ways of understanding our experiences are actually internalized dimensions of ideology. Bourdieu calls this "habitus"; Althusser writes of "our affective, unconscious relations with the world . . . the ways in which we are pre-reflectively bound up in social reality" (Eagleton, 1991, p. 18). So what seems to us to be our idiosyncratic "structures of feeling," to use Raymond Williams's (1977) term, are really social products shaped by the cultural group and social class to which we belong.

Ideologies are manifest in language, social habits, and cultural forms. They legitimize certain political structures and educational practices so that these come to be accepted as representing the normal order of things.

The emphasis of cultural critics such as Williams on how ideology lives within our internal structures of feeling is an important one. Mezirow argues that ideology critique is appropriate for critical reflection on external ideologies such as communism, capitalism, or fascism or for reflection on our own "economic, ecological, educational, linguistic, political, religious, bureaucratic, or other taken-for-granted cultural systems" (Mezirow, 1998, p. 193). But he distinguishes it from critical reflection on and in private intrapersonal domains. However, as Eagleton (1991) has shown, ideology critique has become a much more subtle form of analysis since its early emphasis on the way in which the superstructure of cultural, religious, and political beliefs was framed by the base of economic relationships. Now, as culturalists such as Williams and postructuralists such as Foucault argue, ideologies are experienced as constituent elements of our personalities, framing how we experience the world. From this point of view, ideology critique focuses on how ideology lives within us, pervading our emotional responses. Ideology is not to be understood as pertaining only to our beliefs about social, political, and economic systems, but as something that frames our moral reasoning, our interpersonal relationships, and our ways of knowing, experiencing, and judging what is real and true.

When we do ideology critiques we try to penetrate the givens of everyday reality to reveal the inequities and oppression that lurk beneath. But because of their pervasiveness and persuasiveness, ideologies are hard to penetrate. They are perceived both as representing widely held commonsense understanding and as springing from the unique circumstances of our own lives. However, by turning logic on its head, looking at situations sideways, and making imaginative leaps we realize that things are the way they are for a reason. Through ideology critique what strikes us as the normal order of life is revealed as a constructed reality that serves to protect the interests of the powerful. If what Foucault (1980) calls the "normalizing gaze" is socially constructed, it occurs to us that it can be dismantled and remade by human effort.

This tradition frames my own understanding of critical reflection in adult education by imbuing critical reflection with two distinct purposes, both of which are variations of ideology critique. The first is to understand how considerations of power undergird, frame, and distort so many adult educational processes and interactions. The second is to question assumptions and practices that seem to make our lives easier but that actually end up working against our own best long-term interests—in other words, those that are hegemonic. Before elaborating these purposes in more detail, I want to explore how my understanding departs from Mezirow's use of the term *critical reflection*.

Reviewing Interpretations of Critical Reflection

My interpretation of critical reflection as placed squarely in the tradition of ideology critique differs from Mezirow's in that it is more limited. In his most extended exploration of the centrality of this concept to transformative learning, Mezirow allows for the possibility of implicit critical reflection "as when we mindlessly choose between good and evil because of our assimilated values" (1998, p. 186). I would not allow such a possibility because it denies the intentionality central to ideology critique. For me, critical reflection would focus on making explicit and analyzing that which was previously implicit and uncritically accepted. Mezirow goes on to say that when critical reflection focuses on the investigation of assumptions, which for me would be the only form critical reflection could take, "a different order of abstraction is introduced, with major potential for effecting a change in one's established frame of reference" (p. 186). He proposes a taxonomy of this particular type of critical reflection on assumptions, dividing it into objective and subjective reframing.

Objective reframing focuses on learners doing a critical analysis of the concepts, beliefs, feelings, or actions communicated to them, or pausing to examine assumptions about the way problems of action have been framed. Subjective reframing is characterized as critical self-reflection on assumptions (CSRA). CSRA "emphasizes critical analysis of the psychological or cultural assumptions that are the specific reasons for one's conceptual and psychological limitations, the constitutive processes or conditions of formation of one's experiences and beliefs" (p. 193). Subjective framing itself is split into several subcategories (narrative, systemic, organizational, moral-ethical, therapeutic, and epistemic), of which systemic is the closest to my interpretation of critical reflection. Systemic CSRA "involves critical reflection on one's own assumptions pertaining to the economic, ecological, educational, linguistic, political, religious, bureaucratic, or other taken-for-granted cultural systems. We critically reflect on the canons, paradigms, or ideologies that have generated traditional roles and relationships, and on how they have shaped and limited the development of our point of view and have fostered dependency relationships. Systemic CSRA often leads to some form of collective or collaborative social action" (p. 193).

I am impressed and intrigued by this taxonomy. Like most attempts at creating taxonomies, the carving up of a phenomenon into discrete domains helps delineate the range of the phenomenon and indicate the range of shadings within it. Yet I am uneasy that this CSRA taxonomy risks separating the inseparable if it is taken by researchers and practitioners as a once and for all empirically accurate rendering of the forms critical reflection takes. I accept that sometimes proposing a temporary taxonomy is a good and helpful way to pause and map out a provisional intellectual territory as a way of prompting further debate, refutation, and reformulation. This is something Mezirow is particularly adept at, as the numerous extensions, refutations, and elaborations of his position in the pages of *Adult Education Quarterly* demonstrate. It is also the way he works to develop his theory. By proposing taxonomies and then responding to his critics, Mezirow is engaged in a dialogical (and very public) development of his theory of transformative learning. In this his theory and practice are very consistent. His understanding of critical reflection is that it happens in a community of rational discourse, and a significant element of his theorizing about critical reflection takes place within such a community (of scholars and researchers in adult education).

But we should always remember that the creation of taxonomies springs from the Aristotelian principle of mutual exclusivity. This principle holds that what is contained in one category cannot be evident in another. My experience of critical reflection is that it cannot be carved up in this way. Mezirow himself admits this at various points in his writings. For example, in one response to critiques of his work (1994b) he discusses "whether it is possible and useful to differentiate between transformative learning that deals with sociolinguistic codes and that which deals with psychological codes" and concludes that although it is important to do this "there is obviously a great deal of overlap in learning dicated by these codes and by epistemic codes as well" (p. 243).

More recently, in discussing the first kind of CSRA—narrative CSRA—he acknowledges that "in practice, there may be considerable overlap among these forms" (1998, p. 193). Substitute the word "is" for "may be" and I would agree. Every one of the categories that Mezirow sets up as distinct from systemic CSRA in my view involves some form of ideology critique. For me critical reflection on even the most private matters or in the most unknowable domains is culturally contingent. At the most basic of levels the language and concepts we use to do reflection are culturally framed, transmitted, and learned, thereby representing power formations. So I see ideology critique—or what Mezirow calls systemic CSRA—as the overarching domain of critical reflection, with his other subcategories as different dimensions of this overall activity. Let me illustrate what I mean.

Narrative CSRA, the first of his subcategories, refers to critical reflection that is prompted by the adult's reading a narrative in which the author reflects critically on her own assumptions or poses a set of assumptions that challenges those held by the reader. To me, critical reflection on and about narratives involves a critique of the narrative form itself. It entails understanding how narratives are social constructs in which authors frequently place themselves in the center as the chief protagonists, heroines or villains of the story. Narratives are often expressed in linear developmental forms. For example, a critically reflective teacher writing about her journey as a practitioner might say something like "I used to teach in an unwittingly oppressive way, perpetuating inequities of race, class, and gender. Now—as a result of a disorienting dilemma that caused me to reflect critically on my abuse of power—I have washed my practice free of the stains of racism, classism, sexism, and oppression." Or someone who perceives herself as a member of an oppressed minority might say "I used to live my life according to others' expectations; I didn't know who I was or how to live according to my own assumptions and beliefs. Now I've discovered who I really am—my core self—through critical reflection, and I'm living a more authentic and integrated life."

Postmodernists, particularly Derrida (1978), Lyotard (1984), and Lacan (1979), reject this notion of linear progress. They contend that narratives of critical analysis in which people experience contradictions, are visited by revelations, get better, and come to fuller self-knowledge are necessary palliatives but essentially false. There is no core self waiting to be discovered at the center of these stories, according to these writers. Our narratives of critical reflection and self-discovery are artifices—fictional creations in which we feature as the hero but not to be confused with the chaotic fragmentation of daily experience. As we create these narratives we use socially familiar narrative forms—language, metaphors, and concepts—that are culturally learned. So to do narrative CSRA we must learn how our narrative forms are socially constructed and often distorted. This is one plausible dimension of ideology critique.

Organizational CSRA, as described by Mezirow, is "directed at identifying assumptions that are embedded in the history and culture of a workplace, and how they have impacted on one's own thought or action" (1998, p. 193), a process that seems to me directly to entail ideology critique. Investigating how assumptions are embedded in the history and culture of the workplace means understanding the broader social, political, and economic context that has shaped a particular workplace culture. For example, the principle of merit payments for faculty is a strong feature of many college organizational cultures. The idea that the best and brightest be separated from the masses and rewarded cannot be investigated without realizing how it parallels the competitive ethic of free-market capitalism. Moral-ethical CSRA "involves a critique of the norms governing one's ethical decision-making. This is critical reflection on value judgments one has made or is considering, and is often related to conscience and one's idealized self-image" (Mezirow, 1998, p. 194). As I have written elsewhere (Brookfield, 1998), because the norms, value judgments, and self-images we play with in the process of making moral decisions are socially learned, anytime we critically examine these we are doing a kind of ideology critique.

Similarly, therapeutic CSRA develops "critical insight pertaining to assumptions governing one's problematic *feelings* and related *dispositions*, and their action consequences. . . . [O]ne examines the sources, nature, and effect of assumptions governing the way one feels and is disposed to act upon his or her feelings" (Mezirow, 1998, p. 194). Again I would argue that, because we learn assumptions about what and how we are supposed to feel from media images or through our intimate relationships (which are themselves socially constructed through interpersonal habits and patterns learned in families), this too involves ideology critique.

The final form of CSRA—epistemic—occurs when the learner "sets out to examine the assumptions and explore the causes (biographical, historical, cultural), nature (including moral and ethical dimensions), and consequences (individual and interpersonal) of his or her frames of reference to ascertain why he or she is predisposed to learn in a certain way or to appropriate particular goals" (Mezirow, 1998, p. 195). Mezirow himself identifies the biographical, historical, and cultural background to these assumptions in the first part of this quote. Epistemology is the study of the grounds for knowledge, of how we know that something is true. It seems to me that the epistemologies we hold comprise in large part the standards and criteria we use to judge that we know something correctly. These standards and criteria are often tacit and unproblematized. But that doesn't mean that they exist a priori in our mental structures or consciousness; rather they are socially created and learned.

Mezirow quotes the Dialogue Project at MIT as facilitating this kind of critical reflection in its focus on "the assumptions, taken for granted, the flow of the polarization of opinions, the rules for acceptable and unacceptable conversation, and the methods for managing differences" (Isaacs, 1993, p. 31). This project appears to be an investigation of the social structuring of dialogue and the social creation of rules to govern conversation and difference. Because these rules don't exist independent of human creation (someone gets to propose them, and there is a social process by which some are chosen as more valid than others), critical reflection on them involves an investigation and critique of the way certain intellectual communities gain the power to make and disseminate norms of discourse; in other words, ideology critique.

The Distinct Purposes of Critical Reflection

As I argued earlier, the first important focus of critical reflection is on the uncovering of submerged power dynamics and relationships. As an illustration of how this first purpose can be realized, I want to frame my analysis around what a critically reflective stance toward adult educational practice would involve. The first feature of such a stance would be its focus on identifying and critiquing the (often submerged) power dynamics that permeate adult education practice.

Power is omnipresent in adult education. It is evident in the processes of curriculum decision making and evaluation, in the teaching methods instinctively adopted, in the kinds of discourse allowed in learner speech and writing, even in the way the chairs are set out. The flow of power can be named and redirected or made to serve the interests of the many rather than the few, but it can never be denied or erased. In Foucault's words (1980, p. 141), "it seems to me that power is 'always already there,' that one is never 'outside' it, that there are no 'margins' for those who break with the system to gambol in." Becoming aware of how the dynamics of power permeate all adult educational activities helps us realize that forces present in the wider society always intrude into our work with learners. We come to see that adult education classrooms are not limpid, tranquil eddies cut off from the river of social, cultural, and political life. They are contested arenas—whirlpools containing the contradictory crosscurrents of the struggles for material superiority and ideological legitimacy that exist in the world outside. When we become aware of the pervasiveness of power we begin to notice the oppressive dimensions to adult educational practices that we had thought were neutral or even benevolent. To use Mary Parker Follett's terms (1924a, 1924b), we start to explore how power *over* learners is transformed into power *with* learners.

Externalizing and investigating power relationships (the first purpose of critical reflection) forces us as adult educators to acknowledge the considerable power we exercise in our practice. Many of us would like to believe either that we have no special power over adult learners or that any power mistakenly attributed to us by them is an illusion that can quickly be dissolved by our own refusal to dominate the group. But it is not that easy. No matter how much we protest our desire to be at one with learners there is often a predictable flow of attention focused on us. Although it is important to privilege learners' voices and to create multiple foci of attention in the classroom, it is disingenuous to pretend that as educators we are the same as students. Better to acknowledge publicly our position of power, to engage learners in deconstructing that power, and to attempt to model a critical analysis of our own source of authority in front of them. This involves us in becoming alert to, and publicly admitting, oppressive dimensions to our practice that learners, colleagues, and literature have helped us to see. So critical reflection on power in the adult classroom sometimes leads to a fundamental reordering of how power is named and understood. Learners become transformative agents of their own education, cocreators of knowledge and curricula.

The second purpose of critical reflection is to uncover hegemonic assumptions. Hegemonic assumptions are those that we believe represent commonsense wisdom and that we accept as being in our own best interests without realizing that these same assumptions actually work against us in the long term by serving the interests of those opposed to us. As developed by the Italian political economist and activist Antonio Gramsci (1978), the term *hegemony* describes the process whereby ideas, structures, and actions come to be seen by the majority of people as wholly natural, preordained, and working for their own good when in fact they are constructed and transmitted by powerful minority interests to protect the status quo that serves these interests so well. The subtlety of hegemony is that over time it becomes deeply embedded, part of the cultural air we breathe. One cannot peel back the layers of oppression and point the finger at an identifiable group or groups of people whom we accuse as being the instigators of a conscious conspiracy to keep people silent and disenfranchised. Instead the ideas and practices of hegemony become part and parcel of everyday life—the stock opinions, conventional wisdoms, or commonsense ways of seeing and ordering the world that people take for granted. If there is a conspiracy here, it is the conspiracy of the normal.

Hegemonic assumptions about adult education are those that are eagerly embraced by practitioners because they seem to represent what's good and true about the field and therefore to be in educators' and learners' own best interests. Yet these assumptions end up serving the interests of groups that have little concern for adult educators' mental or physical health. The dark irony of hegemony is that educators take pride in acting on the very assumptions that work to entrap them. In working diligently to implement these assumptions, educators become willing prisoners who lock their own cell doors behind them.

Critical reflection on hegemonic processes becomes transformative when it fosters challenges to hegemony, when it prompts counterhegemonic practices. An example of a hegemonic assumption in adult education is the assumption that adult education is a vocation requiring self-abasement by practitioners on behalf of learners. Embracing this assumption opens adult educators to exploitation by senior administrators who can play on educators' guilt feelings to convince them to take on more and more work, thereby reducing administrative costs. It gets to the point where adult educators pride themselves on a good day's work only when they arrive home completely drained and with no energy to do anything but watch reruns of *The Brady Bunch*.

Problematizing the Idea of Transformative Learning

Having elaborated my particular interpretation of critical reflection, I want now to turn to the concept of transformative learning. In my own work I have consistently refrained from using the concept of transformative learning as a central point of analysis in any discussions of critical reflection. There are several reasons, having mostly to do with what I see as the misuse of the word *transformative* to refer to any instance in which reflection leads to a deeper, more nuanced understanding of assumptions. I should stress that this misuse is one I see in professional conversations at conferences, research seminars, graduate education, and staff meetings, not in Mezirow's work. When one reads Mezirow's careful analysis in his major book (Mezirow, 1991) and his various clarifications and elaborations of the idea (Mezirow, 1992, 1994a, 1994b, 1997), it is clear that he has been consistent in asserting that a transformation is a transformation in perspective, in a frame of reference, in a personal paradigm, and in a habit of mind together with its resulting points of view. For him transformation thereby involves a fundamental reordering of assumptions.

I share this understanding. No matter how much it might be described as an incremental process, transformative learning has for me connotations of an epiphanic, or apocalyptic, cognitive event— a shift in the tectonic plates of one's assumptive clusters. I believe an act of learning can be called transformative only if it involves a fundamental questioning and reordering of how one thinks or acts. If something is transformed, it is different from what it was before at a very basic level. Having a more informed, nuanced, sophisticated, or deeper understanding of something (such as an idea, an assumption, or an educational practice) is not, for me, equivalent to transformative learning. Transformative learning would be learning where the learner came to a new understanding of something that caused a fundamental reordering of the paradigmatic assumptions she held about the idea or action concerned. I believe that many working adult educators have this understanding of the word *transformative*.

Using transformation in this way, however, does raise certain difficulties. For example, it means that when we attach the qualifier *transformative* to some form of practice (as in transformative leadership, transformative counseling, transformative teaching) it immediately becomes imbued with weighty significance. Those who describe themselves as facilitators of transformation thereby place themselves under a burden of guilt. If, for some reason, one's leadership, counsel, or teaching falls short of producing a major change of outlook or commitment in those led, counseled, or taught, then feelings of failure quickly set in. One has not been sufficiently energetic in pushing the envelope to produce the revolutionary change that the term *transformation* seems to call for. Taking "transformative" as the chief descriptor for educational practice means that the main part of our work—which involves engaging people in incrementally deepening their understandings of ideas and actions—becomes, in effect, underestimated and devalued. Of course, if you believe that this kind of learning can accurately be described as transformative, then there is no problem. The problem only occurs if you accept my view that although this learning is crucial and valuable it stops sort of the fundamental reordering that the word *transformative* implies.

The word *transformative*—when indiscriminately attached to any practice we happen to approve of—thereby loses any descriptive or definitional utility. More specifically, it falls victim to the twin dangers of evacuation and reification of meaning. Evacuation describes the process whereby a term is used so often, to refer to so many different things, that it ceases to have any distinctive terms of reference. This is one fate that has befallen the term *empowerment*. To many people empowerment is far removed from the words and actions of Paulo Freire or Myles Horton; rather it is something engaged in by self-help gurus like Susan Powter or Tony Robbins or associated with conservative movements and institutions like Bill Bennett's *Empower America* and Newt Gingrich's *Empowerment TV* network. Reification describes the elevation of a word or idea to a realm of discourse where it appears to have an independent existence separate from the conditions under which that word is produced and used. The word becomes revered, either imbued with mystical significance and placed beyond the realm of critical analysis or accepted uncritically as obviously a "good thing."

I have noticed this happening to the term *transformative*. This word is invoked by practitioners as a form of scriptural signaling to show peers that they subscribe to a certain set of beliefs and practices. Encoded in the term is the message that its user is a sensitive and empathic adult educator, concerned to wreak deep changes in learners who will come to a more accurate understanding of reality. Adult educators working in this self-consciously transformative vein need to take steps to stop "transformative" from becoming a premature ultimate; that is, a term that once invoked forestalls further debate or critical analysis. The most common example of a premature ultimate in adult educational discourse is probably the phrase "meeting needs." Adult educators frequently tell each other that the reason they are doing something is because it meets learners' needs. This invokes a sense of certainty and finality that serves to prevent the asking of inconvenient questions: Whose needs? Are they needs or wants?

Distinguishing Between Critical Reflection and Transformative Learning

So exactly what is the relationship between transformative learning and critical reflection? In terms of the core propositions in Mezirow's transformational theory, critical reflection is integral to transformative learning. The reflective discourse that adults engage in to come to best judgments concerning the accuracy of their interpretations and beliefs cannot happen without a critical assessment of assumptions. Mezirow believes adult learning occurs in four ways—elaborating existing frames of reference, learning frames of references, transforming points of view, and transforming habits of mind—and names critical reflection as a component of all of these. We transform frames of reference through critical reflection on assumptions supporting the content and/or process of problem solving. We transform our habits of mind by becoming critically reflective of the premises defining the problem. Mezirow contends that the two central elements of transformative learning—objective and subjective reframing—involve either critical reflection on the assumptions of others (objective reframing) or on one's own assumptions (subjective reframing). He argues that the overall purpose of adult development is to realize one's agency through increasingly expanding awareness and critical reflection. The function of adult educators becomes to assist this development by helping learners reflect critically on their own and others' assumptions.

So in terms of Mezirow's transformational theory it is clear that transformative learning cannot happen without critical reflection being involved at every stage. Given this, it might seem logical to extrapolate from Mezirow's comments that the two processes are equivalent—synonyms for each other. Yet this would be a mistake and Mezirow carefully avoids it. Critical reflection is certainly a necessary condition of transformative learning, in that the existence of the latter depends on the presence of the former. However, it is not a sufficient condition; in other words, just because critical reflection is occurring does not mean that transformative learning inevitably ensues. An episode of critical reflection on practice does not automatically lead to transformation. As Mezirow acknowledges, the assumptions one holds can be exactly the same after critical reflection as they were before.

For example, one can reflect with colleagues on the hidden dynamics of teacher power and the way in which apparently liberating practices can be experienced by some learners as oppressive.

One can also realize that one's assumptions were more contextually variable than previously imagined, thereby leading to a deepened, new, and more informed understanding of why these assumptions were accurate and valid. For such reflection to be properly labeled transformative, however, the foundational premises that govern one's thoughts or actions would have to be fundamentally changed. Merely understanding better the nuances and multiple realities of an idea or practice does not, in my view, deserve to be called transformative. That term, as Mezirow points out, needs to be reserved for an episode in which the idea or practice concerned undergoes substantial revision to the extent that its new form is qualitatively different from the old. If an episode of classroom research into my own practice had led me to conclude that trust was built best through a charismatic and hierarchical exercise of teacher power, that would have been transformative for me. Transformative learning concerning the use of the circle in teaching would have entailed a wholly new form of democratic seating or a rejection of the importance of furniture arrangements, not a fine-tuning of what went before.

Critical Reflection and Transformative Action

The connection between critical reflection and some form of transformative social action is, for some, self-evident. Building on Freirean interpretations of praxis, this school of thought holds that reflection only becomes truly critical when it leads to transformation. Without consequent social action, critical reflection is castigated as liberal dilettantism, a self-indulgent form of speculation that makes no real difference to anything. This is the heart of critiques of Transformation Theory made by adult educators such as Cunningham (1992) and Newman (1993, 1994) and responded to by Mezirow in the pages of *Adult Education Quarterly* (Mezirow, 1992, 1994a, 1994b, 1997).

In these responses Mezirow has distinguished between transforming habits of mind and transforming structures and has written that "significant personal and social transformations may result from this kind of (critical) reflection" (1998, p. 186). He has also pointed out that a changed way of understanding the world and one's place within it represents a singularly important form of mental action. He writes that "deciding is an action in transformative learning. Upon reflection, one can decide not to change one's behavior. Or a change in behavior to implement the decision to act upon a reflective insight may be delayed because the immediate situation does not permit it or because one lacks dependable information, requisite skills, or the emotional commitment to proceed" (1992, p. 251). He distinguishes between the educational tasks of critical reflection—helping adults become aware of oppressive structures and practices, developing tactical awareness of how they might change these, and building the confidence and ability to work for collective change—and the broader scale political mobilization needed to force economic change (Mezirow, 1990, p. 210).

Here Mezirow is in good radical company. His distinction between the tasks of education and those of political mobilization echoes Myles Horton's insistence (1990) on the difference between organizing and education. Horton argued that organizing a specific political initiative required working toward specific limited goals. Education, by helping people become better analysts, could prepare people to organize, and organizing (if it was done democratically) could be educational, but sometimes the goals of organizing stood in opposition to the educational process. Paulo Freire, in conversations with Horton (Horton and Freire, 1990) and Ira Shor (Shor and Freire, 1987), also emphasized the limits of education where large-scale social, economic, and political transformation were concerned. Freire observed that "systematic or formal education, in spite of its importance, cannot really be the lever for the transformation of society" (Shor and Freire, p. 129). He urged teachers to be "critically conscious of the limits of education. That is, to know that education is not the lever, not to expect it to make the great social transformation" (p. 130).

However, this did not mean that education for critical reflection was somehow unimportant or that it had no wider social or political significance. In terms close to Freire's idea of teachers as cultural workers (1998), Mezirow (1999) has stated that we should think of adult educators as cultural activists. Freire argued that an awareness of the contradictions in society and a commitment to engaging in transformation could be fostered in classrooms. Echoing Freire's comments, Shor (Shor and Freire, 1987) agreed that "critical curiosity, some political awareness, democratic participation, habits of intellectual scrutiny, and interest in social change are realistic goals from inside a dialogic course" (p. 132). Importantly, for Freire an understanding of the limits of education helps us "avoid a certain naive optimism which can lead us in the future to a terrible pessimism. By avoiding naive optimism at the beginning we prevent ourselves from falling into despair and cynicism" (p. 130).

It is important to acknowledge that critical reflection's focus on illuminating power relationships and hegemonic assumptions can be the death of the transformative impulse, inducing an energy-sapping, radical pessimism concerning the possibility of structural change. It is undeniable that raising the consciousness of adult educators can easily produce negative effects on their practice. Knowing about the forces that use adult education to preserve and transmit dominant cultural values can leave its practitioners feeling puny and alone. Knowing that challenging the dominant ideology risks bringing isolation and punishment down on our heads is depressing and frightening. We can easily become demoralized by our awareness of the strength of the opposition and by the realization that questioning common sense may lead to our being excluded from the groups and communities that give us our sense of identity. Who has the courage, or foolhardiness, to commit cultural suicide in the cause of social transformation? So an unresolved question concerns how we remain critical yet optimistic while practicing a transformative pedagogy of hope (Freire, 1994).

The ravages of radical pessimism are felt most destructively by those who perceive themselves to be isolated, as the only sane ones in the madhouse struggling without help to transform their life-worlds, institutions, and communities. As Freire said, "[A]cting alone is the best way to commit suicide" (Shor and Freire, 1987, p. 61). I believe that critical reflection must be a collaborative project. Indeed, I am unable to see how it can be anything other than an irreducibly social process. Any critically reflective effort we undertake can only be accomplished with the help of critical friends. We need others to serve as critical mirrors who highlight our assumptions for us and reflect them back to us in unfamiliar, surprising, and disturbing ways. We also need our critical friends to provide emotional sustenance, to bring us "reports from the front" of their own critical journeys. One of the most deeply felt elements in tales from the dark side of critical reflection is the crucial importance that a community of peers has to sustaining people's commitment to the critical journey and the transformations it involves (Brookfield, 1994). It is thus entirely appropriate that the conference that prompted this book, and the book itself, represents a collective effort to understand, and live, the transformative learning process.

References

Adorno, T. W. *Negative Dialectics*. New York: Seabury Press, 1973.

Althusser, L. *For Marx*. New York: Vintage Books, 1969.

Brookfield, S. D. "Tales from the Dark Side: A Phenomenography of Adult Critical Reflection." *International Journal of Lifelong Education*, 1994, *13*(1), 203–216.

Brookfield, S. D. "Understanding and Facilitating Moral Learning in Adults." *Journal of Moral Education*, 1998, *27*(3), 283–300.

Bourdieu, P. "Cultural Reproduction and Social Reproduction." In J. Karabel and A. H. Halsey (eds.), *Power and Ideology in Education*. New York: Oxford University Press, 1977.

Cohen, S. *Folk Devils and Moral Panics*. London: MacGibbon and Kee, 1972.

Cunningham, P. "From Freire to Feminism: The North American Experience with Critical Pedagogy." *Adult Education Quarterly*, 1992, *42*(3), 180–191.

Derrida, J. *Writing and Difference*. New York: Routledge, 1978.

Eagleton, T. *Ideology: An Introduction*. London: Verso Press, 1991.

Follett, M. P. *Creative Experience*. New York: Longmans, Green, 1924a.

Follett, M. P. *Dynamic Administration*. New York: Longmans, Green, 1924b.

Foucault, M. *Power/Knowledge: Selected Interviews and Other Writings, 1972–1977*. New York: Pantheon Books, 1980.

Freire, P. *Pedagogy of Hope: Reliving Pedagogy of the Oppressed*. New York: Continuum, 1994.

Freire, P. *Teachers as Cultural Workers: Letters to Those Who Dare Teach*. Boulder, Colo.: Westview Press, 1998.

Giroux, H. A. *Theory and Resistance in Education: A Pedagogy for the Opposition*. Westport, Conn.: Bergin and Garvey, 1983.

Gramsci, A. *Selections from the Prison Notebooks*. London: Lawrence and Wishart, 1978.

Hebidge, D. *Subculture: The Meaning of Style*. New York: Routledge, 1979.

Horkheimer, M. *Eclipse of Reason*. New York: Oxford University Press, 1947.

Horton, M. *The Long Haul: An Autobiography*. New York: Doubleday, 1990.

Horton, M., and Freire, P. *We Make the Road by Walking: Conversations on Education and Social Change*. Philadelphia: Temple University Press, 1990.

Isaacs, W. *Taking Flight: Dialogue, Collective Thinking and Organizational Learning*. Cambridge, Mass.: Organizational Learning Center, Massachussetts Institute of Technology, 1993.

Lacan, J. *The Four Fundamental Concepts of Psychoanalysis*. London: Penguin, 1979.

Lyotard, J. *The Postmodern Condition: A Report on Knowledge*. Minneapolis: University of Minnesota Press, 1984.

Marcuse, H. *One Dimensional Man*. Boston: Beacon, 1964.

Mezirow, J. (ed.). *Fostering Critical Reflection in Adulthood*. San Francisco: Jossey-Bass, 1990.

Mezirow, J. *Transformative Dimensions of Adult Learning*. San Francisco: Jossey-Bass, 1991.

Mezirow, J. "Transformation Theory: Critique and Confusion." *Adult Education Quarterly*, 1992, 44(4), 250–252.

Mezirow, J. "Understanding Transformation Theory." *Adult Education Quarterly*, 1994a, 44(4), 222–232.

Mezirow, J. "Response to Mark Tennant and Michael Newman." *Adult Education Quarterly*, 1994b, 44(4), 243–244.

Mezirow, J. "Transformation Theory Out of Context." *Adult Education Quarterly*, 1997, 48(1), 60–62.

Mezirow, J. "On Critical Reflection." *Adult Education Quarterly*, 1998, 48(3), 185–198.

Mezirow, J. Dialogue with Cohort 2 of the Doctoral Program in Adult Education, National Louis University, Chicago, Feb. 12, 1999.

Newman, M. *The Third Contract: Theory and Practice in Trade Union Training*. Sydney, Australia: Victor Stewart, 1993.

Newman, M. *Defining the Enemy: Adult Education in Social Action*. Sydney, Australia: Victor Stewart, 1994.

Shor, I., and Freire, P. A *Pedagogy for Liberation: Dialogues on Transforming Education*. Westport, Conn.: Bergin and Garvey, 1987.

Williams, R. *Marxism and Literature*. New York: Oxford University Press, 1977.

II

Fostering Transformative
Learning in Practice

6

Teaching with Developmental Intention

Kathleen Taylor

*I am the first woman in my family to get a divorce
and the first to pursue a college education— I don't
know which is harder for my mother to accept. What
I know is I must step outside the boundaries of my
culture and learn to make my own way in the world.*

*In response to the Vietnam draft my family moved to
Canada, where I finished high school. I tried higher
education but dropped out because I couldn't conform. I didn't want to listen to some stuffy professor;
I wanted to change the world! What I finally realized
was I would have to have more education to make the
kind of contribution to society that's important to me.*

*I was raised in an extremely abusive environment.
After high school, I worked as a lab technician but
developed an increasing addiction to alcohol and tried
suicide more than once. Then I got pregnant, stopped
drinking, and realized I had to get serious about bringing some financial security and stability into my son's
life and mine.*

For their contributions to conceptualizing this chapter I gratefully acknowledge
my research collaborators, Catharine Marienau and Morry Fiddler.

These returning adult learners have diverse backgrounds but have something important in common: they are "in grave danger of growing" (Kegan, 1994, p. 293). This potential growth is described by Mezirow's learning theory (Mezirow, 1990; Mezirow and Associates, 1991; and Chapter One of this book) in terms of "transformation of meaning schemes" and by Kegan's developmental theory as "transformation of consciousness."

Most adult educators no doubt find that Mezirow's notion of transformation ably describes what they desire for their learners: to "understand and order the meaning of [their] experience . . . [by] becom[ing] more aware of the context of their problematic understandings and beliefs, more critically reflective of their assumptions and those of others . . . more fully and freely engaged in discourse[,] and more effective in taking action on their reflective judgments" (Chapter One). Adults who by these means come to understand their role and responsibility in constructing knowledge are likely to become more effective members of a pluralistic, changing society; such outcomes might well be considered meta-objectives of higher education (Taylor and Marienau, 1997).

But as any adult educator will attest, such changes are not easily accomplished. Learners can attend classes and seminars, perform the tasks assigned to them by instructors, do well on typical assessments (exams, papers), and still not develop the capacity to "critically reflect on the validity of their assumptions or premises" (Mezirow, Chapter One). Even when the assessment is a more demanding lengthy analytical paper, many adults can persuasively present ideas that turn out to be only superficially understood. For example, J., a doctoral student, wrote a convincing eighty-plus–page survey of case study methodology yet could not apply these ideas to her own protocol; B., an undergraduate who earned high marks for a paper on the merits of affirmative action in the workplace, later said, with no awareness of the irony, that having lived in the southern United States as a child she "knew" that certain groups of people were "just lazy and didn't want to work hard." Each learner had examined her topic thoroughly and had "acquired" relevant knowledge, yet both had failed to connect that information to her own situation. They are hardly unique nor are they limited to the American system of education (Gibbs, 1992).

How does this happen? Mezirow might say that these learners had not been involved in "a critique of previously unexamined premises regarding one's self" (see Chapter One). Kegan suggests more explicitly that, though such learners have increased their fund of information, the underlying *form* of their relationship to knowing remains unaltered (see Chapter Two). This chapter describes how a scheme of explicit developmental intentions may support adult educators who wish to encourage transformative outcomes, meaning that learners will not only know *more* but know *differently*. First, however, I examine ways in which transformational learning theory and constructive development theory intersect, using a particular learner's experiences as illustration and bridge.

A Study of Transformation

S. was forty years old, married, and the father of six children when he entered a degree completion program for a B.A. in management, having completed two years of community college general education courses. On the first night of class, when all the participants were briefly describing themselves to the group, S. identified himself as a born-again Christian. He was also a former professional athlete and currently employed as a middle-level manager.

The focus of the course, the first in the program, was to compile a portfolio of experiential learning to be submitted for possible award of college credit. If students were successful in petitioning for credit they would accelerate completion of their degrees. Adults therefore had to demonstrate learning comparable to what a traditional-aged undergraduate might obtain though coursework. This required documenting not only their experience but also the college-level learning acquired from that experience. Doing this successfully meant critically examining their own (and others') relevant experiences through a suitable disciplinary lens and forming appropriate generalizations from that analysis. Because previous academic or work experiences typically do not prepare learners for the complexity of this task, they revise essay drafts after receiving feedback from the instructor and their peers.

Among other topics, S. chose to write on marriage and family and on parenting. His first drafts amounted to a series of biblical injunctions on family matters combined with a narrative of how he had raised his children accordingly. In response he was advised that, however valuable these guidelines might have been for him, a college-equivalent course would include more than one perspective. It was suggested that he examine other families' approaches, contrast and compare various ideas, describe the strengths and weaknesses of each, and include psychological and sociological analyses.

This was taxing for S. When he reflected on other models of parenting and family life he could see that they had possible strengths, but he was initially stymied by the idea that his own perspective might have weaknesses. Fortunately, class exercises included exchanging papers with other learners writing on similar topics. This enabled S. to read and to discuss with their authors a variety of ideas from many perspectives.

By the end of the course S. produced a portfolio of adequate essays. More significantly, however, in his written end-of-course self-assessment he thoughtfully observed, "I have learned to put myself on the other side of what I believe." This suggests an important, even remarkable, change in his point of view in the space of three months—a change that seems to echo Mezirow's transformed meaning schemes. It does not, however, appear to encompass the complexity of Kegan's transformation of the very form of knowing, though it may well be an early move in that direction. Where particular perceptions may be challenged and changed within one or a few courses (Taylor, 1997), the transformation that Kegan describes takes place, if at all, over a longer time period (1994, pp. 187–197). It would seem, then, that transformational learning is one important route to the development that is transformation of consciousness (psychotherapy would be another). Continuing with the example of S., I will explore some of the ways that both transformational learning theory and constructive-developmental theory speak to our practice as adult educators.

Learning and Transformation

According to Mezirow, transformative learning begins with a "disorienting dilemma"—some experience that problematizes current understandings and frames of reference. For S., the assignment to critically examine his own ideas from a variety of unfamiliar perspectives created such a dilemma; his assumptions, beliefs, and values were no longer self-evident truth.

Though Kegan's constructive-developmental theory does not depend on particular trigger events, he does point to ways in which living in a modern, diverse, rapidly changing society demands of its citizens increasingly complex ways of making meaning (1994). By contrast, when people lived their lives within a few miles of where they were born, patterned their spousal relationships and child-rearing practices on what their parents had done, rarely met people of different cultures or with significantly different value systems than their own, and worked at the same job (perhaps even for the same company) until retirement, there was less pressure to acknowledge or examine one's assumptions about self, others, and society.

However, Kegan underscores the effects of two potentially growth-inducing experiences that are specifically part of most adults' return to school: first, that it often requires renegotiation of relationships with others (with regard to, for example, family roles and responsibilities); and second, that many adult-focused programs provide the kinds of support and challenge that, taken together, have been shown to facilitate new ways of thinking and knowing. For instance, "being taken seriously, acknowledged, attended to, and treated as a responsible, self-governing adult" is support; and "being asked to make decisions, design your own program, formulate, act, resolve, . . . master a discipline, and contend with competing values, theories, and advice" is challenge (Kegan, p. 294).

For S., being asked to explore his own experience as a parent and spouse within a framework of just such competing values and theories was that challenge. As many adults do, S. first attempted to stay within his established frame of reference by clearly and coherently detailing the ways in which he had applied his spiritual beliefs within his family. Then, however, he was asked to further examine his beliefs using methods that invited him to become critically reflective of his assumptions and constructions—in Mezirow's terms, to "expand [his] options, and facilitate [his] taking the perspectives of others who have alternative ways of understanding" (1991, p. 200). At the same time, he was supported by a learning environment that exposed him to others' ideas in a setting of open discussion and mutual respect. Neither his instructor nor his peers directly challenged S.'s existing viewpoint nor did they characterize it as wrong—merely as insufficient to the task. Kegan describes such careful attention to the learner's existing meaning perspectives as a bridge—a structure firmly anchored both in a learner's current frame of reference and in the one toward which he or she is growing. Such a bridge fulfills the essential requirement, if transformation is the intended outcome, of meeting learners where they are and then guiding and accompanying them on the journey of change (Kegan, 1994; Daloz, 1999).

Because S. was not expected to abandon his values, only to broaden the context within which he examined them, he was able to "negotiate his . . . own purposes, values, feelings, and meanings" (Mezirow, Chapter One). Indeed, this enabled him to make new meaning—he came to understand that others' beliefs and values, though different from his own, were nevertheless supportable and that systematic criteria for certain life choices could reasonably be based on something other than religious conviction (the "other side" of his belief). He was able to try on other points of view and, in so doing, to elaborate and even transform an existing frame of reference. Subsequent discussions revealed that his new perspectives had led him to examine both his own and others' assumptions in a variety of settings beyond the classroom, including in his religious community.

Challenges to Transformational Learning

Would S. have had a similarly transformative experience in a standard college course on parenting or marriage and the family? Perhaps. But, as noted, a considerable body of research suggests that learners can fulfill the requirements in many traditional learning environments yet fail to integrate the learning in a way that challenges their existing ideas (Gibbs, 1992; Entwistle, 1984; Säljö, 1982; Schneps, 1989). Some adults simply reject outright new information that does not fit their established beliefs. But most adult educators are more troubled by adults whose concept of learning is to "give the teacher what he or she wants" and thus only appear to engage with new ideas. Still other learners unconsciously compartmentalize ideas that might contradict their core beliefs. They "isolate [the] discovery in the world of academics alone and never allow it to raise questions about [their] own life and purposes" (Perry, 1970, p. 37).

As an adult educator I am very much focused on Mezirow's challenging question: How does an adult learn to use "a prior interpretation to construe a new or revised interpretation of the meaning of [his or her] experience in order to guide future action" (p. 162)? What kind of learning leads to a deepened understanding of oneself, one's responsibility, and one's capacity to act in the world—to the potential for "transformation of consciousness . . . toward self-authorship" and self-definition (Kegan, 1994, p. 300–301)? How can adult educators encourage the kind of learning that has the potential to transform the very way one perceives and understands?

Research on how learners approach the task of learning offers clues (Marton and Booth, 1997). Those learners who perceive that knowledge is primarily bits of information, and that their task is to get, store, and retrieve this knowledge, are identified with a surface approach to learning. They can often summarize a text reasonably well and can answer factual questions about what they have read, but they tend to focus on the details of the content and may not distinguish effectively between important and unimportant details. They do not see their task as learners as being to "confront their preconceived assumptions . . . [or to] *change their conceptions of reality* (Säljö, 1982, p. 186). By contrast, those who think of knowledge as something that has the potential to change the way they perceive the topic, and even perhaps the way they perceive themselves, are identified with a deep approach. It is interesting to note, particularly in light of most undergraduate assessment practices, that those who take a deep approach may be less effective at short-answer tests than those who take a surface approach. Because they have integrated the material, they no longer recall details but are more likely to see connections among ideas.

Learners who take a deep approach intend to understand for themselves rather than to passively accept ideas and information presented to them (Entwistle and Entwistle, 1991), but empirical evidence suggests that they are in the minority (Kegan, 1994). Most supposedly self-directed adult learners do not start out prepared to "read actively (rather than only receptively) with [their] own purpose in mind," or, more generally, to "take initiative; set [their] own [learning] goals and standards," using teachers as resources and guides rather than as the source of knowledge to be acquired (p. 303).

Developmental Intentions

What particular elements of teaching, then, might encourage learners to approach for understanding, for meaning, and for transformed perspectives? In researching this question, two colleagues and I explored the literature of adult learning and adult development, reflected on our practice, and consulted adult educators on three continents. Some have international reputations; others, less renowned, we knew to be developmentally focused. First, we asked about their goals: What do you want your adult learners to walk away with at the end of your time together, developmentally speaking?

Dimensions of Development

We organized the rich and varied responses into five overarching dimensions comprising thirty-six discrete elements (Taylor, Marienau, and Fiddler, 2000). However, we found that these elements interacted across the dimensions: some overlapped, some were sequential, and some seemed to enhance the potential for others to emerge. As a result, assigning each element to a particular dimension became a somewhat arbitrary exercise. Taken as a whole, however, they describe an evolving, growing self who can engage with the world of ideas and learn from experience; who can examine and challenge assumptions; who can, through self-reflection, arrive at thoughtfully considered commitments; and who relates to others from a place of mutual enhancement rather than need. To underscore the sense of movement, we chose to express the individual characteristics as actions (for example, reflecting) rather than as conditions (reflection). These elements are also, in some sense, indicators. As people learn and are more able to engage in these actions comfortably and consistently, one would say they are developing. Development is, of course, an ongoing process and not a destination; at some point, however, adults may look back and discover that the totality of their experience seems somehow greater than the sum of the small shifts that have accrued—that they have, in some substantive way, changed. As Daloz observed, "Nothing is different, yet all is transformed" (1999, p. 27).

Adult learners engaged in this process are actively questioning heretofore invisible assumptions about self, society, role, and responsibility that were internalized at the transition between adolescence and young adulthood (Kegan, 1994). Consequently this shift is often associated with midlife change. For example, adults who begin by asking themselves "Am I in a job I really enjoy?" may go on to wonder, "Does the kind of work I do reflect my values?" This may lead to "What are my values, anyway?" and "Are they really *mine*, or are they values I accepted unquestioningly from others before I was capable of formulating my own?" This, in turn, may lead to the realization that ideas of all kinds must be examined, evaluated against criteria that must first be constructed, and then either accepted or rejected. Such changes can leave adults feeling extremely vulnerable. They have spent most of their lives committed to particular ways of thinking, doing, and being, and now may find these approaches inadequate, unsatisfactory, or unworkable. Indeed, one area in which Mezirow's (1990) otherwise informative scheme for facilitating adult learning could be more helpful is in examining the emotional complexities and psychological costs of transformation, which he mentions only in passing (pp. 199–205). In fact, developmental growth is enormously challenging. Though it may be experienced as exhilarating and energizing it is also, at times, traumatic and overwhelming. Changing how one knows risks changes in everything one knows about: personal and professional relationships, ideas, goals, and values—in short, the totality of one's adult commitments.

The Dimensions from Learners' Perspectives

The elements within each dimension are explored in detail elsewhere (Taylor, Marienau, and Fiddler, 2000) and only summarized here (see Exhibit 6.1).

Learners moving *toward knowing as a dialogical process* are becoming aware of how they construct knowledge, beginning to recognize the sources of the ideas they hold, and increasingly able to reconstruct knowledge as new experiences and reflection warrant. Similarly, those moving *toward a dialogical relationship to oneself* are starting to

Exhibit 6.1. Development: Movement Along Five Dimensions.

I. Toward Knowing as a Dialogical Process

1. Inquiring into and responding openly to others' ideas
2. Surfacing and questioning assumptions underlying beliefs, ideas, actions, and positions
3. Reframing ideas or values that seem contradictory, embracing their differences, and arriving at new meanings
4. Using one's experience to critique expert opinion and expert opinion to critique one's experience
5. Moving between separate and connected, independent and interdependent ways of knowing
6. Paying attention to wholes as well as the parts that comprise them
7. Associating truth not with static fact but with contexts and relationships
8. Pursuing the possibility of objective truth
9. Perceiving and constructing one's reality by observing and participating
10. Tapping into and drawing on tacit knowledge

II. Toward a Dialogical Relationship to Oneself

1. Addressing fears of losing what is familiar and safe
2. Engaging the disequilibrium when one's ideas and beliefs are challenged
3. Exploring life's experiences through some framework(s) of analysis
4. Questioning critically the validity or worth of one's pursuits
5. Exploring and making meaning of one's life stories within contexts (for example, societal, familial, universal)

III. Toward Being a Continuous Learner

1. Reflecting on one's own and others' experiences as a guide to future behavior
2. Challenging oneself to learn in new realms; taking risks

Exhibit 6.1. (continued)

3. Recognizing and revealing one's strengths and weaknesses as a learner and knower

4. Anticipating learning needed to prevent and solve problems

5. Posing and pursuing questions out of wonderment

6. Accepting internal dissonance as part of the learning process

7. Setting one's own learning goals, being goal-directed, and being habitual in learning

8. Seeking authentic feedback from others

9. Drawing on multiple capacities for effective learning

IV. *Toward Self-Agency and Self-Authorship*

1. Constructing a values system that informs one's behavior

2. Accepting responsibility for choices one has made and will make

3. Risking action on behalf of one's beliefs and commitments

4. Taking action toward one's potential while acknowledging one's limitations

5. Revising aspects of oneself while maintaining continuity of other aspects

6. Distinguishing what one has created for oneself from what is imposed by social, cultural, and other forces

7. "Naming and claiming" what one has experienced and knows

V. *Toward Connection with Others*

1. Mediating boundaries between one's connection to others and one's individuality

2. Experiencing oneself as part of something larger

3. Engaging the affective dimension when confronting differences

4. Contributing one's voice to a collective endeavor

5. Recognizing that collective awareness and thinking transform the sum of their parts

see themselves not only through the lenses of their prior experiences but through reflection on those experiences. They come to understand more clearly why they are who they are, and can therefore imagine how they might choose to be some other way. Those moving *toward being continuous learners* are realizing that learning is ultimately the result of their own actions and choices. Though they may call on others for advice, expertise, or directions, they must decide their learning goals, seek appropriate resources, and be actively involved in the learning process. Those moving *toward self-agency and self-authorship* increasingly recognize their responsibility for their actions, choices, and values and for the decisions they may make based on those values. Finally, those moving *toward connection with others* are learning to bring themselves fully into relationship and community while still maintaining their integrity as individuals.

Teaching with Developmental Intentions

Because the thirty-six characteristics in Exhibit 6.1 were extrapolated from responses to our question about goals, my collaborators and I next asked experienced adult educators how they achieved these goals. In analyzing their replies, we discovered that what we had thought of as *outcomes* were, in our colleagues' view, *intentions*. Though they could not be certain that learners' ways of thinking would change, educators nonetheless designed their courses with the potential for transformation in mind. For example, if the educator intended that adults learn to take multiple perspectives or to explore ideas and beliefs through some framework of analysis, then activities were devised that required them to engage in just those ways. Rather than depend on information *about* something, learners were encouraged to *experience* something. These adult educators' primary, if tacit, strategy was to have adults learn by doing. As in the case of S., if provided appropriate supports the challenge to actively explore new ways of doing and being seemed to move learners toward new ways of thinking and knowing.

Three Activities

To demonstrate how this experience-based strategy plays out in specific learning encounters, following are synopses of three activities informed by developmental intentions. (The activities can be found at the end of this chapter, starting on page 168.) Though each is described in terms of the particular educational setting or course for which it was created, these activities can be adapted for other applications.

In a literature course, Roberta Liebler (2000) organizes reading assignments around ethical dilemmas. Learners write short essays describing their individual opinions about a guiding ethical question (several such questions are introduced as new units throughout the course). This is followed by small-group activities and additional reading and writing assignments. Small groups are sometimes arranged to encourage exchange of diverse views and at other times to deepen understanding of a particular perspective.

In their discussions learners examine both their ethical views on a given question and their understanding, supported by textual evidence, of the views of a character chosen from the readings. They are also encouraged to articulate and examine the criteria they have used to formulate their own ethical beliefs. In large- and small-group activities learners explore their reasons for agreement and disagreement with one another.

Given their tendency to seek the "right answer," adults are initially uneasy with these activities and are challenged by the requirement to construct criteria to help them decide among various possibilities. Over time, however, they explore new ethical positions, support their positions with text, and come to appreciate that others can hold reasonable opinions that are nevertheless different from their own. They also come increasingly to understand the contextual, constructed nature of knowledge and how they might contribute to that knowledge. A variant of Liebler's activity could be used in most courses requiring interpretation of textual material designed to illuminate values rather than to provide facts.

Carolyn Clark and Deborah Kilgore's activity (2000) begins with instructors and learners writing their educational life histories, which are then made available to everyone in the class via the Internet, as a springboard to extensive on-line dialogue. When learners read the course texts and write papers, they are invited to weave together themes from their readings with those that emerged in the life histories and Web-based dialogue. At the end of the course learners revisit their initial histories and note how the course may have helped them to reinterpret those events. By reflecting on both formal texts and self-as-text, learners can observe the development of their own and others' ideas and interpretations. In a women's studies course, sociocultural themes would also be included. Other variations would work well in psychology courses.

David Boud's activity (2000) has been used in graduate and undergraduate courses in a variety of subjects. It is based on principles of self-assessment and invites learners to establish the criteria used to judge their work. Though the final form of the criteria may depend on the nature of the course and its content, this exercise helps learners not only think through what counts as "good work," but shifts their perception of who is in charge of the quality of their learning.

Boud first creates an environment in which all voices are heard and then facilitates, rather than directs, the process of constructing the criteria. Once agreed upon, these outcomes are used by learners to evaluate their own and others' work.

He finds that learners who have thought in this way about quality in learning are less inclined to do "what the teacher wants" and more willing to take responsibility to meet their own standards. Though no one exercise is sufficient to change learners' embedded assumptions about learning and assessment, continuous moves in this direction help learners develop more complex learning skills.

Teaching with Developmental Intentions

Though these exercises may at first appear dissimilar, each makes learners' existing ideas and beliefs the initial focus of the learning process. Learners then reflect on these ideas using frameworks of analysis that are in part constructed from learners' interpretations of their own and others' ideas. The instructor's job is less to provide answers than to act as partner, catalyst, resource, or poser of questions that sharpen learners' thinking.

As Boud did, the educator may also provide information that creates a context for the activities that follow. This is still markedly different from the traditional approach wherein the instructor is the primary source of information. Instead learners work together in groups to articulate their existing beliefs, try out new ideas, and explore the contradictions that may ensue. In this way, as well as through instructor-facilitated discussion, learners can work toward constructing new meaning that takes into account a variety of perspectives. Paradoxically, providing authoritative ready-made meanings (such as those of the teacher or texts) may not challenge adults' existing beliefs, whereas using their ideas as a starting place for further exploration is likely to raise to awareness the assumptions that are often hidden even from themselves, thus encouraging self-questioning. This does not imply that individual experience is the only appropriate text for adult learning; on the contrary, such an approach can leave adults mired in their subjective beliefs (Belenky, Clinchy, Goldberger, and Tarule, 1996; Perry, 1970). It does, however, underscore the significance of the reciprocal nature of using experience to critique expert opinion *and* expert opinion to critique experience.

Adult educators familiar with Kolb's (1984) experiential learning theory will no doubt see its implications for teaching with developmental intentions. Though Kolb does not require that the cycle begin with concrete experience, we were intrigued to note that most of the contributors to our volume, including these three educators, chose to do so. Learners are then invited to reflect and, based on that reflection, to try to formulate ideas, theories, or principles while also taking expert opinion into account.

Deep approaches to learning focus on meaning and include the possibility of change in the learner as a person (Marton and Booth, 1997). Teaching with developmental intentions appears to support learners in adopting deep approaches; it seems also to encompass Mezirow's call for learning that is emancipatory. Adults who develop— that is, whose meaning-constructive systems transform—are likely to become more deliberative, responsible, and competent in carrying out the work of society. They may also be less reactive and more considered in personal, workplace, and political decisions as well as better able to adapt to changing circumstances. They are better able to recognize the need for more just, humane, and equitable economic and social structures and to work toward achieving those goals.

In sum, though many adult educators no doubt have tacit goals for their learners that are reflected in the list of developmental intentions (Exhibit 6.1), we suggest (Taylor, Marienau, and Fiddler, 2000) that explicitly teaching with developmental intentions is more likely to encourage adult learners' potential for transformational growth, hence the kinds of changes that, in Mezirow's view as expressed in Chapter One, "are central to the goals of adult education in countries that aspire to democracy."

Stimulating Cognitive and Ethical Development

Roberta Liebler, Aurora, Illinois
E-mail: raliebler@yahoo.com

Roberta Liebler is the director, Center for Continuing Professional Education and Center for Organizational Effectiveness, Aurora University.

Developmental Intentions

I.   Toward knowing as a dialogical process.

    2. Surfacing and questioning assumptions underlying beliefs, ideas, actions, and positions.

    3. Reframing ideas or values that seem contradictory, embracing their differences, and arriving at new meanings.

II. Toward a dialogical relationship to oneself.

    3. Exploring life's experiences through some framework(s) of analysis.

IV. Toward self-agency and self-authorship.

    1. Constructing a values system that informs one's behavior.

V.   Toward connection with others.

    1. Mediating boundaries between one's connection to others and one's individuality.

Context

This activity has been used in a course on global literature in a community college.

Description of Activity

Purpose. To broaden students' global literary horizons, guide them through a cognitive adventure by developing their facility for analysis, and help them observe critically and commit intellectually without dependence on certainty.

Format-steps-process. Unit structure: The syllabus organizes modern global literary readings around ethical dilemmas. At the beginning of each unit, each student writes a short personal essay answering the thematic ethical question of the unit. This essay serves as a baseline for how the student views the ethical question before the course exploration. For a unit exploring the individual's responsibility toward the needy, for example, a student might write about his response to being asked for money by a homeless person. For a unit on balancing private and public responsibilities, a mother might examine her dilemma of choosing between staying home with a sick child or making a presentation to an important client.

At the start of the next class, in small groups, students briefly share their personal viewpoints. During the unit, students answer the same ethical question from the point of view of one character in each literary work.

Frequently I divide the class into groups, each of which views the ethical question from the perspective of a different character. Other times I bring together students with a similar perspective in order to develop a deeper understanding as a group than they could individually. All "answers" must be supported with textual material. Individually or in groups, students must support their perception with evidence from the literary work or background materials. Class discussion often focuses on groups explaining or justifying the actions of the character they are representing.

Specific exercise—role taking: This exercise assists students in considering the feelings of characters and authors. I divide the students into small groups to analyze an ethical dilemma in the literature from the perspective of different characters.

I.   Questions for the small group discussions include (fifteen minutes)

   A. What is the principal ethical issue the character faces?
   B. What are the facts?
       1. What are the claims placed on this character?
       2. How can the claims be weighed against one another?

C. What principles are at issue (for example, justice, mercy, duty)?

D. How can the principles as formulated apply to this case? What circumstances would change the principles?

E. What are the options?

F. What choice does the character make?

1. Why does the character select this option?
2. What is the principle that determined this decision?
3. Do you think the character made the "right" decision?

G. What choice would you make under these circumstances?

1. Why did you select this option?
2. What is the principle that determined your decision?
3. Why did you and the character make the same (or a different) choice?

H. As a group, what is the decision you advocate?

II. Each group then reports to the whole class (two to three minutes each group, about ten minutes total) on the following questions.

A. What did your group decide was the best choice from the perspective of this character?

B. How did you arrive at your decision to act, given the situation described?

III. The whole class then engages in discussion around these questions (twenty-five minutes).

A. What was your group's ethical decision?

B. How did you arrive at your decision to act, given the situation described?

C. If members in your group agreed on the choice:

1. What underlying principle(s) did you apply to making your decision?
2. If more than one principle was applied in this decision, what was the connection between them?

   D. If members in your group disagreed on the choice:
   1. What underlying principle(s) did you apply to making your decision?
   2. How did these underlying principles result in differing choices?
   3. Now that you understand another's perspective, can the two positions be reconciled?

Processing Tips

During the first few times students engage in this exercise, they require much encouragement. Since initially they are seeking the "right answer," they look to the instructor for verification. The instructor, however, offers help by asking questions that facilitate the students' exploration. Willingness to argue an opinion not one's own, ability to use textual support of one's argument, and appreciation of other cultural perspectives are encouraged. With practice, students become more comfortable in arguing viewpoints other than their own. Eventually, many become more articulate in arguing their own views through having learned how to explore the basis of other perspectives.

Contributor's Commentary

Though many of my students are ill prepared to face the rigors of the traditional academic regime, they respond eagerly to concepts they deem meaningful. Their lives are complex (nearly everyone holds a paying job and many have families); their academic expectations are vague (almost all are first-generation college students); and their future is indeterminate (though they hope to go on to a four-year college, they don't know how or where).

My dialectical approach emphasizes process (the how) rather than providing answers and solutions (the what). My goal is to assist students in overcoming the uncritical thinking of most undergraduates. I attempt to confront "students with the reality that experts disagree, that their finds may be studied and tested, and that one can, with effort, work one's way to some reasonable conclusions"

(Plummer, 1988, p. 79). The implications of this process extends far beyond content into a different mode of thinking and perhaps living.

Educational Autobiographies

M. Carolyn Clark and Deborah Kilgore, College Station, Texas, and Ames, Iowa
E-mail: cclark@tamu.edu; dkilgore@iastate.edu

M. Carolyn Clark is associate professor of adult education at Texas A & M University. Her research focuses on transformational learning and identity development of marginalized women. Deborah Kilgore is assistant professor of adult education at Iowa State University.

Developmental Intentions

I.   Toward knowing as a dialogical process.

   4. Using one's experience to critique expert opinion and expert opinion to critique one's experience.

II.   Toward a dialogical relationship to oneself.

   3. Exploring life's experiences through some framework(s) of analysis.

III. Toward being a continuous learner.

   8. Seeking authentic feedback from others.

IV.   Toward self-agency and self-authorship.

   6. Distinguishing what one has created for oneself from what is imposed by social, cultural, and other forces.

   7. "Naming and claiming" what one has experienced and knows.

Context

This activity has been used in a five-week summer session course for women graduate students.

Description of Activity

This approach evolved from a single reflective exercise to a structured modality for the entire course.

Purpose. To encourage learners to identify and reflect on specific life events, in this case, educational experiences; construct a cohesive interpretation of those experiences in an integrated way and present it authoritatively as text for use by others; critically assess their own interpretations by bringing them into dialogue with other texts (both from class participation and from the formal texts); and be in dialogical relationship with their own growth and the process of their ideas.

Format-steps-process.

1. We begin by each of us writing our educational life history. In this particular course we had nine students (all women) and two instructors, so there were eleven educational life histories to read. No page limits were given. Histories ranged from approximately eight to fifteen pages, single-spaced.

2. We post our document on our FirstClass site (a Website) and each of us reads all the other documents.

3. We next read the texts for the course (Aisenberg & Harrington, 1988; Belenky, Clinchy, Goldberger, and Tarule, 1996; Goldberger, Tarule, Clinchy, and Belenky, 1996; Middleton, 1993).

4. The students write several short papers in which they identify key ideas in each text and put them in dialogue with relevant themes within the educational life histories. These are posted on FirstClass and read by everyone, with their comments posted. (It should be noted that this class met face-to-face twice each week for three hours and that there was extensive and ongoing discussion of the on-line dialogue as it unfolded.)

5. At the end of the course, each student revisits her educational life history and writes an addendum that assesses the

course's impact on her interpretation of her educational life experiences.

Processing Tips

We gave only sketchy guidelines for the first step (writing the educational life history), as we want each person to have maximum freedom to construct this narrative in the way that makes the most sense to her.

Contributors' Commentary

The process generates new insights into the self (a core developmental goal), but it also generates insight into the nature of knowledge constructions. Learners enter into dialogue with their experience, begin to explore the complexities and ambiguities of that engagement (for example, as shaper and shaped), and begin to put their experiences in dialogue with the experience of others. To frame this for women specifically enables them to recognize the impact of particular sociocultural forces on the lives and consciousness of women. The self-assessment further enhances the concept of personal and group knowledge construction, further underscoring the provisional nature of knowledge construction, its tentativeness, and the need for ongoing review and critique.

Development Through Self-Assessment

David Boud, Sydney, Australia
E-mail: David.Boud@uts.edu.au

David Boud is professor of adult education and associate dean (research) in the faculty of education at the University of Technology, Sydney. He has written extensively on teaching, learning, and assessment in higher and adult education.

Developmental Intentions

II. Toward a dialogical relationship to oneself.

    4. Questioning critically the validity or worth of one's pursuits.

III. Toward being a continuous learner.

    3. Recognizing and revealing one's strengths and weaknesses as a learner and knower.

    8. Seeking authentic feedback from others.

IV. Toward self-agency and self-authorship.

    2. Accepting responsibility for choices one has made and will make.

    7. "Naming and claiming" what one has experienced and knows.

Context

This activity has been used in graduate courses for adult educators and in undergraduate courses in law. It has also been used at all undergraduate and graduate levels other than in introductory courses.

Description of Activity

Self-assessment involves a range of different practices in which learners take responsibility for making their own judgments about their work. Self-assessment does not occur in isolation from others; learners need to draw upon teachers, practitioners, and peers. What characterizes self-assessment is that learners themselves make decisions. In formally accredited courses, self-assessment has been used as part of a mix of assessment activities, which includes teacher-determined, self-determined, and negotiated assessment, depending on the context.

Purpose. To involve students in the process of actively engaging with what counts as "good work" and to apply these ideas to their own assignments. (The assignment may be a paper, a research proposal, or the report of project work. The process works well in each case.)

Format-steps-process.

1. A few weeks after students have identified a topic for their major assignment, I mention that the following week we will spend some time in class focusing on what constitutes good assignments and that they should come prepared with ideas of their own.

2. I start the next class by discussing the notion of self-assessment, giving a rationale for its use in the present context. I then invite each student in turn to offer one idea about what distinguishes good from not-so-good work with regard to their assignment. The round continues until all criteria are covered. (I write these on large sheets of paper, so that all can see and I have a record.) Once all the ideas have been displayed and numbered, I seek clarification from the class on any item that is unclear. Some items are thus modified or reworded, and identical ideas are collapsed together.

3. I then pose a question: "Are there clusters or groupings of items?" Invariably there are, and I create a list of major headings as identified by the students, with the numbers of the specific items that they associate with each.

4. I then ask: "Would you be happy to have your work judged on the basis of the criteria before us?" Normally there is rapid assent, but occasionally discussion arises when students believe that some criteria are relevant in certain circumstances but not in others. These items are starred and marked "only as relevant."

5. In classes where students are graded, students commonly say, "It may be OK for us to use these criteria, but which criteria are you going to use when you make your judgments?" I normally have no difficulty in agreeing to use their criteria, as they are often more thorough than I would have adopted anyway.

6. Following the class, I take the paper and transcribe the list of criteria into the following format: major heading, list of criteria under that heading (using the exact words from class discussion). A large area of blank space is included so that students can later add their own comments on the extent to which they have met these criteria in their assignment.

7. An optional stage is for students to exchange drafts of their assignments and use the criteria to provide qualitative feedback to each other prior to final revision.

8. Students finish their assignments and return their completed self-assessment sheets on the due date.

Processing Tips

It is vital that the teacher does not intrude her or his own views about criteria or make judgmental remarks during the generation stages (steps 2 and 3). When I think that important criteria may be overlooked, however, I will join in at the end of each round and add a statement to the list in the same way as any other member of the group.

Contributor's Commentary

Self-assessment in adult and higher education involves much more than self-administered and self-marked tests. Self-assessment skills of learners are developed when learners are more actively involved in understanding and formulating the criteria used for judgment. My experience, and that of colleagues in other disciplinary areas who have used this approach, is that the quality of students' work improves. The reason for this is simple: Students have a ready-made checklist in their own language that they can use to judge the quality of their work. In addition, they have engaged in a process of questioning what counts as good work, thus becoming involved with deeper questions of academic standards in the subject area and standards of presentation.

A single exercise involving systematic self-assessment does not in itself foster the development of the skill, but it can lay the foundation for its development if reinforced elsewhere. If the self-assessment is repeated in different ways in other classes, it is likely to lead to habits of questioning criteria for performance and noticing the extent to which one's own work meets these criteria.

The process described is effective in classes of up to forty; it is less effective in groups of less than six to eight, as the group may be too small to generate ideas of sufficient diversity.

This activity is but one of many self-assessment activities. Experience shows the importance of designing self-assessment to fit the particular context (discipline, nature of group, class size, degree of sophistication in self-assessment) and to introduce it in ways that illustrate the educational value of the process. Self-assessment involves a set of complex educational skills. Development of these skills needs to be embedded in classes in diverse ways. Further discussion and many examples of using self-assessment in higher education contexts can be found in my book on self-assessment (Boud, 1995).

Self-assessment can be used to

- Self-monitor and check progress

- Promote good learning practices (learn how to learn)

- Self-diagnose and self-remediate

- Practice alternatives to other forms of assessment

- Improve professional or academic practice

- Consolidate learning over a range of contexts

- Review achievements as a prelude to recognizing prior learning

- Achieve self-knowledge and self-understanding

References

Aisenberg, N., and Harrington, M. *Women of Academe: Outsiders in the Sacred Grove*. Amherst: University of Massachusetts Press, 1988.

Belenky, M. F., Clinchy, B. M., Goldberger, N. R., and Tarule, J. M. *Women's Ways of Knowing*. (2nd ed.). Boston: Basic Books, 1996.

Boud, D. *Enhancing Learning Through Self-Assessment*. London: Kogan Page, 1995.

Boud, D. "Development Through Self-Assessment." In K. Taylor, C. Marienau, and M. Fiddler (eds.), *Developing Adult Learners: Strategies for Teachers and Trainers*. San Francisco: Jossey-Bass, 2000.

Clark, C., and Kilgore, D. "Educational Autobiographies." In K. Taylor, C. Marienau, and M. Fiddler (eds.), *Developing Adult Learners: Strategies for Teachers and Trainers*. San Francisco: Jossey-Bass, 2000.

Daloz, L. *Mentor: Guiding the Journey of Adult Learners*. San Francisco: Jossey-Bass, 1999.

Entwistle, N. J. "Perspectives on Learning." In F. Marton, D. Housell, and N. Entwhistle (eds.), *The Experience of Learning*. Edinburgh, Scotland: Academic Press, 1984.

Entwistle, N. J., and Entwistle, A. "Contrasting Forms of Understanding for Degree Examinations: The Student Experience and Its Implications." *Higher Education*, 1991, *22*, 205–227.

Gibbs, G. *Improving the Quality of Student Learning*. Bristol, U.K.: Technical and Educational Services, 1992.

Goldberger, N. R., Tarule, J. M., Clinchy, B. M., and Belenky, M. F. *Knowledge, Difference, and Power*. Boston: Basic Books, 1996.

Kegan, R. *In Over Our Heads: The Mental Demands of Modern Life*. Cambridge, Mass.: Harvard University Press, 1994.

Kolb, D. A. *Experiential Learning: Experience as a Source of Learning and Development*. Englewood Cliffs, N.J.: Prentice Hall, 1984.

Liebler, R. "Stimulating Cognitive and Ethical Development." In K. Taylor, C. Marienau, and M. Fiddler (eds.), *Developing Adult Learners: Strategies for Teachers and Trainers*. San Francisco: Jossey-Bass, 2000.

Marton, F., and Booth, S. *Learning and Awareness*. Hillsdale, N.J.: Erlbaum, 1997.

Mezirow, J. *Transformative Dimensions of Adult Learning*. San Francisco: Jossey-Bass, 1991.

Mezirow, J., and Associates (eds.). *Fostering Critical Reflection in Adulthood: A Guide to Transformative and Emancipatory Education*. San Francisco: Jossey-Bass, 1990.

Middleton, S. *Educating Feminists: Life Histories and Pedagogy*. New York: Teachers College Press, 1993.

Perry, W. G. JR. *Forms of Intellectual and Ethical Development in the College Years: A Scheme*. Austin, Tex.: Holt, Rinehart and Winston, 1970.

Plummer, T. "Cognitive Growth and Literary Analysis: A Dialectical Model for Teaching Literature." *Unterrischtspraxic*, 1988, *21*(1), 79.

Säljö, R. *Learning and Understanding: A Study of Differences in Constructing Meaning from Text*. Goteburg Studies in Educational Science, no. 41. Acta Universitatis Gothoburgensis, 1982.

Schneps, M. H. "Private Universe: Misconceptions That Block Learning." Santa Monica, Calif.: Pyramid Film & Video, 1989.

Taylor, E. "Building Upon the Theoretical Debate: A Critical Review of the Empirical Studies of Mezirow's Transformative Learning Theory." *Adult Education Quarterly*, 1997, *48*, 34–59.

Taylor, K., and Marienau, C. "Constructive-Development Theory as a Framework for Assessment in Higher Education." *Assessment and Evaluation in Higher Education*, 1997, *22*(2), 233–243.

Taylor, K., Marienau, C., and Fiddler, M. *Developing Adult Learners: Strategies for Teachers and Trainers*. San Francisco: Jossey-Bass, 2000.

7

Individual Differences and Transformative Learning

Patricia Cranton

A few years ago in an adult education course for college teachers, students were engaged in a lively discussion of how critical self-reflection led to transformative learning. Peter, usually at the center of any discussion, was oddly quiet. I was about to nudge Peter into the conversation with a well-placed question when he burst out with obvious emotion, "I don't do this! I don't reflect! But I for sure have transformed perspectives." We asked Peter questions about the process he went through. We checked to see if we all understood transformation in the same way. Though Peter was unable to articulate exactly what his process was, he was sure it was neither logical nor analytical. Change in a frame of reference "came to him" directly as a "result of an experience," he said. The discussion with Peter set us all to thinking about how people are different in their learning processes.

Transformative learning involves reconstructing a frame of reference so that it is more dependable and better justified. People with different learning styles, cognitive styles, and personality traits both assimilate and reconstruct frames of reference in distinct ways. It is my intent in this chapter to encourage practitioners, researchers, and theorists to consider differences among people as they foster, investigate, and write about transformative learning.

Our frames of reference are complex webs of assumptions, expectations, values, and beliefs that act as a filter or screen through which we view ourselves and the world. Our cultural background, the knowledge we have acquired, our moral and spiritual beliefs, and our own psychological makeup all influence how we interpret and make meaning out of our experience. A frame of reference can become problematic when we encounter new and different viewpoints or information. We can be led to question what we believe or assume to be true, talk about it with others, and potentially change our way of seeing things.

Different people go about this in different ways. Psychological predisposition—our very nature—forms one kind of habit of mind. There are two intertwined dimensions at work here. First, as we grow, develop, and gain self-awareness we not only come to understand our own nature but we individuate: we separate ourselves from the collective of humanity as we learn who we are. This process is transformative; it is a reconstruction of a frame of reference related to the self. On a second dimension, our psychological predispositions influence the way we engage in transformative learning. We can only see ourselves, our experiences, and others through our own eyes. Whether we are questioning a frame of reference of a sociolinguistic, moral, epistemic, or philosophical nature, we do it using our own psychological traits. Even when we try on another person's point of view (as Mezirow suggests in this book) it is perceived in our way; we can never see that point of view exactly as another person would.

In this chapter I first use Jung's ([1921] 1971) theory of psychological type to describe differences in learners' psychological habits of mind. In describing psychological preferences as habits of mind, my intent is to integrate my thoughts with Mezirow's work (Chapter One) rather than to challenge his theory. Second, I discuss the development of psychological type preferences as transformative learning and argue that the adult educator has a responsibility to encourage individuation and personal growth. Third, I examine how people with different psychological predispositions engage in transformative learning. Finally, I consider how the adult educator can use a knowledge of psychological type preferences as a basis for fostering self-awareness, encouraging personal development, promoting transformative learning, and increasing her own self-awareness as a teacher.

Differences Among Learners' Psychological Predispositions

Mezirow (1991) describes a meaning perspective as a habitual set of expectations that constitutes an orienting frame of reference. It serves as a system for interpreting and evaluating the meaning of experience. Among the influences that shape psychological meaning perspectives, or frames of reference, he lists characterological preferences. In Chapter One of this volume, Mezirow lists psychological characteristics as habits of mind. Habits of mind are seen to be one dimension of a frame of reference, the dimension that acts as a broad, orienting predisposition filtering the interpretation of the meaning of experience. I understand this to mean that personality preferences act as one filter for the way we see ourselves, others, and the world around us.

Although there are many theoretical models of personality preferences, I choose to work with Jung's ([1921] 1971) psychological types for three main reasons. First, Jung is explicitly constructivist in philosophy, which is in harmony with transformative learning theory. Boyd (1991), among others, has used a Jungian approach to understanding transformative learning. Second, Jung's model has been popularized through the availability of several assessment techniques (Cranton and Knoop, 1995; Keirsey and Bates, 1984; Myers, 1985), making the concepts and terminology familiar to most adult educators. Third, unlike other approaches to personality, psychological type theory has been clearly linked to learning style and cognitive style (Cranton, 1998; Kolb, 1984; MacKeracher, 1996).

Here I choose to work with Jung's original theory rather than with the perhaps more familiar assessments derived from his theory.

In doing so I hope to avoid the rigid categorization and labeling that I see as counterproductive to the developmental goals of transformative learning.

Jung describes two attitudes or ways of relating to the world. Introversion is a preference for the self or the inner world; extraversion is a preference for the world external to the self. The introverted attitude leads to a personalization or subjectification of experiences. When a person hears, sees, reads, or experiences something she interprets it in relation to herself—how it makes her feel, how it affects her, what it means to her personally. Mezirow's (Chapter One) notion of subjective reframing seems to be especially relevant to introversion. The extraverted attitude is demonstrated through an objective reaction to experiences. The person does not internalize or personalize what happens but rather relates it to other objects, people, or events in the world. Mezirow's description of objective reframing in Chapter One would seem to be a more natural process for those people who tend toward an extraverted attitude. Introversion and extraversion form a continuum, not a dichotomy. People prefer one attitude over the other to varying degrees.

Jung ([1921] 1971) delineates four functions of living that, when combined with the two attitudes, form eight distinct patterns of personality or psychological types. He defines two judgmental or rational functions and two perceptive or irrational functions. The words *rational* and *irrational* have a slightly different meaning in Jung's work than they do in Mezirow's writing, so we must be careful in our interpretation here; yet I believe that this is a critical point in understanding individual differences in transformative learning, so I do not avoid the terms.

When making judgments a person uses one of the rational functions. Use of the thinking function involves a logical, analytical process in which pros and cons of a problem are considered and weighed, alternatives considered, and a conclusion reached. Use of the feeling function relies on deep-seated, value-based reactions of acceptance or rejection in which logic plays no part. Jung does not use the term *feeling* to refer to emotion; he describes both thinking and feeling as rational processes. He defines the rational as "the reasonable" and then goes further to say that the reasonable "conforms with thought, feeling, and action to objective values" ([1921] 1971, p. 458). Making judgments, whether by logic or values, is in accordance with laws of reason. Thinking and feeling are rational functions, he says, as they are "decisively influenced by reflection" (p. 459).

The irrational or perceptive functions, sensation and intuition, serve only to perceive. In order to attain the most complete perception of events, reason (or judgment) must be dispensed with. When we make sense of what we perceive based on prior comparable sense perceptions, we have already switched to using the thinking or feeling function. Jung uses the word *irrational* to mean not "contrary to reason" but rather "beyond reason," or "not grounded on reason" (p. 454). If we were to perceive a series of events or facts, there is no "reason" involved in the actual perception. These things just are. When we start making judgments about what we are observing we are no longer using the perceptive functions but moving on to the judgmental process. Although these functions seem to be operating simultaneously in everyday life and the distinction, therefore, seems artificial, it is important to pull these threads apart in order to understand differences among individual psychological preferences. A person who prefers using a perceptive function perceives without judgment for longer periods of time and more often than a person who prefers using a judgmental function.

The sensing function perceives through the five senses, and the intuitive function follows hunches, images, or possibilities rather than relying on concrete reality. A person using the sensing function focuses on what is, the present. Someone who prefers intuition is concerned with what could be, the future. Perception that comes through intuition seems to come out of nowhere or from the unconscious.

Although most psychological type inventories tend to label or pigeonhole people as one type or another, Jung was quite clear that this was not his intent. Each of the eight types exists to varying degrees and manifests itself in different ways (including unconsciously) in each person. I prefer to present psychological type results in a profile format and to avoid categorization. However, most people do have a dominant or preferred function, one of extraverted thinking, feeling, sensing, or intuition, or introverted thinking, feeling, sensing, or intuition. This is their first choice, their most comfortable way of being, their most well-established habit of mind. It does not mean that they are unable or unwilling to use other functions.

Similarly, most people have an auxiliary or secondary function. The auxiliary function is complementary to the dominant function. If the first preference is judgmental, either through thinking or feeling, then the second preference is perceptive, either through sensing or intuition—this because we all both judge and perceive and have a favored way of doing each.

Jung calls the least developed, most primitive or archaic function the inferior function. It is the opposite to the dominant function (for example, introverted feeling is opposite to extraverted thinking). It is almost entirely unconscious and tends to be the source of personal anguish. The normally logical and analytical thinking person who falls foolishly and obsessively in love with an inappropriate person may have "fallen into" his inferior feeling function.

Not everyone has clearly developed preferences. Jung describes this as being not well differentiated from the collective. The person has not "found herself," has not formed her identity as separate from that of others. When one function is fused with another it is "in an archaic condition, not differentiated, not separated from the whole as a special part and existing by itself" (Jung [1921] 1971, p. 424). The individual appears to be inconsistent, unreliable, or unsure of herself as she vacillates between two preferences or experiences conflict between two different ways of functioning. Jung proposes that a person must first differentiate the various components of the psyche and then consciously develop the functions, one aspect of the process of individuation.

Underlying this approach is Jung's concept of a unified self. Unlike some postmodern thinking that postulates many selves and no single integrating entity, Jung (p. 460) says that the "self designates the whole range of psychic phenomena in man. It expresses the unity of the personality as a whole" even though it can be described only in part because it is composed of conscious and unconscious components.

Developing Psychological Preferences as Transformative Learning

I have two goals in including a section on developing psychological type preferences in this chapter. First, self-awareness is the foundation of mindful transformation, and becoming conscious of how we function psychologically is pivotal to self-awareness. Included in the process of increasing self-awareness should be critical reflection on the assumptions implicit in psychological type theory (or any other approach that is used to understand oneself). Second, I do not believe that psychological preferences or learning styles are static. Our growth as human beings depends on psychological development and individuation; this development is often transformative, and educators have a role to play in fostering it.

Increasing Self-Awareness

Increasing self-awareness as to how we function in the world involves more than taking a test and acquiring a label. In fact, many approaches to personality and learning and cognitive style become dysfunctional when individuals use their category or label as a justification for not changing. People who say "I am a converger" or "I am a thinker" and, therefore, "I cannot be expected to be imaginative" are doing themselves a great disservice. Jung did not feel that psychological type preferences could or should be assessed quantitatively at all, but if an instrument is used as a starting point for discussion, interpretation, and critical questioning it can be the beginning of a fruitful journey. Jung (1964, p. 215) writes that "whenever a human being genuinely turns to the inner world and tries to know himself . . . then sooner or later the Self emerges. The ego will then find an inner power that contains all the possibilities of renewal." Daryl Sharp (1987), who closely follows Jung's work, encourages us with the statement, "In the area of typology, as with any attempt to understand oneself, there is no substitute for prolonged reflection" (p. 94).

In order to increase self-awareness as a basis for transformative learning, using a psychological type inventory may be a good first step. However, it must be followed with personal interpretation, individual critical questioning of the results, reflective discourse, and serious consideration of its meaning.

Individuation

Jung ([1921] 1971, p. 448) defines individuation as "the process by which individual beings are formed and differentiated; in particular, it is the development of the psychological individual as a being distinct from the general, collective psychology. Individuation, therefore, is a process of differentiation, having for its goal the development of the individual personality." Individuation incorporates further and more complex processes, such as developing a dialogue with our unconscious, and understanding our shadow, animus or anima (masculine or feminine soul), the presence of archetypes in our psyche, and the psychological projections we engage in. Although these aspects of individuation are intriguing to explore in relation to transformative learning, here I choose to focus on the separation of the individual from the collective as this process most closely and clearly parallels critical self-reflection, the core concept in transformative learning theory.

The early psychological condition is one of fusion with the psychology of the parents; the individual is only potentially present. Sharp (1995) writes that education should "contribute toward the growth of individual consciousness" and that "without such consciousness, one is doomed to remain dependent and imitative, feeling misunderstood and suppressed, unwittingly victimized by a collectively acceptable persona" (pp. 75–76). Mezirow (Chapter One) describes our frames of reference as often representing collectively held frames of reference, learning that is unintentionally assimilated from the culture or from our primary caregivers. As we grow up and become socialized to our community and culture, we adopt, without reflection, the frames of reference from those around us. We become a part of the collective of the humanity we know.

Individuation takes place as we break from that collective and come to critically question the habits of mind of which we have been unaware. The differentiation and definition of our psychological preferences and the formation of our psyche is an integral part of this process. It is not a onetime event. Jung describes individuation as a lifelong journey. Neither is it the "sole aim of psychological education" (Jung, 1971 [1921], p. 449); that is, the goal is not to become only separate but to continue to group, differentiate, and regroup with other social collectives as we grow and develop. Yet as Sharp (1995) says, we cannot develop unless we choose our own way, consciously and with moral deliberation. The development of the personality means "fidelity to the law of one's own being," "the segregation of the individual from the undifferentiated and unconscious herd," and this means isolation (p. 48).

One goal of adult education, and transformative learning in particular, is individuation, the development of the person as separate from the collective, which in turn allows for the person to join with others in a more authentic union. If people run with the herd, if they have no sense of self as separate from others, there is no hope for finding one's voice or having free full participation in discourse, as Mezirow puts it in this book. Our democratic values of freedom, equality, and justice depend on the participation of individuals who are differentiated from the aggregate. Differentiation from the aggregate is grounded in the conscious development of psychological type.

Differences in the Ways People Transform

It is commonly acknowledged that people learn in different ways. Preferences for using the right or left hemisphere of the brain; being field dependent or independent; preferring visual, auditory, or kinesthetic modalities; or working best with the concrete experience, reflective observation, abstract conceptualization, or active experimentation stages of the learning cycle have become a part of the way we talk about adult learning (for example, see MacKeracher, 1996). Yet it seems when we come to transformative learning we do not expect people to exhibit varied styles or preferences. Although different kinds of transformative learning are being discussed—for example, epochal and incremental transformations (Mezirow, Chapter One)—these are not distinguished on the basis of learner characteristics but rather in relation to the type of insight people have or the situation they are in. Transformative learning is seen to be a process in which we become critically reflective of our own assumptions or those of others, arrive at an insight, and justify our new perspective through discourse (Mezirow, Chapter One). Imagination plays a role in the examination of alternative interpretations of experience.

Not that there is anything wrong with or missing in transformative learning theory as it is currently described, but I suggest that people, due to their psychological makeup, vary in how they experience the process. Our psychological preferences are a habit of mind. They filter how we see the world, make meaning out of our experiences, and determine how we reconstruct our interpretations. In her thesis, Mary Lou Arseneault (1998) conducted in-depth interviews with seven individuals who reported they had engaged in critical self-reflection. Although she was not studying transformative learning directly, several aspects of the transformative process—disorientation, self-examination, critical assessment, exploration of options, engaging in discourse, planning a course of action—were mentioned by most participants. It was also the case that not all participants experienced transformative learning. Perhaps it is the movement from critical self-reflection to transformative learning that is most clearly related to psychological preferences. The extent to which participants saw themselves as involved in aspects of transformative learning varied greatly, and the degree to which they were introverted or extraverted or preferred rational or irrational functions (using this terminology as does Jung) seemed to play a role in explaining the variations. In the years that I have worked with transformative learning in courses and workshops, I have observed these and other differences among people on countless occasions.

In the general literature, too, we find these strands in the interpretation of transformative learning. Mezirow describes a rational problem-solving process. But Dirkx (1997, p. 81) writes that framing this learning as "a problem of critical-self reflection understates the affective, emotional, spiritual, and transpersonal elements." Scott (1997, p. 46) describes transformative learning as "fundamentally extrarational and intensely personal." The "'sitting' (listening or waiting)," she writes, "with the images requires us to descend into a kind of darkness." Scott has a depth-psychology orientation to transformation based on Jung, as does Boyd (1991). In this interpretation it is the unconscious and the collective unconscious where emotional work, as transformative learning is seen to be, starts.

Similarly, we may be able to understand some of the common criticisms of transformative learning theory for not fully incorporating social action (see, for example, Newman, 1993) if we consider psychological habits of mind as filters for viewing the theory itself. It may well be that people with different preferences see social structures or react to oppression or authority in different ways. Writers, theorists, and those critical of theory are no exception.

Those who call for empirical support for such claims are usually referring to objective experimental or scientific evidence, a methodology inappropriate to understanding transformative learning. However, if we use the broader definition of empirical—that which is derived from observation or experience—most would agree that in their practice, personal lives, and reading they have seen individual differences in the transformative process.

I argue that it is not the case that one philosophical orientation or another is more valid but rather that individuals who undergo transformative learning do so in different ways. Their psychological habits of mind influence the way they reconstruct frames of reference. Using psychological type theory as the framework, I speculate on how this may be, keeping in mind that a person is never of one type but has attitudes and functions integrated within the psyche.

Preferences for the Rational Functions of Thinking and Feeling

A preference for the thinking function is displayed in a well-organized, problem-solving approach to decision making. Judgments are made on the basis of logic and reason. Becoming critically reflective of problematic frames of reference and generating interpretations that are more justifiable fall readily into the purview of the thinking function.

Judgments made using the feeling function are based on values, the goal being to remain in harmony with the norms, expectations, and values of others in the community or culture. So although the feeling function is rational as Jung defines rational, it is not critical rationality, and although it is based on reflection, it is not critical reflection as it is for the thinking function. For a person who prefers to use the feeling function, questioning of a frame of reference would occur when he finds himself in conflict with others' values, and the goal of the process is to return to a state of harmony with others. Trying on another's point of view would come easily as a way of resolving conflict, and I suspect habits of mind would be readily revised. However, the way this is done and the motivation behind it are different than for the person using the thinking function. A frame of reference is problematic when it leads to discord; the primary goal is to eliminate the discord rather than come to a better judgment or a truth through the objective assessment of arguments. It may be that the transformation appears to be epochal, in that it is sudden and reorienting, not a careful, progressive series of changes in points of view.

For both thinking and feeling, an orientation to introversion or extraversion is related to the direction of the energy, whether it is channeled to the inner self or outer world. A tendency toward subjective reframing follows from the introverted attitude, objective reframing from the extraverted attitude.

When thinking or feeling is backed up by a secondary preference for intuition, easily imagining alternatives would also be a part of the process. This would be a more difficult activity for a person whose secondary function of sensing grounded her in present and concrete reality.

Preferences for the Irrational Functions of Sensing and Intuition

A person who is more perceptive likes to continue to take in information and impressions, either through the senses or intuition, and postpone judgment or closure. By definition, the perceptive functions cannot engage in critical reflection on assumptions or belief. This is a judgmental process *aided by* perception. When a person prefers to operate in a perceptive mode, she is less likely to critically judge. The insights that come solely through intuition are not transformations of frames of references as Mezirow defines them. Neither are the changes in perception that come about solely through immersion in an experience and the absorption of facets of that experience through the senses. When Peter, whom I describe at the beginning of this chapter, said he transformed but did not reflect we do not know for sure if he truly did not reflect or if the process was so secondary to his nature that he could not articulate it. He may have assimilated changes as a result of experience and labeled that transformation. Or he may have engaged in a judgmental process that was not entirely conscious.

When Sue Scott (1997) says that transformation is not a rational process, "although it includes rational abilities" (p. 44), we can interpret this as an illustration of how a secondary, rational psychological type function backs up or assists a preference for intuition. Boyd's (1991) suggestion that discernment rather than critical reflection is the basis of transformative learning similarly integrates the extrarational with the rational, though the emphasis is on the former. Discernment begins with openness to images and symbols and leads to illumination through sorting, relating, and bringing images into consciousness—extrarational processes assisted by rational processes. Intuition is dominant here, and thinking backs it up.

When a person prefers either intuition or sensing, the actual transformation of frames of reference occurs through the use of the auxiliary rational function of thinking or feeling. Following the activities of the irrational function, it is the judgmental process of thinking or feeling that leads to the change. Change requires a decision or judgment by definition. However, the process appears quite different on the surface as a result of the dominance of intuition or sensing. It is different enough that individuals who undergo transformation in this way argue that there is no rationality involved at all. It is also different enough that theorists propose it is not a rational process. I suggest this is not an either-or issue. For those individuals who have a first preference for the perceptive irrational functions, the rational component of the process is buried underneath the more visible perceptive process, often partially unconscious but clearly acting as a reflective judgmental mechanism.

When the perceptive functions are extraverted in attitude, they focus on the outside world—what is or what could be. An objective reframing or reconstruction of frames of reference could describe the transformative process, but it would not be "task-oriented problem solving" (Mezirow, Chapter One) in the same way that it would be for a person who works with the thinking function. Envisioning alternatives would precede and dominate task orientation. When the sensing or intuitive function is more introverted, the process is personalized and subjectified. Use of the introverted sensing function attaches personal meaning to observations and experiences; subjective reframing would come more easily to a person who had this preference. Introverted intuition yields images, fantasies, and hunches that seem to come out of nowhere, from the unconscious, and trigger subjective, almost inexplicable reactions to things in the external world. To some extent, Dirkx's (1997) concept of soul in learning mirrors that which comes forth from introverted intuition.

The Educator's Role

Fostering transformative learning involves helping learners bring the sources, nature, and consequences of taken-for-granted assumptions into critical awareness so that appropriate action can be taken. I see three distinct but interrelated educator roles in this endeavor. First, given that our psychological predispositions form a habit of mind that influences how we make meaning out of experience, educators have a responsibility to assist learners in becoming aware of their psychological preferences. Second, because we are involved in a continuous lifelong process of developing and individuating as human beings, educators have a role to play in encouraging critical questioning of psychological habits of mind and supporting the differentiation of the individual from the collective. Third, if our psychological preferences influence the way we engage in reconstructing frames of reference, educators need to help create learning experiences that involve learners of different predispositions in that process. Integral to each of these roles is the educator's own self-awareness of her psychological predisposition and how it influences her work with learners.

Fostering Self-Awareness of Psychological Predispositions

The better we understand how we learn, the more likely we will be to work with our nature to consciously develop, interpret our experiences, and reconstruct faulty frames of reference. Epochal transformations that arise out of traumatic personal experiences or dramatic insights are not often within the scope of the educator's responsibility, though they may sometimes be stimulated by something an educator says or does. More often we work, as educators, with incremental change based on a careful examination of a variety of perspectives, the consideration of new alternatives, reflective discourse, critical questioning of expressed points of view, and nurturing the first tentative forays students make into a new way of seeing things. To do this well, people need to understand how their minds work. Helping learners become fully aware of their preferences assists them in seeing their strengths, their blind spots, their prejudices against others different from themselves. As long as people believe that their way of being in the world is the only or the best way, it is very difficult for them to see alternative perspectives or to engage in reflective discourse.

Educators can foster increased self-awareness of psychological predispositions in many ways. The selection of specific strategies would depend on the context and discipline, but I list some general approaches and examples here.

- A variety of published inventories assessing psychological type preference are available and provide a good starting point for discourse. They should always be used to assist in self-discovery and understanding alternative predispositions, never as an end in themselves. After students complete an inventory, I often form like-minded groups where people can discover their similarities, then turn to mixed groups to enhance the appreciation of differences.

- Games and icebreaker activities focusing on differences among individuals can raise students' awareness of their preferences and those of others. For example, I use a "Trading Statements" activity in which I list individual characteristics such as "I am an organized person," "I learn best through collaboration," and "I am the kind of person who always notices details." Students receive two or three of these statements at random and are asked to trade the statements with which they do not agree with a person who does agree.

- Being conscious of psychological type preferences during general discussions and pointing out differences among people as they come up will not only raise awareness among individuals but will also set up an atmosphere in which everyone notices how the various temperaments are related to learning styles.

- Dialogue journals can be useful in some settings. In pairs, students keep a journal of their reactions, insights, thoughts, and feelings related to class activities, each writing in the same journal as well as commenting on their partner's entries. It is ideal if members of the pair are dissimilar in psychological type preferences and have an understanding of their own profile.

Encouraging Individuation

In order to participate fully and freely in discourse and to question uncritically assimilated social norms and values, people must see themselves as separate from the social collective. If we have no separate identity, no clear sense of self, we cannot pull back from the messages we have absorbed from others in order to see which frames of reference belong to us as individuals and which have been absorbed without reflection. Mezirow (1998, p. 70) writes, "Transformative learning is about emancipating ourselves from these taken-for-granted assumptions about social being."

Individuation is in large part a personal journey. Sharp (1998, p. 53) puts it well when he says "individuation is a kind of circular odyssey, a spiral journey, where the aim is to get back to where you started, but knowing where you've been and what for." Educators can have an important role to play in this developmental process. Their role is not to push in a certain direction, or to encourage people to develop one set of preferences over another, but to help people separate their own views from collective views to see what has been uncritically accepted. In a sense individuation leads to increased autonomy and as such is a universal human goal. It is always a developmental process and as such should be both a learning goal and a goal of adult education. Regardless of students' psychological preferences, our goal is to encourage them to view experiences from alternative perspectives. Here are some examples of what educators can do to foster individuation:

- Activities that put people into a position where they must go against social or group thinking can be enlightening. For example, debates where students argue for a point of view with which they normally disagree can break into routine, uncritically assimilated thought. Similarly, writing a letter to an expert or politician or developing a short position paper arguing against a perspective can encourage students to separate their thoughts from commonly espoused views.

- Critically analyzing socially or professionally accepted theories, models, or perspectives on issues assists students in distinguishing their beliefs and values from those put forth by a society, community, or other collective. It is useful here to choose not a controversial issue but rather one where everyone agrees with a socially acceptable view, then to search for ways of criticizing it.

- Exercises in which students describe themselves as different from others can facilitate individuation. For example, people can work in pairs or small groups to identify only those things that are different between individuals. Journals, personal narratives, or autobiographies that focus on the unique qualities of the writer or differences between the writer and his family, community, or peer group can also help to create a sense of identity.

Promoting Transformation

Good strategies for promoting transformative learning are suggested in the literature. Brookfield (1995), for example, suggests autobiographies, critical incidents, and collaborative problem solving. Activities and discussions that encourage learners to become aware of their habits of mind, engage in discourse and reflection, and critically question their perspectives have the potential for fostering transformative learning. What we need to keep in mind are people's psychological predispositions and their importance in the way individuals react to various learning experiences. If all the activities we use focus on logical, analytical thinking, a good proportion of our students will not be touched by our efforts. Here are examples of strategies that may be useful for learners of different psychological type preferences:

- Case studies, debates, critical questioning, and analyses of theoretical perspectives work well to help students with a preference for the thinking function uncover underlying assumptions and beliefs and question them. Whether students are working as a whole class or in groups, pairs, or individually, such activities provide the stimulus for critical reflection.

- Students who prefer the feeling function do not enjoy the potential conflict inherent in debate and critical analysis. Their temptation is to smooth over discord by adopting others' points of view. In order to foster transformative learning, I have found that it is helpful for learners with this predisposition to work together in harmonious groups in which the group as a whole examines a frame of reference. There is no conflict within the group, and individuals can venture into the difficult arena of being critical with support from their peers.

- Concrete experiential strategies can assist students who prefer the sensing function to encounter and examine alternative viewpoints. Field trips, simulations, and role playing can be used to immerse people in an experience where the underlying assumptions, values, and beliefs are different from their own. In follow-up discussion, journal writing, or position papers, the auxiliary rational function of thinking or feeling can be engaged to yield critical analysis and reflection.

- Games, metaphors, imaging, brainstorming, or any activities that encourage imagination, visioning, or flights of fancy appeal to learners who prefer the intuitive function. It is in the debriefing that follows the activity that critical reflection can be encouraged.

Most groups or classes include individuals of all psychological type preferences, though sometimes the discipline or subject area automatically draws people of certain natures. Unless we are absolutely sure that learners in a group are of one type, we should always maintain a balance among activities that appeal to each function. Just as it is important that every student has the opportunity to engage in learning experiences that are in tune with her nature, it is equally important that we do not only match activities to personalities. Facing something different from what one prefers can assist in individuation and critical questioning of one's psychological habits of mind.

Educator Self-Awareness

As are all human beings, we as educators are inclined to expect others, including our students, to think like us, to share our preferences. When they do not we can be quite critical of their learning process. Why is this student always relating personal anecdotes when I am trying to focus on theory? Why does that student demand examples and practical illustrations when this is not the point of the discussion? Why are there always students who go off on tangents? We all have such thoughts and questions.

When we know something about our own psychological preferences and understand how they influence our teaching style, we can overcome the expectation that all students should be or should become like us. Even if we actually do not do anything different in our practice, we will be able to give up the idea that our own way of learning and making meaning of experiences is the only or best way. Ideally, increased self-awareness also helps us to recognize exactly how others are different and to create learning experiences that better meet the needs of others. The adult educator who has a good understanding of herself can become an authentic teacher, working with her strengths rather than trying to be what she is not, while respecting and valuing that her learners are different from her. I strongly recommend that adult educators take some steps toward increased self-awareness:

- Completion of psychological type inventories or teaching style assessments is a helpful first step in understanding our preferences. It should not be the only step, and we definitely should not label ourselves as a particular kind of teacher in order to rationalize our approach. Instead such information can become the foundation for a more critical examination of teaching style and personal educational philosophy.

- Videotaping teaching or having a peer observe teaching with a view to determining our dominant style and questioning it can go a long way toward increased self-awareness.

- Keeping a journal or log of teaching experiences, then reviewing the writing to look for patterns, repetitive strategies, and implicit teaching values can be helpful for some educators.

- Discussing teaching with our peers gives us alternative frames of reference on teaching.

- In class, having students design activities or learning experiences that suit their nature and leading a session in which they are used can introduce variety and cater to different psychological predispositions.

In summary, one of our habits of mind is our psychological predisposition. You may be an imaginative, creative learner, interested in following all flights of fancy until you tire of them. I may be an organized, focused learner who wants to solve the problem without any interruptions. You may like people, be genuinely interested in their perspectives and values, and want to keep all exchanges at a congenial and agreeable level. I may be more interested in concrete, practical experiences and care less about people or social values. Our psychological predispositions both influence the way we engage in transformative learning and are frames of reference that we should examine and reconstruct.

I use Jung's ([1921] 1971) theory of psychological type to explore psychological frames of reference, but this is only one of many means of understanding differences among human beings. What matters is knowing our students and ourselves and how we learn and teach. Psychological type theory suggests there are two attitudes toward the world: introversion, focused on the inner self, and extraversion, focused on the world external to the self. These attitudes are combined with four functions of living—thinking, feeling, sensing, and intuition—to form eight distinct types. However, each person has a profile of preferences in which both attitudes and all four functions play varying roles.

Individuation, the process of delineating one's identity as separate from the collective of humanity, is a lifelong transformative process. I propose that the educator has a role to play in individuation and that until people are clear as to their sense of self they will be limited in the extent to which they can fully and freely participate in reflective discourse.

An awareness of individual differences among learners in the transformative process helps us to provide opportunities for everyone to use his or her preferred approach to critical reflection and discourse. Similarly, an awareness of our own preferences as educators allows us to see when we get on a one-track path to teaching and learning. I encourage all educators to get to know their students' preferences as well as their own in order to best foster transformative learning experiences.

References

Arseneault, M. L. "Adult Education Experiences with Critical Self-Reflection." Unpublished M.Ed. thesis. University of New Brunswick, 1998.

Boyd, R. *Personal Transformations in Small Groups*. London: Routledge, 1991.

Brookfield, S. D. *Becoming a Critically Reflective Teacher*. San Francisco: Jossey-Bass, 1995.

Cranton, P. *No One Way: Teaching and Learning in Higher Education*. Toronto: Wall & Emerson, 1998.

Cranton, P., and Knoop, R. "Assessing Psychological Type: The PET Type Check." *General, Social, and Genetic Psychological Monographs*, 1995, *121*(2), 247–274.

Dirkx, J. M. "Nurturing Soul in Adult Learning." In P. Cranton, (ed.), *Transformative Learning in Action: Insights from Practice*. New Directions for Adult and Continuing Education, no. 74. San Francisco: Jossey-Bass, 1997.

Jung, C. *Man and His Symbols*. London: Aldus, 1964.

Jung, C. *Psychological Types*. Princeton, N.J.: Princeton University Press, 1971. (Originally published 1921.)

Keirsey, D., and Bates, M. *Please Understand Me*. Del Mar, Calif.: Prometheus Nemesis, 1984.

Kolb, D. A. *Experiential Learning: Experience as a Source of Learning and Development*. Englewood Cliffs, N.J.: Prentice Hall, 1984.

MacKeracher, D. *Making Sense of Adult Learning*. Toronto: Culture Concepts, 1996.

Mezirow, J. *Transformative Dimensions of Adult Learning*. San Francisco: Jossey-Bass, 1991.

Mezirow, J. "Transformative Learning: Theory to Practice." In P. Cranton (ed.), *Transformative Learning in Action: Insights from Practice*. New Directions for Adult and Continuing Education, no. 74. San Francisco: Jossey-Bass, 1997.

Mezirow, J. "Transformative Learning and Social Action: A Response to Inglis." *Adult Education Quarterly*, 1998, 49(1), 70–72.

Myers, I. *Gifts Differing*. (7th ed.) Palo Alto, Calif.: Consulting Psychologists Press, 1985.

Newman, M. *The Third Contract: Theory and Practice in Trade Union Training*. Sydney, Australia: Stewart Victor, 1993.

Scott, S. M. "The Grieving Soul in the Transformative Process." In P. Cranton (ed.), *Transformative Learning in Action: Insights from Practice*. New Directions for Adult and Continuing Education, no. 74. San Francisco: Jossey-Bass, 1997.

Sharp, D. *Personality Types: Jung's Model of Typology*. Toronto: Inner City Books, 1987.

Sharp, D. *Who Am I Really? Personality, Soul and Individuation*. Toronto: Inner City Books, 1995.

Sharp, D. *Jungian Psychology Unplugged: My Life as an Elephant*. Toronto: Inner City Books, 1998.

8

Transformation in a Residential Adult Learning Community

Judith Beth Cohen, Deborah Piper

I found the voice I'd never used.
I tapped into a part of myself that had been asleep
for so long.
I discovered that I could create theories myself.

Over and over again we hear the language of personal transformation from adult students who complete bachelor's degrees in our residential learning community, a program based upon a nine-day retreat held every six months. Our understanding of transformative learning resonates with Jack Mezirow's theory as described in Chapter One. From our own disciplines of literary studies and psychology, respectively, we add a narrative theory perspective (Bakhtin, 1981; Iser, 1978; Bruner, 1990; Polkinghorne, 1988) that suggests that we create meaning through recounting our life events in a narrative form. Images of transformation give us rich linguistic metaphors for human experience. We're intrigued that our students often use the same images of discovery and awakening found in myths and fairy tales when they speak of this particular educational experience. In his critical review of transformative learning theory, Edward Taylor (1997, p. 48) suggests that transformative learning can be driven by nonrational elements such as dreams and visions. The questions he raises direct attention to the neglected role of context and environment in perspective transformations. When Jean

Anderson Fleming (1998, p. 260) studied the residential learning experiences of adults, she found a lack of empirical research on such models. The absence of participant voices was especially remarkable. Building upon these helpful observations, we have examined the elements of a residential learning community that contribute to students' perceptions of personal transformation.

The adults in our study share the common theme of an unfinished education. Often they assume themselves to be the one person in their peer group or workplace who has never finished college, and thus conceal this part of their history. For others, life circumstances, perhaps parenting, poverty, illness, or addiction, kept them away from formal education and they feel ashamed of their history. This "interrupted narrative" (Cohen, 1996) and its accompanying feelings of unfinished business contribute to the disorienting dilemma (Mezirow, 1991) they bring to their college studies. As Mezirow explains, "transformation refers to a movement through time" in which we "reformulate reified structures of meaning by reconstructing dominant narratives" (see Chapter One). Through both telling their stories in the learning community and then weaving these stories into their studies, they combine interpersonal and academic discourse to reflect upon, and then rewrite their failure narratives. Peers and mentors create a dialogue as they revise their subjective interpretations of life events and construct a more critical perspective. Then, as if they had physically moved to a different vantage point, they begin to see themselves from another place, through others' eyes. We argue that this process encompasses both transformations in habits of mind and points of view as described by Mezirow.

Our program weds two contradictory aspects of American life: our hunger for community and our often competing commitment to radical individualism. The learning community (designated Intensive Residency Option or IRO) is one alternative open to students in the Adult Baccalaureate College of Lesley College in Cambridge, Massachusetts. This is how it works: a group of forty to fifty students and seven faculty members representing different disciplines convene for a nine-day residency at the beginning of each semester. During this residency or "retreat," as we have come to call it, students and faculty meet in formal and informal groups that focus on identifying each student's interests, experiences, and existing areas of expertise. Students leave the residency with an individualized study plan designed to cover a full semester's college course work. Between sessions of the learning community, students carry out their studies at home with the guidance and collaboration of a faculty mentor. The number of learning community residencies each student attends depends upon her previous college work or college equivalent credits (128 credits are required for a bachelor's degree). Students typically participate in three or four nine-day residencies over the course of two years. Overall, approximately one hundred students per year go through two residencies, offered at four times.

In this examination of the learning community we try to tease apart the ingredients of a complex, long-simmering concoction. As faculty advisors for more than twelve years, we have been immersed in this educational process. Just as adult learners reflect back on their experiences to make meaning of them, we have followed a similar retrospective examination of our program. Heeding the new interdisciplinary paradigms, we've resisted trying to analyze intellectual, emotional, and spiritual components as neatly divisible entities and thus we have not designed a linear "objective" study. Instead we have built on our local knowledge (Geertz, 1983) to paint a holistic picture of the learning community. Though we can't precisely measure the transformative learning we have witnessed, we still try to tell its allusive tale. Using narrative accounts gathered from interviews, on-site observations, and student writing, we demonstrate how this educational model functions and how it embodies both Mezirow's propositions as set forth in Chapter One and factors Taylor (1997, p. 52) identifies as significant to perspective transformation, such as affective learning, nonconscious learning, and the importance of relationships.

The four critical components of our learning community are the setting, the breakdown of roles among those attending (including faculty and staff), the element of time, and the structural paradoxes of the curriculum. (A recent dissertation by Jean Anderson Fleming [1996] discusses these as well as a number of other features of residential learning for adults.). Through the eyes of Ben, a Vietnam veteran who completed his degree at the age of forty-three, we explore the process of weaving a personal narrative into a course of study. In a retrospective interview we examined his personal transformation six years after he completed the program.

The Setting

The nine-day retreat has been held at two different estates in northeastern Massachusetts, each the former home of a wealthy New England family. Though the polished elegance of their heydays may be gone, the mansions and grounds still hold a sense of history. Paneled rooms evoke past times when privileged mill owners and their servants entertained guests. The quotes that began our essay contain images of discovery: "a found voice," "an untapped source . . . asleep for so long," awakened like the princess in the fairy tale. Myths and folktales abound with images of transformation: wheat is spun into gold, frogs turn to princes, beggars become kings. Though we cannot guarantee such dramatic shifts, we do see transformation as an apt image for what our students report, and after twelve years and at least thirty residencies we too still experience this atmospheric magic when we drive up that long road to find the hidden old house surrounded by trees.

In adult life we may have lost this sense of adventure, but when we engage with that mythic quality of wonder, not knowing what may be around the next corner, we experience a tingling sense of anticipation. The estate itself evokes a sense of childlike curiosity mixed with intrigue. Students often experience a keen desire to explore the many rooms or discover where the outdoor paths lead.

Their responses to this environment show how a physical setting can enhance or inhibit the learning experience. One student spoke of the setting this way: "It's really difficult to get there. The forest on the top of a hill makes me feel I'm in a story from the brothers Grimm." Another student took the wrong path from the parking area and finally arrived a bit breathless. "I felt like Hansel and Gretel," she said. "There are so many paths you can take and you don't know where they will lead."

These observations underscore how the setting itself, with its many paths and many rooms to explore, serves as a metaphor for the educational journey students embark on in the learning community. From wondering about the place students move on to wonder about themselves, each other, and the larger world. They bring this infectious sense of curiosity when they sit down to plan their intellectual work, thus infusing rational inquiry with a mythic sense of quest and discovery.

Breakdown of Roles

Trying to isolate and identify the ingredients of the learning community is like taking apart a grandmother's stew. She's adjusted the seasonings again and again as each spice or legume affects the mix. A central ingredient of residential learning identified by Schacht (1960) and supported by Fleming (1998) is the dynamic of detachment. Students must leave their regular routines and familiar circumstances to attend the nine-day retreat. Left behind are the suits, ties, briefcases, and outward badges of work identity, as well as children, spouses, homes and extended families. They arrive in casual clothing without those accouterments of their daily lives to become peers in a learning adventure. When an adult can step out of her regularly held roles, hidden aspects of her personality can emerge: she may be a secret artist, writer, political activist, even an intellectual theorist. Without the mask of everyday life to hide behind, the more creative, expansive aspects of the self can come out of hiding or "wake up from a long sleep," as one student phrased it. Like the adults in Fleming's study of residential learning, our students loosen up; they begin to write or draw, to sing or dance (1998, p. 266).

The breakdown of roles also affects the faculty and helps to level the playing field. The usual hierarchies seem to vanish. Students, faculty, and staff share sparse, camplike rooms and bathrooms. Students remark on how hard it is to sort the students from the professors until we are formally introduced. We too come casually dressed and use our first names. This role diffusion adds to the mystery of the setting by both destabilizing expectations and building confidence. Curiosity and inquiry begin right away: Who are you? Where are you from? What is your life like? Why are you here? A student may be deep in conversation with a faculty member at supper before she realizes that her companion is a teacher. Their exchange may begin with talk about children or gardening. From there it's not such a huge step to meeting about a study idea, but now the professor is someone you've socialized with; a relationship has begun even before the formal mentoring ensues. As the week progresses and work on study plans becomes more focused, student-to-student and student-faculty conversations move from personal matters to issues discussed at workshops, book suggestions, Internet sites, and other forms of resource exchange. These dialogues continue during walks, over early morning coffee, or late into the night before the fireplace.

It is particularly during these informal moments of the residency that students begin to tell their stories and listen to others. It's almost impossible to avoid reflecting on one's own life and to begin considering new interpretations of these long-lived life narratives. Schacht (1960) noted how the elements of a residential learning community expose adults to different values and perspectives. The atmosphere of discovery is enhanced by learning about other people, their differences as well as their obvious commonalities. Comparing others' stories to one's own begins the process of reflection and informed reinterpretation that eventually leads to transforming one's own perspectives and assumptions.

Ben's First Residency

Ben's words helped us to understand the impact of both the setting and the role breakdown we have been describing. He arrived at his first residency one crisp October afternoon with low expectations, certain that he'd be an "old man" among the students. A Vietnam veteran of forty-three, he hadn't attended college for over twenty years. Ben sat around a table with a dozen other new folks and noted that he was one of only five male students present. (When we interviewed him six years later, he still remembered all their names.) Hearing students and instructors introduce themselves over cookies, juice, and yogurt, Ben wondered about the atmosphere. It was supposed to be college but it felt like someone's home. The competition he was so accustomed to in male-dominated settings was gone. Though his skepticism didn't disappear, he was intrigued. The setting itself had created a disorienting dilemma for him. He recalled it in these words: "I had always been in that machismo environment, but here it was different, and despite all the women, I wasn't on the make. In a lot of ways that's when everything started to change for me."

Ben's sense of himself as the aggressor, the one to make the moves, shifted and he could begin to allow himself to take in what he heard, to be reflective rather than defended. The egalitarian ambience, the shared stories, and the nurturing setting, elements usually associated with women, triggered a response that led Ben to a serious reconsideration of gender roles. But we're getting ahead of our story.

The Temporal Aspect of the Learning Community

Time is another important dimension of the learning community. Historically, time to sit, read, and reflect was a luxury reserved for wealthy people able to hire servants for life's daily tasks. With today's technology making communication nearly instantaneous, we all work even harder to make every moment count. Ironically, time has again become a luxury, yet creativity and thoughtful reflection require us to move slowly. Letting go of our daily responsibilities clears the way for what Schacht (1960) calls "concentration of learning" (as cited by Fleming, 1996, p. 57). The focus on education becomes central, uninterrupted for many days. Someone else does the cooking; someone else is caring for children or covering the office; someone else mows the grass and empties the trash. There is no commute. Living in an atmosphere that has traditionally been reserved for those of the privileged classes, even if we are temporary residents, gives students permission to take time for themselves. The value-laden nature of our choices was expressed by a woman who confessed that she felt shame when her in-laws found her studying. In her working-class family, to sit and read was equated with being lazy; it was almost decadent. In the learning community, she could focus on her studies without apology. As writers we experienced the luxury of extended time for reflection and collaboration ourselves when we spent several days together working on this chapter at a summer house. There we could reread, reflect on, and rewrite our work in a much more immediate and richer way than if we had worked in segmented meetings interspersed with other demands.

Residential education by design includes time for reflection as an integral component. Although a student-centered classroom can include reflective activities and peer collaboration, an illusion of infinite time is difficult to maintain. By contrast, the residency offers many interstitial moments for quiet reflection. After a stimulating group session one can go off and sit under a tree or find a quiet corner and get lost in thought. A student can approach a peer or a faculty person for further conversation during a walk or a meal. There is time to consider how the material covered relates to someone's own passionate interests. The residential retreat thus becomes what Simpson and Kasworm (1990) have called a "learning sanctuary" (Fleming, 1996, p. 60). Fleming emphasizes the "continuity" that comes from extended time away as an overarching theme of residential learning (1998, 260). This compression of time can be compared to the aesthetic element of dramatic unity that makes fiction, film, and theater satisfying. These art forms appeal to us on many levels, just as the experience of being in a residential learning community speaks to our unconscious as well as our rational selves.

Some of the best studies we have facilitated grew out of long walks where we left the books behind and simply wondered aloud with the student. Jeff, a competent man in his personal life, had been out of school for over twenty years. He doubted that he had any ideas. When Jeff's faculty mentor heard his frustration she suggested they take a walk together. As they passed an old stone wall, he mentioned his abiding interest in these structures. This seemingly trivial reference grew into a semester-long project in which Jeff surveyed and researched the history and construction of the stone walls in his northern Maine town. He also investigated the spiritual and cultural aspects of other rock constructions. To earn art credit he constructed a complicated stone arch on his property. His interest expanded until he was creating balanced rock sculptures near his home. When a neighbor called his attention to some "amazing rock formations" on a nearby beach, Jeff quietly acknowledged that he had built them.

Jeff's barely articulated idea could emerge and evolve because of the extended time of the learning community residency. Grundtvig's research on residential learning in the 1840s indicated that it was not simply residing together, but that "a maturity of viewpoint" develops out of close communion between tutor and student (Fleming, 1996). In our residency the close communion between peers has a similar effect. Adults may have more to offer each other in the form of life experience than the traditional-age students Grundtvig studied. Furthermore, the days of literally living together allows them to develop relationships that could not occur when everyone retreats to his or her home after classes end. Here students are able to continue a discussion later the same day or the next morning over breakfast rather than waiting for the next class or some future appointment with the instructor. Conversations can go deeper and the dialectical process that moves thinking forward can have a more flowing quality.

Ben and Everett

By returning to Ben's experience at his first residency we can observe how his connection with a student even older than himself triggered a process of reflection for him.

"Meeting Everett was a lucky stroke for me," Ben recalled. "You go to small groups with four or five students and one faculty person where we each get the chance to speak." These groups, where students share aspects of their stories during the extended time of the residency, inspire conversations that spill over to other sessions. Ben was amazed when Everett admitted that he'd once been a drunk, sitting on the curb. The calm Alaskan native, administrator of a large substance abuse program for the Athabascan community, appeared to be so self-confident. At the age of fifty-two he had returned to school because he needed to know more about management, about addictions, and about his own culture. For Ben, who had been a perennial outsider, Everett provided a bridge to the community of adult learners. They had both struggled with drugs and alcohol, but before meeting Everett, Ben thought he had bottomed out.

"I'd never gone as far down as he had," Ben told us. Though Ben said very little about himself in that first group, hearing Everett helped Ben revisit his own story. Bruner (1990) notes how listening to someone else can begin a process of reflection, reorganization, and reinterpretation of one's own narrative. As a "reader" of Everett's text, Ben was practicing skills he would later apply to reauthoring his own narrative, a process we explore soon.

Everett wondered how he could reach clients who seemed so resistant to the dominant culture's approach to substance abuse. Ben's conversations with Everett about addictions, treatments, and native culture continued at meals and long into the night with or without faculty present. Ruby (1982) describes reflexivity as "the ability of any system of signification to turn back upon itself, to make its own object by referring to itself." Reflective discourse that involves a critical assessment of our assumptions is central to Mezirow's transformation theory. In this process one is able to "step aside" from the discourse one was initially engaged in and view it from another perspective. Such a habit of mind contributes to expanded constructions and new understandings of one's world. In the learning community such thinking is fostered when students have the necessary space and permission to wonder out loud with each other. This Vygotskian "dialectical process" (Vygotsky, 1978), modeled in a group by a faculty facilitator, encourages both speakers and listeners to respond in their own voices. Each person is encouraged to contribute from his or her own situated knowledge by asking questions and making suggestions. In the learning community students are thus plunged into the academic conversation and it is nearly impossible for them to hide. Before they know it they are engaged in discussions that stimulate their critical faculties.

Curriculum Design

The design of the learning community curriculum is somewhat of a structural paradox. Though each day is clearly scheduled the student's own study plan is individually designed. The faculty do not arrive with planned courses. Instead the nine days are dedicated to helping students identify their interests and setting academic goals. We open the residency with a community meeting, a ritual that takes place in a circle where everyone introduces herself, students, faculty, and household staff. In smaller groups and during informal exchanges faculty try to create an environment in which all questions are honored. Ideally students should feel safe to ask questions they may have labeled as "silly" or unworthy of intellectual discourse. "Who was Freud anyway?" a younger student blurted. "I know he had something to do with sex, but when people talk about him, I don't have a clue about what he did." Those very questions can be potential paths toward learning.

The learning community's curriculum design must provide what Winnicott (1965) refers to as a "holding environment." When so much about the experience is unstructured, feeling safe is critical. Students must learn to tolerate the stress of not being told what to do. Moving away from a teacher-directed format to becoming the active subject who creates her own curriculum is a powerful transition to make. For many of our students this requires a perspective shift. A student may arrive in a place of silence or may defer to the professor's authority, but she must plan her own study before she leaves the retreat. This requirement accelerates movement to a more independent perspective, what Belenky and her colleagues call "constructed knowing" (Belenky, Clinchy, Goldberger, and Tarule, 1986). Students are encouraged to experiment with a different mode of thinking, almost like trying on dress-up costumes, but they do this with the support of faculty willing to tolerate mistakes and peers engaged in a similar endeavor. As Mezirow argues in Chapter One, "feelings of trust, solidarity, security, and empathy are essential preconditions if we are to expect free and full participation in discourse."

The Study Plan

We return to Ben's experience with his faculty mentor to demonstrate how a study plan begins to take shape. By the second day Ben was wondering what his focus would be. In his faculty-led study group he said that most of his earlier college work had been in writing, but that was ages ago.

"What would you like to write about now?" his faculty advisor asked.

He drew a blank. The four other students in the group waited patiently as he formed his answer. "I've worked on documentary films in my job at a television station," he said. "I've always been interested in film. Could I write about films?"

Other students expressed interest in his work; they were impressed when he described the TV documentaries he had worked on. "What films do you admire?" the advisor asked when there was a silence.

He laughed. "Not documentaries," he admitted. "I loved *The Last Picture Show*. It was my favorite movie of all time but I've never really analyzed why."

"Tell us about what you remember," the instructor said. As he described the characters and the setting Ben began to unpack his own critical tool kit. Asked to explain his intuitive reaction, he had to move toward a critical stance, using his own experience as the subject matter. He didn't clam up because he knew they weren't waiting for a right answer. Both the instructor and his peers seemed genuinely curious about his ideas. As faculty in the learning community, we must move away from the position of expert that we usually bring to our courses and assume what psychologists Goolishian and Anderson (1992) have called a "not knowing stance." We try to model the curiosity and wonder we wish to inspire in our students. The more we initially presume we know, the fewer questions we will ask. Without these queries we won't get close to what we refer to as the student's "passion." A "not knowing" position encourages the critical reflection that Mezirow regards as so important to transformative learning. Asking questions about our own experiences helps us to build connections between emotional and rational processes.

Study planning in the learning community takes the form of a dialectical process that constructs meaning in a manner similarly noted by both literary critics and psychotherapists. Just as authors and audiences collaborate to produce meaning in a literary text (Iser, 1978), so too do patients and narrative therapists work to reconstruct the patient's life story. Psychotherapist Kenneth Gergen (1991) argues that critical reflection helps dissolve the distinctions between object and subject, mind and world. Individuals come to see that words are not external signs of internal meanings and as "the object of the individual's words is deconstructed . . . the individual slowly disappears into the greater dance of communal life" (p. 110). In dialogue groups, students imaginatively try on other points of view; as Mezirow points out, this playing with other perspectives works along with critical reflection through discourse. In these learning community study groups, students collaborate with peers and faculty to design their own custom-tailored studies, yet their personal learning plans fold in others' ways of seeing. As active subjects who author their own curriculum they are at the center rather than the periphery of the learning experience.

Though the pressure is on to come up with a study plan, peer collaboration and opportunities for creative expression are ever present, maintaining a balance between challenge and support. While students labor at the computers to finish on time, there are freshly baked chocolate-chip cookies to snack on. They can release tension in late-night gossip sessions in dorm rooms or find someone to help when the printer jams. Each student has seven faculty and forty to fifty peers to draw ideas from, as well as computer technologies to help them with research and study design. Each faculty member represents a different discipline, but all are available as collaborators and consultants during both the nine-day residency and the following six months. A management major might sit with the psychology faculty to discuss possible readings on women's development to complement a business study, giving her an interdisciplinary perspective on her chosen field. She isn't handed a book list but is encouraged to talk through her own particular focus. The student then brings these ideas back to her own mentor, a management instructor, for further refinement. By the end of the nine days all students have developed a comprehensive study plan that includes a bibliography and a schedule for submitting written work to their faculty mentors at three-week intervals. For many, producing the study plan itself brings a sense of accomplishment even before any work has been submitted.

A regular learning community ritual is a student-driven evening of readings, skits, and music where all are encouraged to share some part of themselves, whether it be a hidden talent like singing or performing, reading original poetry, or even passing family pictures around. Faculty often perform silly skits or watch themselves lampooned in parodies of the "process." Students are also brought into the governing structure of the residency. Each semester they elect the "Voice," a representative who functions as an omsbudsperson with the faculty and residence staff. Students meet without faculty to list their suggestions and complaints and elect a new Voice for the coming retreat six months hence. The learning community ends as it began, with the ritual of a community meeting where anyone is free to speak about the past week.

Bringing the Community Home

We return to Ben's experience in the program to follow the learning community process in more detail. Through his story we can observe the way students' narratives are woven into their academic work during the independent study period.

"When people are interested in what you have to say, it's transforming, it makes life more whole," he said, looking back at his first residency. His connection of transformation with wholeness underscores the importance of weaving affective and unconscious elements into the rational discourse of academic study. Wholeness became a metaphor Ben took away from the residency that gave him an image for connecting the pieces of his own history. What had seemed like a random series of events now began to take shape, revealing new interpretations. In our retrospective interview he went back to the most pivotal moment of his youth.

"When that letter from my draft board came in spring of 1965, I'd never been so frightened by anything—to me it was the end of my life. It wasn't Vietnam, I knew nothing about Vietnam. I barely knew who the President was," Ben said. "After I got back, people didn't want to hear about it."

He had thus assumed the stance of silence. Ben went on to explain that his return to school after twenty years came from a desire "to make something positive happen" in his life. Dropping out of college when he was nineteen had interrupted his formal educational narrative and began a sequence of events that landed him in Vietnam as a helicopter pilot. In the years since his Vietnam service he had neither examined his experience nor put it in any context. Life seemed like a series of accidents, unconnected fragments without a shape.

Ben's life story, from his parents' divorce and his subsequent loss of contact with his father through his Vietnam service, failed marriage, and hippie ramblings, can be seen as a tale of his generation. Many intelligent men, be they former warriors, manual laborers, or self-proclaimed bad boys, reject higher education yet they continue to wonder if they're smart enough to earn a college degree. Though much attention has been focused on women who struggle against the dominant, limiting narrative to finally speak in their own voices, a similar culturally constructed myth of gender was constricting Ben. In a setting like the learning community, these gender barriers could be challenged.

Ben had listened as his new friend Everett developed his idea for creating a unique treatment program for native substance abusers. He was impressed that Everett's study plan involved exploring the cultural history of his own tribe. To reach his clients Everett needed to understand their traditions, as the dominant culture's methods weren't working. Because Everett had learned very little about his own heritage as a child, he was eager to reconnect with his personal and cultural history. Ben admitted his surprise at discovering that personal issues and academic studies, the so-called "objective" and the "subjective," need not be polarized.

When it was his turn, Ben spoke haltingly about his past. For the first time he publicly acknowledged his Vietnam service. "Things happened that I didn't want to be part of" was about as much as he could manage to say. Other students encouraged him to speak about his history. Recapitulating his past in a group dedicated to thoughtful discourse helped him to begin reenvisioning his experiences through the multiple perspectives of his audience.

"People listened to me. . . . I wasn't being told what to do," he said, his voice still reflecting amazement six years later. Simply being heard was clearly a breakthrough experience for Ben. In the military he had followed orders; back home his experience had seemed shameful—something to hide. Freed of the automatic need to censor himself, his thinking could come out of its shackles. By the fourth day of the retreat Ben began to formulate his own study plan as his self-selected faculty mentor and peer group chimed in. Building on his work in film, he thought about comparing novels with their film adaptations. But what films should he choose? This question led him to wonder about the cowboy and war movies he had loved growing up in Oklahoma. Why had those heroes affected him so profoundly?

The essays Ben wrote over the next six months covered film history and criticism, and gradually moved from the cowboy to the subject of war. "I think I had been searching for a male mentor ever since Dad left," Ben told us in his interview. "Dad and I didn't know how to behave around each other."

That mutual discomfort stopped being a mystery after Ben analyzed the forces that had shaped them both. Those films he had loved so much as a child equated masculinity with war and toughness.

"I had no male role model so I based my ideas on John Wayne and Audie Murphy. It's that fifties upbringing—if you're going to test me, test me good," he said.

Mezirow notes that habits of mind can be transformed through an incremental process, and we can observe this type of change in Ben. He gradually revised his unspoken assumptions about manhood and the military as one essay built upon an earlier one. Through his writing about the male images in the films of his boyhood Ben reconnected with his absent father. He recognized why the world had seemed to split after his parents' divorce and why the tough, macho world of his father, so remote and so different from the soft, permissive world of his mother, had seemed so desirable to him. Those cultural myths of male destiny had continued to drive him throughout his Vietnam experience. Without a real father in his life he had pushed himself to fulfill an abstract heroic ideal so fiercely that his imaginative and intellectual life were stifled. Though Ben had doubts about the Vietnam war he had nevertheless signed on for another tour of duty stateside and had seriously considered a career in the military. When he finally left the service he regarded his decision as a failure of will rather than a positive moral choice.

A sense of irony colored Ben's reflections when he spoke to us six years after his graduation. Taking apart those male icons allowed him to subvert his own macho stance; he was then able to reexamine the meaning of his father's departure. He came to see that his profound hunger for male closeness had reverberated throughout his Vietnam service, continuing to hover as he completed college twenty-five years later. Ben's investigation of cultural images of masculinity had led him to a different understanding of his own needs and a different notion of what might be possible between fathers and sons. If their rigid macho roles were cultural products, then he could choose to break down the barriers and redefine their relationship before it was too late. As he applied this critical perspective to his life Ben became a different kind of man. With his transformed perspective he was able to reach out to his father and reestablish a connection that had been dormant for over thirty years. Fortunately his father welcomed his overtures, and they began taking yearly hikes together in the western mountains they both love. The two men have continued to grow closer as the years pass.

Not only did Ben revise his personal views on masculinity, he also came to a different understanding of his own place in history. During his first semester he viewed the World War I film *All Quiet on the Western Front* and then read the novel by Remarque (1929). Surprised to find his own war experiences reflected in that early work, he went on to read World War I poet Wilfrid Owen, whose writing left him breathless. He phoned his advisor to tell her how "blown away" he was to find his own Vietnam experiences mirrored so movingly by a poet writing fifty years earlier: the soldiers Owen described as "bent double . . . coughing like hags" cursing "through sludge"

(Owen, 1963) could have been his own buddies. In that moment Ben saw himself as part of history rather than an insignificant soldier in a despised war. The very personal questions he had been asking about his own life had led him to larger questions about the impact of war on human history. Throughout his studies, personal narrative and academic writing were never separated. In his essays he would write about his own experiences and then reflect on them in light of what he read. Moving back and forth between these modes of discourse, Ben became immersed in the dialectic that constitutes Vygotsky's web of meaning, "in which the personal and social are rendered virtually indistinguishable" (DiPardo, 1990, p. 62). Rather than encouraging self-indulgence, a claim made by some critics of narrative writing, we believe with DiPardo and others that the construction of a personal narrative awakens the critical faculties of reflexivity and comparative evaluation.

Through her comments and responses, Ben's advisor entered into a dialogue about his work, becoming a collaborator as he reauthored his narrative. Bodily, students are no longer in the learning community once they leave the residency, but the virtual interpretive community continues to function throughout the independent study period. There were many voices: those of Ben's mentor, other professors he had consulted during the retreat, and his peers. The voices lived on in his inner dialogue, reflecting what Russian literary critic Bakhtin (1981) calls the heteroglossic (or multivoiced) nature of narrative. When we understand that our self-stories are formed through participation in the culture we can become active in reinterpreting and reauthoring them.

Ben came to recognize his need for community as well as his hunger for a male mentor. He reread his war experience, seeing the horror as well as the exhilarating effect of being with other men in a life-threatening situation. In one of his narratives he wrote: "Being shot at in a helicopter, the connection with your buddies, the adrenalin high—it's something I've never felt again—as awful as war is, you miss those feelings."

His participation in the learning community, where the bonding was connected to an adventure of the mind, might be less intense than trying to survive a war but it gave Ben an alternative model of community. He could look back at his combat experience in a more realistic way, accepting his own ambivalence.

Graduation

Students in the learning community must complete a senior thesis in their last semester. This project contains forty to sixty pages of written work, including an analytical component. Those working in the arts may do a shorter paper to accompany an exhibition or performance. As Ben had decided on a writing major it made sense for him to produce a memoir about his Vietnam experience. At his final residency he presented his work to the learning community, (also a requirement for all culminating students). In a darkened room Ben read from his essay in a shaky voice while a slide showed a fatigue-clad, crewcut, twenty-year-old standing beside a helicopter. His hair might have thinned, but he hadn't lost his old Oklahoma drawl so it almost seemed as if the young Ben were speaking.

"There's plenty to tell, but you never asked," he read. "I was drafted at nineteen, barely old enough to have a background. . . . The average age in Vietnam was twenty. In World War II the average age was twenty-six. But that's the tragedy of war, isn't it? It steals our youth."

The room nearly vibrated as the community responded. Many had protested the war; others had lost relatives; some hadn't even been born.

"I suppose the most difficult thing about Vietnam was coming home," Ben concluded. "I was marked with something I could never shed. I wanted to be alive every single day and began to look for whatever I could find to make me feel that way."

In Ben's multimedia production he synthesized the many strands of his narrative while further developing his skills in media and writing. The experience of reconstructing his story and acknowledging the value of his history allowed him to accept his past rather than conceal it. This process released energy for creative, intellectual work that took him beyond the limits of his autobiography. Two milestones, reconciliation with his aging father and the completion of his college degree in midlife, were connected by more than co-incidence. Finally he could put the war behind him and turn to his attention to photography and writing, interests he'd pursued only sporadically before returning to school. His interrupted story could finally move forward. At fifty, six years after completing his bachelor's degree, Ben was involved in a film project for public television that he described as "the biggest thing I've ever worked on." No longer does Ben view himself as the lone cowboy who blindly confronts the enemy. Today Ben is actively helping to raise his two daughters, something he has said he could not have done at the time he returned to school. The protagonist of his narrative is a softer, more reflective man.

Discussion

A great challenge in conducting research on transformative learning is to get beyond language and be able to spot transformation in action rather than through verbal or written responses. When we follow students for five to ten years after they leave us, we can determine whether or not their lives are different than they were before their studies. Along with the changes Ben reported, he also indicated that older, less functional patterns continue to hamper his life. His efforts to go to graduate school never coalesced; often he feels stuck in his job or disappointed in relationships. Does that mean that transformation is too strong a word to describe what has taken place? Rather, we think that such knowledge of our student's lives reveals the messiness of our concepts.

Transformed perspectives do not necessarily change all aspects of such complex lives. Yet as we continue to follow students who have completed this program our enthusiasm for the residential community model as a vehicle for transformative learning continues to deepen. We have come to appreciate more fully how the setting facilitates the rekindling of wonder and curiosity. We have seen more clearly just how the breakdown of roles allows for group discourse that is not distorted by power and influence but rather encouraged through mutual inquiry. Students have used the extended time away for taking imaginative leaps and trying on other points of view. These program ingredients all blend into the curriculum design, which is student driven and informed by both peers and faculty. Art, music, dance, and other expressive modes are woven into both the residential and nonresidential components so that non-linguistic ways of meaning-making as well as active, embodied learning are part of each student's education. These combined elements encourage adults to bring their own stories into the academic conversation. The transformations we see cannot be neatly pinned down to either the nine days of the residency or the months of independent study but are a result of the entire process. Repeating the cycle every six months allows for further solidification and integration of a student's life experience and academic work. As we saw in Ben's story, incremental shifts prepare the ground for larger transformations in habits of mind. As they examine their own narratives, students become aware of personal frames of reference and meaning schemes outside their consciousness. This complex process promotes critical inquiry and, ideally, leads students to a constructivist stance. Finally, though autonomy is central to this educational process, connection to a learning community keeps individualism in balance. We would love to see this powerful model replicated in other settings where a learning community can be formed, such as a housing project, neighborhood center, or common workplace. Indeed, for many adults leaving the classroom behind may be the first step toward transformative learning.

References

Bakhtin, M. M. "Discourse in the Novel." In M. Holquist (ed.), *The Dialogic Imagination*. Austin: University of Texas Press, 1981.

Belenky, M. F., Clinchy, B. M., Goldberger, N. R., and Tarule, J. M. *Women's Ways of Knowing: The Development of Self, Voice and Mind*. New York: Basic Books, 1986.

Bruner, J. *Acts of Meaning*. Cambridge, Mass.: Harvard University Press, 1990.

Cohen, J. B. "Rewriting Our Lives: Stories of Meaning-Making in an Adult Learning Community." *Journal of Narrative and Life History*, 1996, 6(2), 145–156.

DiPardo, A. "Narrative Knowers, Expository Knowlege: Discourse as Dialectic." *Written Communication*, 1990, 7(1), 59–95.

Fleming, J. A. "Participant Perceptions of Residential Learning." Unpublished doctoral dissertation. Boulder: College of Education, Division of Educational Leadership and Policy Studies, University of Colorado, 1996.

Fleming, J. A. "Understanding Residential Learning: The Power of Detachment and Continuity." *Adult Education Quarterly*, 1998, 48(4), 260–271.

Geertz, C. *Local Knowledge*. New York: Basic Books, 1983.

Gergen, K. J. *The Saturated Self: Dilemmas of Identity in Contemporary Life*. New York: Basic Books, 1991.

Goolishian, H., and Anderson, H. "The Client Is the Expert: A Not-Knowing Approach to Therapy." In S. McNamee and K. J. Gergen (eds.), *Therapy as Social Construction*. Newbury Park, N.J.: Sage, 1992.

Iser, W. *The Act of Reading: A Theory of Aesthetic Response*. Baltimore: Johns Hopkins University Press, 1978.

Mezirow, J. *Transformative Dimensions of Adult Learning*. San Francisco: Jossey-Bass, 1991.

Owen, Wilfrid. *Collected Poems*. New York: New Directions, 1963.

Polkinghorne, D. E. *Narrative Knowing and the Human Sciences*. New York: SUNY Press, 1988.

Remarque, E. M. *All Quiet on the Western Front*. Boston: Little, Brown, 1929.

Ruby, J. (ed.). *A Crack in the Mirror: Reflexive Perspectives in Anthropology*. Philadelphia: University of Pennsylvania Press, 1982.

Schacht, R. H. *Weekend Learning in the United States*. Brookline, Mass.: Center for the Study of Liberal Education for Adults, 1960.

Simpson, E. G., and Kasworm, C. E. *Revitalizing the Residential Conference Center Environment*. San Francisco: Jossey-Bass, 1990.

Taylor, E. "Building Upon the Theoretical Debate: A Critical Review of the Empirical Studies of Mezirow's Transformative Learning Theory." *Adult Education Quarterly*, 1997, 48(1), 34–59.

Vygotsky, L. *Mind in Society: The Development of Higher Psychological Processes*. Cambridge, Mass.: Harvard University Press, 1978.

Winnicott, D. W. *The Maturational Processes and the Facilitating Environment.* New York: International Universities Press, 1965.

9

Creating New Habits of Mind in Small Groups

Elizabeth Kasl, Dean Elias

O ur purpose in this chapter is to encourage adult educators to expand their epistemic assumptions to include group learning. In the United States, where strong Eurocentric cultural traditions of individual autonomy prevail, educators' usual conceptual frame for learning is that it is an individual process. In her review of several adult educators' perspectives on learning in groups, Susan Imel observes that for most adult educators "the emphasis is primarily on the group as a vehicle that supports the learning of individuals" (1996, p. 92). She argues that, instead of proceeding with this perspective as an unexamined assumption, adult educators should become aware that the idea of group learning can also refer to the possibility that the group as an entity learns.

We believe that groups can learn and, further, that the health and effectiveness of our organizations and communities depend on the capacities of small groups to be transformative learners. Here we hope to stimulate conversation about groups as learning entities and to invite adult educators to embrace the cultivation of learning in groups and other collectives as a central domain of practice. By using a case study of a particular group, we illustrate how concepts describing transformation in individuals can also apply to groups. Before we delve into our case analysis, we explain our beliefs about group learning and transformative learning.

Worldview About Group Learning

Our practice as adult educators is based on the premise that groups have the capacity to learn. We find support for our belief in two concepts from systems thinking. The first is isomorphism among levels of human systems—for example, the individual, group, and organization. "If the object is a system, it must have certain systems characteristics, irrespective of what the system is otherwise" (von Bertalanffy, 1968, p. 85). The second concept is the idea of group mind. As defined by Gregory Bateson, groups and organizations satisfy the criteria for mind (1979, p. 97). Accepting the validity of isomorphism and group mind, we conclude that if an individual can learn, so can a group, organization, or community.

Given the premise that groups are able to learn and postulating that theories about learning in individuals can also apply to groups, we turn to theories of individual learning for guidance in how to understand and facilitate group learning.

Key Concepts for Understanding Learning

As practitioners, we have found two theories of individual learning particularly useful in understanding group learning. The concepts of transformative learning and of constructivist-developmentalism each provides a lens for understanding evolution of consciousness. We draw on Jack Mezirow's theory of transformative learning and two perspectives on constructivist-developmentalism (Kegan, 1994; Bennett, 1992).

Mezirow, Kegan, and Bennett are constructivists. They believe that meaning is socially constructed or, as Mezirow (1991, p. 11) has observed, that "making meaning is central to what learning is all about." From a constructivist perspective, human growth is the reconstruction or transformation of systems of meaning. All three theorists believe in the evolution of consciousness. For Mezirow, evolution means that perspectives are increasingly "more inclusive, differentiated, permeable, and integrated" (p. 155). For both Kegan and Bennett, evolution refers to predictable stages of capacity for constructing meaning.

Transforming the Content of Consciousness

Mezirow focuses primarily on transformation of the content of consciousness—that is, on assumptions or premises that form the content of a person's frames of reference, meaning schemes, or meaning perspectives. In Chapter One Mezirow describes four ways that transformative learning takes place: elaborating existing frames of reference, learning new frames of reference, transforming frames of reference or points of view, and transforming habits of mind.

Our practice as facilitators teaches us that transformation in the context of consciousness is facilitated most effectively when we nurture interdependent processes of discernment and critical reflection. Critical reflection is a process of precipitating transformation in frames of reference by surfacing and challenging uncritically assimilated assumptions about oneself and one's world (Mezirow, 1991). Discernment is a process of seeing patterns of relational wholeness that begins with an attitude of receptivity and appreciation. Frames of reference are transcended rather than analyzed; new frames of reference emerge. The interdependence of these two processes is illuminated by David Kolb's theory of how people learn from their experience. Discernment cultivates what Kolb calls apprehension, "a registrative process transformed . . . by appreciation," whereas critical reflection cultivates comprehension, an "interpretive process transformed . . . by criticism" (Kolb, 1984, p. 103). Each way of knowing is valorized by Kolb; neither, he argues, is complete without the other. We agree.

Transforming the Structure of Consciousness

Kegan and Bennett focus primarily on transformation of the structure of consciousness. Kegan argues that consciousness evolves through successive orders or structures that emerge in response to demands of a changing environment. As the environment becomes more complex, consciousness evolves and becomes more complex.

For example, because the consciousness compatible with traditional culture (Order 3) didn't match demands taking shape in industrial capitalism and democratic nation-states, a new form of "institutional" consciousness (Order 4) emerged. Order 4 consciousness is oriented toward self-authorship, identity, autonomy, and individuation, in contrast to Order 3 consciousness, which is oriented toward culturally determined identity.

As we face the demands of a postmodern environment, Kegan asserts that our capacity to flourish depends on the emergence of a new structure of consciousness in which the self has capacity for self-reflection and correction, for reflecting on and changing its relationship with its identity. In this new structure of consciousness, the self no longer *is* its identity, as in Order 4 consciousness; instead the self *has* an identity or identities. Kegan names this new pattern of relationship within the structures of consciousness Order 5.

We believe that evolving complexity in the structure of consciousness not only enables expansion of learning capacity but is also a necessary precondition.

In addition to Kegan's model, we draw insight from Bennett's point of view on constructivist-developmentalism. He suggests that growth in capacity to empathize and experiment with different cultural lenses is a developmental trajectory that moves from ethnocentrism, the source of hegemonic attitudes and practices, to ethnorelativism. Within ethnorelativism, developmental stages are learning to appreciate differences, then learning to relate and communicate with people of other cultures, and finally integrating "disparate parts of one's identity into a new whole" (1992, p. 65). According to Bennett, a primary catalyst for developing toward ethnorelativism is the experience of being marginal to a mainstream or dominant culture.

Defining Transformative Learning

Mezirow primarily addresses the content of consciousness; both Kegan and Bennett address the structure of consciousness, especially the structure that engages a system with understanding its own identity. We seek a definition of transformative learning that includes both of these concepts as well as our initiating premise that groups learn. In Chapter One of this volume Mezirow defines transformative learning as a process of exploring, assessing, and working to change limiting frames of reference and habits of mind. We expand Mezirow's definition as follows.

Transformative learning is the expansion of consciousness in any human system, thus the collective as well as individual. This expanded consciousness is characterized by new frames of reference, points of view, or habits of mind as well as by a new structure for engaging the system's identity. Transformation of the content of consciousness is facilitated when two processes are engaged interactively: the process of critically analyzing underlying premises and the process of appreciatively accessing and receiving the symbolic contents of the unconscious. Transformation of the structure of consciousness is facilitated when a learner is confronted with a complex cultural environment because effective engagement with that environment requires a change in the learner's relationship to his or her or the group's identity.

A Case History of Group Learning

We now illustrate the elements of our definition by interpreting, through the lens of transformative learning, the experience of a group to which we both belong, the Transformative Learning Collaborative.[1] This group, an independent praxis collective, has emerged from its originating identity as a faculty group in a small institution of higher education in California, which we will call The Center.[2]

1. We acknowledge the contribution of all members of the Transformative Learning Collaborative: Liz Campbell, Dean Elias, Dorothy Ettling, Joanne Gozawa, Taj Johns, Connie Jones, Masai Jones, Lewis Jordan, Elizabeth Kasl, Terri O'Fallon, Ken Otter, and Linda Sartor.
2. We use pseudonyms for the institution and the school within the institution.

The Center was founded with the vision that a world order of peace, freedom, and justice can emerge only from a new global vision of humankind's common destiny. Until 1992, Center curricula were in philosophy, religion, and the social sciences. In 1992 a new entrepreneurial venture was launched within The Center as the School for Holistic Education (SHE). The flagship program for the new School was a doctorate in transformative leadership, an innovative approach to studying transformative change in individuals, groups, communities, and cultures.

The case history we offer as an illustration of transformative learning traces the group life of the transformative leadership faculty as it evolved into the Transformative Learning Collaborative. The case is conveyed through three different but interrelated stories. As part of each story we discuss how our understanding is enhanced by applying concepts about transformative learning. Our assumption is that other practitioners can more easily apply these concepts to group learning if they see them come to life through concrete example.

Although these stories relate the life history of the Transformative Learning Collaborative, they are told from the perspective of two group members: this chapter's authors. Therefore, the narratives that follow are given in their own words.

Structures of Consciousness and Marginality: Dean's Perspective

I trace how the program faculty learned—that is, how it increased its capacity for learning—through changes in the structure of its group consciousness. In the succeeding story, Elizabeth describes what the group learned; she traces change in the content of the group's consciousness. My story of how the group learned is interpreted through the conceptual lens of constructivist-developmentalism. It is a story of how the group developed in response to its environment.

The Roots of Our Marginality

At the invitation of the Center president, I came in the summer of 1992 to help create a new school within The Center, the School for Holistic Education (SHE). SHE's first disorienting dilemma took shape six months after it was initiated and before it yet had either faculty or a student body. A budget shortfall of over $1 million precipitated faculty and staff reductions across The Center, with one exception: the SHE budget was untouched because SHE had been initiated as a potential long-term profit maker. Faculty and students most harshly affected by the cuts were enraged at the perceived inequity, and SHE thereafter was the target of ongoing animosity.

Born from financial crisis, the animosity that continued toward SHE was also a reaction to our "otherness." Our school brought not only new curricular content to The Center but also new formats and pedagogies. We organized our students into self-contained cohort groups; our pedagogy emphasized learning from experience in highly collaborative processes; we pioneered the on-line medium. Whether coming for three-day weekends or studying at a distance, our students were an anomaly in an institution organized for students who could attend weekday classes. Another factor that set us apart was our ethos as a school. We were committed to collaboration and full participation by faculty and staff, but to others it seemed simply that we spent a mysterious and inordinate amount of time in meetings.

Another factor in our otherness was our relative success in achieving diversity. With leadership from newly admitted students in our first year, we recruited a cohort with a majority of students of color. Our ongoing effort in recruiting students and faculty of color made us stand out in The Center, a school sometimes caricatured in the community as a refuge for the wealthy, white, and privileged. Our diverse student body and faculty, our cohort organization in weekend and on-line curriculum formats, our experiential pedagogy, our school's way of work all marked us as different. We commonly were described in the larger Center as "not spiritual enough." My interpretation is that, because the Center prides itself as embracing spiritual dimensions of reality, labeling us "not spiritual" was a way of expressing judgment that we were markedly different.

From our perspective in SHE these factors that made us different were marks of educational vision. We were quite full of ourselves and sometimes a bit arrogant, thus exacerbating the animosity and our position in the institutional margins.

Reorganizations and Shifting Frames of Reference

In response to chronic financial troubles, in 1996 the board and administration began an aggressive effort to downsize. The three-school organization was dismantled and reformed into five divisions, thus removing the cost of a level of management. Although shaken by the loss of our school, as a division faculty we continued our bold commitment to our own values and vision. Concomitantly, we continued our life in the margins, perceived by many faculty and administrators as alien.

The following year, the board mandated another downsizing to achieve further fiscal stability. By January 1998 our program, which had begun as a separate transdisciplinary Ph.D. program, was reconstituted as one among several concentrations in a single Ph.D. awarded by The Center. In the short space of thirteen months we had moved from having our own school, with a unique vision and the autonomy necessary to actualize that vision, to being dependent on partnerships with faculty who held many beliefs radically different from our own.

Although our frame of reference as an autonomous group no longer fit our reality, we did not change our frame but instead attempted to preserve it by changing our reality. We scheduled off-site, all-day retreats that we devoted to theory building about transformative learning and facilitative practices. We tried to find a new institutional home for our program. While pursuing these venues for holding onto our autonomy we also engaged in good faith with our new Center faculty partners: we initiated meetings for mutual planning, accepted a degree title that gave primary status to another program's academic discipline, and negotiated a mutually agreeable common core curriculum.

Our dual activities sharpened our capacity to articulate our vision. We were identifying what conditions we would need if we were to transplant our program to another institution and what programmatic values we held as nonnegotiable in blending our program with others at The Center. Our retreats provided an environment that supported reflective conversation.

In September 1998 we met for a three-day retreat in an idyllic rural setting. The outcome was unanticipated and transforming. A clear vision emerged along with an intuitive sense of excitement and well-being. In short, we agreed that we no longer would base our group's identity on our role as faculty but rather on our activity as a learning community committed to generating new knowledge about transformative learning. Our identity would be linked to shared praxis; our relationship with each other would be independent of any particular project or employing institution. This rather homely realization was a revelation to us and we felt exhilarated, as if a new being. Our frame of reference for our collective identity was transforming.

Evolution of Consciousness

We find the constructivist-developmentalist perspective useful in making meaning of this experience. We begin with Kegan's lens, then turn to Bennett's.

Our group operated, by and large, at a fourth-order level of consciousness oriented toward the group's sense of self-authorship, identity, autonomy, and individuation. Feeling proud of our accomplishments, deeply committed to our values and pedagogy, our response to marginalization was to take refuge in our fourth-order consciousness. When we no longer had the status of a separate program faculty we held onto our fourth-order identity by moving out of The Center psychologically, pursuing our common values and vision in a series of retreats.

Our experience in grappling with the challenges that the Center's downsizing thrust upon us created moments of Order 5 consciousness. As we participated in good faith with new colleagues in crafting a blended program, we grew less attached to the particulars of our curriculum design and more articulate about our basic values and pedagogical beliefs. The tight bond between our group's sense of identity and the academic program we had created began to loosen. Our insight at our September 1998 retreat, that we could separate our group's identity from the institution, dramatically accelerated this loosening process. The realization that our inquiry about transformative learning theory could transcend institutional context changed our relationship with our identities, prodding us away from Order 4 structure, where a group *is* its identity, toward Order 5 structure, in which a group *has* identities that can be the object of its own self-reflection.

Bennett's model (1992) of ethnorelativism also helps construe the meaning of this experience. Bennett describes the ethnorelative person as always in the process of becoming a part of and apart from a given cultural context (p. 64). The experience of being marginal stimulates capacity to use frames of reference of various cultures as situations demand. In our group the faculty learned to function with goodwill in the Center system while becoming increasingly aware of how marginal our deepest values were to that system. Our capacity to inhabit different identities that matched the challenge in different situations is akin to what Bennett calls "constructive marginality."

Content of Consciousness and Transformation: Elizabeth's Perspective

Dean uses constructivist-developmentalism to describe the changing structures of our group's consciousness and the way these changes were linked to our position in the margins of the larger system. He described *how* we increased our capacity to learn. I now tell *what* we learned, using Mezirow's lens of transformation as a process in which learners elaborate existing frames, learn new frames, and transform their points of view. Additionally, I show how critical reflection and discernment facilitated the group's movement to a more inclusive, differentiated, permeable, and integrated perspective.

A New Faculty Forms

In 1993 our fledging doctoral faculty met frequently to share our experiences with implementing a curriculum created before we arrived. Although we did not understand it at the time, we had little mutual understanding of either the program's vision or its intended pedagogical strategies. We all used the phrases "learning community" and "transformative learning" as if we shared common concepts, yet our disparate interests and academic training led us to quite different practices with our students. Dean, the program initiator who might have shown us how our differing perspectives contributed to an integrated vision, had been drafted for administrative duties related to the Center's financial woes. As a consequence, he rarely attended faculty meetings and was not an influence in our group.

Elaborating Our Frame on Faculty Identity

By 1995–96, our third full program year, we were a significantly different group. Two of the original group were gone, but we had five new core faculty, including two persons of color, as well as two teaching fellows (advanced doctoral students who served as half-time faculty with entering cohorts). With a new provost in place, Dean was free to be an active participant and assumed a leadership role.

Our group's experience during this third year is marked by a growing sense of efficacy as we took increasing initiative for the shape and content of the program. Through discussion we explored our individual perspectives on the meaning of learning community and transformative learning. Through cycles of full-group reflection on written position statements drafted by small work teams, we gradually forged mutual understanding about the program's content and pedagogical intentions. By the end of our third year we had a curriculum authored synergistically by the full faculty, to which most of us felt strongly committed.

As our doctoral faculty deepened its understanding of its curricular intentions, we also participated in SHE faculty development gatherings where engaging multiple ways of knowing was the norm. For example, in one meeting we created individual drawings that represented personal goals for growth as scholar-practitioners, then shared the drawing's meaning. On another occasion we painted a group mural in which the theme was "learning community," then engaged in critical reflection about how the experience unveiled our assumptions and beliefs. In another, two faculty staged a dramatic reading about race and communicating across racial difference. These activities tapped intuitive knowledge and emotional energy that led us to discover differences we had not surfaced in faculty business meetings where analytic discussion and critical reflection were the dominant modes. We also grew in our empathic appreciation of each other.

Our impulse for learning manifested outside the workplace. For over three years several of us participated in a biweekly evening study group devoted to deepening our understanding about transformative learning. We experimented, trying out activities such as word-for-word "close text analysis" of Mezirow's writing and role play within Kegan's orders of consciousness.

Incubating a New Frame on Identity

Just as we achieved a sense of efficacious identity, The Center was mired in tumult related to its financial stability. Faculty became absorbed by the challenge of helping shape a necessary downsizing. In January 1997, midway through our fourth academic year, the organization of three quasi-autonomous schools changed to five less-autonomous divisions. Our transformative leadership doctoral program became part of the graduate Division for Holistic Education.

Although our school was dismantled, our impulse for learning was unchanged. Among our transformative leadership faculty, two ideas took form. The first was that faculty must protect time for generative learning. During our intense participation in planning for reorganization we had grown increasingly frustrated that development activities invariably were crowded off meeting agendas. The group resolved that half of all meeting time would be reserved for professional learning. The second emerging idea concerned the group's identity. We began to attend more consciously and critically to the proposition that, like the student cohorts we led, faculty should be developing capacity to form and nurture itself as a learning community. We reshaped business meetings to include more reflective pauses and to be more participatory. Dean continued to chair but we distributed authority and responsibility for planning and facilitation.

Apprehending a New Frame on Identity: Learning Community

As part of our resolve to develop capacity as a generative learning system, we held an end-of-year two-day retreat in June 1997. This retreat marked a special moment in our development. We were all there—eight core faculty, four teaching fellows, three adjunct or associate faculty. We gathered in a beautiful setting, a colleague's home on a bluff above the Pacific Ocean.

Sprawled on couches, chairs, and floor pillows, we went round the circle with a personal check-in, a traditional beginning for both our own meetings and our student cohorts. Then Dean walked to the easel and uncovered his planned agenda. I was dismayed. The agenda seemed overscheduled and usurped by program tasks, with little trace of the participatory leadership that was the emerging norm when I left on sabbatical three months earlier. Wondering how others felt, I said nervously, "I invested money and time to come cross-country during my sabbatical, and this agenda is not what drew me here." Others murmured agreement. After a few exchanges about the pace and content of the planned agenda, Dean walked across the room and sat in the chair he had vacated moments earlier, now just another member of the group.

We were in the process of trying to articulate our hopes for the retreat when another member of the group, Tingli, uncharacteristically burst out that he thought we should spend time sharing experiences. Without pause he then spoke at length about his own experience, pouring out disappointment as a Chinese man who had expected the espoused global philosophy of The Center to make him feel welcome. Instead he felt isolated by cultural difference and racism within the center and within our faculty group.

From that moment the retreat took on a life of its own. We moved organically, addressing some items on the original agenda and creating other unanticipated conversations. Although the idea that faculty was a learning community—just like the student cohorts—had been percolating for months, we came during these two days to know this identity experientially. Our learning became full-bodied when we apprehended what we had been espousing as a somewhat abstract comprehension. We experienced ourselves as self-directing when we rejected the agenda. We experienced ourselves as being "just like the cohorts" when we realized how imperfect we were as a community, having created a context of racism that inflicted pain on a member of our group.

To capture our new sense of identity we decided to name ourselves, settling on the name "Cohort 13." Tingli observed with pleasure that, in Chinese culture, thirteen is a lucky number. As we left the retreat all agreed that something magical had happened. We were a new group, qualitatively different from the one that had arrived at the retreat. We felt hopeful and strong.

Two months later, in August 1997, a new financial crisis enveloped The Center and the board decreed another downsizing. By January the five divisions, in existence for only a year, were disassembled and surviving programs reassembled into two schools.

Although we had lost institutional autonomy, we maintained our commitment to our inquiry about transformative learning. Our end-of-year retreat in June 1998 was particularly engaging. Students of color had challenged our most core assumptions about effective pedagogy; our reflections about their challenge revealed surprising differences. Enlivened by the vitality of our discussion, we planned a three-day retreat for fall. This fall 1998 retreat would become our moment of transformation, what Dean identified in his story as the emergence of clear vision and new identity, the growing intimation of Order 5 consciousness.

Birthing the Transformative Learning Collaborative

We gathered in September 1998 at a small retreat center nestled among the golden hills of northern California. We had assigned ourselves summer homework so that we could deepen our discussion about how our pedagogy perpetuated white hegemony. From that discussion we moved seamlessly into an exploration of members' spiritual practices. The day was full, the evening luxurious with personal storytelling.

On the second day we turned our attention to our efforts to find a new institutional home for our program. In the morning we spoke thoughtfully about many troubling complexities but found no resolution. We chose to reconvene after lunch under a huge oak tree that overlooked the rolling hills. As we resumed discussion under the peaceful embrace of the spreading oak, an intuitive knowing that had been incubating became articulate. The idea seemed to spring full-blown that our work as a learning group did not have to be linked to our work as a faculty. Within moments we birthed and named the Transformative Learning Collaborative—separating the identity of Cohort 13, which we associated with our role as Center faculty, from the identity of the Transformative Learning Collaborative, which we conceptualized as a group of scholar-practitioners engaged in an inquiry about transformative learning. When we made this separation it became clear to us that our survival as a group did not depend on moving our academic program to a more supportive institutional environment.

We created a name for this new conceptualization of identity, "praxis collective," and committed ourselves to three annual retreats. Since that time we have been actively engaged in inquiry about what it means to be a praxis collective.

Frames and Transformations

Mezirow's conceptualization of ways that transformative learning happens is useful in interpreting the evolution of the group's meaning perspective on its identity. Our group's *initial frame* about its faculty identity focused on the role of teaching. Gradually we *elaborated our frame*, expanding the content of our point of view about faculty roles to include shared responsibility for program development and leadership in directing our own work. However, our frame on our identity was still as faculty. When we named ourselves Cohort 13 in June 1997 we were manifesting the process of *learning a new frame*. The content of our new frame was "learning community." This new frame was discerned when we rejected Dean's planned agenda and when we learned from Tingli about our own racism. We apprehended experientially that we were a group like our student cohorts, facing the same challenges of learning-in-relationship.

Fifteen months later, in September 1998, we imagined ourselves as a praxis collective. This new identity was not an elaboration of our existing frame of learning community, but a *transformation in our point of view* because we changed our perception about the locus of our identity. Cohort 13 was a group of faculty who challenged themselves to learn together within a relationship of community; as a faculty group Cohort 13 derived its identity from its institutional context. When we realized that our inquiry about the theory and practice of transformative learning could transcend institutional context, we realized that our locus of legitimacy was conferred by our own inquiry agenda, not the institution and its curricula. Our point of view about our identity was transformed. The startling revelation was emancipatory because it freed us from our assumption that the survival of our initiating vision depended on moving the program to a new institutional context.

More traditional academics, who collaborate in pursuing scholarly interests not connected to their faculty roles, may be surprised that we found this insight revelatory. But we had been immersed for five years in actualizing a praxis-based curriculum about transformative learning. Our realization that we could detach our own inquiry about praxis and transformation from the institutional context in which we had been pursuing it with such intensity was transformative.

Each of the apparently sudden insights that manifested at the two extended retreats had actually been taking form for some time. The June 1997 insight that we were a cohort had been voiced two years earlier by a new teaching fellow who observed that the faculty "was a cohort too." During the next year a new faculty member, still holding an outsider's perspective, began to observe that the faculty ought to be working as hard as the students to practice the skills of learning community. Although we talked periodically about the idea of being a learning community, we did not learn this new frame until we also discerned it—when we apprehended the meaning of rejecting Dean's agenda, of discovering our complicity in Tingli's pain. The pattern repeats itself in our September 1998 insight that we would transform ourselves into a praxis collective. Although naming ourselves as a praxis collective seemed sudden and full-blown, the intuitive knowing that our inquiry had intrinsic merit had been guiding us as a faculty for some time—when some of us formed an extracurricular study group during our first year, when we stubbornly protected half of our meeting time for generative learning, when we made time for numerous off-site, all-day retreats that grew increasingly detached from institutional duties and identities.

Our experience illustrates how discernment interacts with critical reflection to catalyze learning and transformative learning. In this narrative about our evolving identity I described examples of activities, such as visual or dramatic arts inquiry, that invite discernment.

In addition to planned activities, planned conditions also are important facilitators of discernment. Our increasing numbers of one-day, off-site retreats were our attempt to create an environment that nurtured exploration and reflection. In our longer residential retreats in June 1997 and September 1998 we carefully created a caring, relational environment with freedom for meandering contemplation, thus enabling us to be open to apprehending our experience.

Transforming Our Understanding of Race and Cultural Diversity: Elizabeth's Perspective

Our faculty, and now the Transformative Learning Collaborative, perceives capacity to engage diversity creatively as a cultural imperative. We evolved to our current understanding through a painful process of transforming our individual and collective frames of reference.

Disorienting Dilemma: Faculty Perceives Its Own Inadequacies

During our first three years we developed a sense of competence and deep devotion to the value of our enterprise. Gradually our sense of well-being and competence eroded, precipitated by an understanding of our relationship to diversity. During our faculty retreat at the close of our fourth program year, in June 1997, our dilemma came into focus.

I have already described one triggering event that happened during that retreat. On the first morning, Tingli spoke with despair about his sense of isolation and the incongruence between espoused commitments and actions. We had heard Tingli speak many times about his disappointment in the larger Center's failure to actualize synergy among global perspectives, but we had not understood that Tingli's anguish included his feelings about our group and its context of racism.

Our second triggering conversation related to one of our cohorts that, at the end of its second year, was in serious trouble. Dean convened a conversation about the troubled cohort. We listened as the cohort's two core faculty described a very difficult year, fraught with conflicts related to race and cultural difference. As we asked questions about the cohort's situation, I became aware, as I imagine others did, that there was serious tension and disagreement between the cohort's two faculty.

Over the course of the next year our faculty group gradually confessed to each other that we all had difficulties in our cohorts and often felt very unsure about what we were doing. We needed each other's help.

Toward Congruence

A year after our faculty discussed the cohort so troubled by the conflict related to culture and race, we attended that group's culminating curriculum event. In our program cohorts are required to demonstrate competency as learning systems at the end of the third year. This cohort's demonstration focused on the group's difficulties and the learning that evolved from them.

An entirely unplanned outcome was precipitated by this event— our cultural consciousness project. With this group of students lighting our way, our faculty organized a learning project open to the full Center community. It included several activities. One was a cooperative inquiry in which faculty, both white and of color, pursued the question, How can we increase our understanding of the ways in which our curriculum is embedded in white supremacist consciousness?

This cohort's analysis prodded our faculty to examine our most fundamental beliefs about learning. The students argued that the program's constructivist assumptions about the communicative domain of learning cannot be viable in the context of unexamined white privilege, that our basic strategies for facilitating transformative learning perpetuate systems of domination. This critique profoundly challenged our habits of mind about participation and discourse. As the Transformative Learning Collaborative, with a mission of developing theory about transformative learning, we grapple with this challenge.

Diversity and Transformative Learning

Our experiences have provoked reflection on our individual and collective assumptions about diversity and its relationship to transformative learning. As a faculty, the content of our initial meaning perspective about transformative learning theory did not include race and ethnic diversity as an integral component. Rather we thought of race and ethnicity as two of many sources for potential disorienting dilemmas that could precipitate transformative learning processes. Our frame of reference has changed: we now assume that, in U.S. culture, habits of mind are permeated with hegemony of white (and male) privilege that must be consciously confronted in all our interactions.

Space does not allow me to relate the multitude of incidents that would bring alive how the interaction of discernment with critical reflection facilitated the evolution in our understanding of diversity. Both learning processes were indispensable to our changing perspectives.

Implications for Theory and Practice

In this final section we have two tasks: first, to review the extent to which theories of individual learning seem able to illuminate the experience of a group; and second, to spell out the implications for adult education practice.

The case study illustrates how models developed for the purpose of describing individual learning also are lenses for interpreting the group's learning. In terms of the content of consciousness, the group changed its premises about its identity first by elaborating its frame of reference for faculty, then by adding a new frame of learning community, and finally by transcending both of these identities and creating a new identity as a praxis collective. In relation to race and diversity, the group moved through a series of perspectives. Initial pride of leadership in advocating for a more diverse student body and faculty was later tempered by dismayed realization that the group participated in perpetuating white hegemonic consciousness.

In terms of the structure of consciousness, the group began by forming an Order 4 consciousness through clearly defining its identity. As the environment grew more turbulent and the group more marginal in the institution, the group vacillated between hanging onto identity as a faculty striving to ensure survival of a particular curriculum and evolving to an identity as a praxis collective detached from any specific curriculum application of its beliefs. The group's experience of constructive marginality helped it move through Order 4 consciousness into the beginning stages of Order 5.

Although limited to the example of one case, we proceed with the premise that theories of individual learning are applicable to groups and suggest implications for practice.

The first implication for practice applies to transforming the content of group frames of reference. The case study demonstrates the importance of creating processes and conditions that can facilitate both discernment and critical reflection. Critical reflection enables current reality to be assessed; discernment generates insights about current reality and images of new possibilities. Adult education practitioners are relatively well schooled in how to facilitate critical reflection but relatively unprepared to facilitate discernment. We need to acquire competence and comfort in evoking and processing the imaginal, the archetypal, the mythic, the affective, the somatic. We have allies in the expressive arts (Lewis, 1993; Stromsted, 2000) and archetypal psychology (Boyd, 1991; Boyd and Myers, 1988; Johnson, 1986) who can provide assistance.

The second implication applies to transforming the structure of group consciousness. Using Bennett's concept of constructive marginality and Kegan's assumption about how consciousness evolves, the case study demonstrates the importance of understanding that consciousness develops in response to demands from the environment. Our interpretation is that, short of intentionally precipitating institutional crisis, adult educators can help groups develop capacity for learning by helping them pay ongoing attention to their identity and to their environment. The function of clarifying a group's relationship with its identity can be facilitated by challenging a group to clarify its mission, and the alignment of individuals' visions with the group's vision. In Peter Senge's view, "[t]eam learning is the process of aligning and developing the capacity of a team to create the results its members truly desire" (1990, p. 236). Groups will also be helped by becoming clear about the field of forces in which they exist—ecological, social, and cultural. Adult educators can deepen their skills in helping groups assess mission and contextual forces by turning to colleagues who focus on organization learning (Kasl, Marsick, and Dechant, 1997; Raelin, 1999).

The third implication for practice applies more broadly to group learning. In the case study, the group worked hard to articulate core values and operating principles. In so doing it deepened a context for relationship that inspired trust, self-disclosure, and empathic listening. As it took ownership of the curriculum it engaged in cycles of full-group brainstorming, small-group writing tasks, and full-group critique of draft documents until consensus was reached. In effect, the group produced the conditions for group learning spelled out by Kasl, Marsick, and Dechant: appreciation of teamwork, freedom for individual expression, and operating principles that are both commonly developed and consensually adopted (p. 230). Adult educators can develop tools for creating these conditions—cultivating interpersonal communication competence, creating group norms, developing consensual decision-making processes.

The fourth implication challenges cultural norms. Transformative learning takes time—meeting time for the group to develop, calendar time for insights to gestate. This group was immersed in the tasks of developing a new program and leading a time-intensive curriculum; time devoted to reflection and development had to be a fiercely held priority to survive busy schedules. Further, the group's transformation required sustained effort across many years. It was well into its third year when the group consolidated an elaborated frame on its identity, the end of the fourth year when it added a perception that it was a learning group akin to a student cohort, and the beginning of the sixth year when it transformed its point of view. Commitment to investing a substantial amount of time has far-reaching implications. For the case study group, its use of time was contrary to norms in the larger institutional culture. The Center's environment is typical of many organizations. Sustaining group effort when the larger culture is not supportive requires great capacity and tenacity. Adult educators can become advocates within organizations about the long-term benefit of creating cultural norms that support groups in their needs for time.

The fifth implication from the case study is more for the practitioner than for any specific practice, a matter of personal mastery in Senge's framework (1990, p. 139), and derives from the group's engagement with the issue of diversity. Given the changing demography of the United States, we believe that adult educators are obligated to become competent to function effectively in multicultural environments. We believe that in American culture we all are socialized into a system of white and male privilege (to name just two sources of status privilege), a system based on distorted and limiting assumptions that disadvantages a growing percentage of our diversifying population. Adult educators who are members of groups near the center of hegemonic systems (most particularly, educators who are white or male) must aggressively undertake their own transformations of consciousness if they are to be competent in a diverse society. We believe it imperative that adult educators embrace an exploration of how diversity interrelates with transformative learning theory and practice.

We are left with particular curiosity about what conditions seem to evoke and sustain the capacity of groups (especially groups with diverse members) to evolve to Order 4 consciousness and beyond. We look forward to receiving suggestions about this and other areas of theory and practice that illuminate the phenomenon of group learning. Our hope is to draw adult educators into conversation about group mind and the facilitation of transformative learning in groups, institutions, and communities.

References

Bateson, G. *Mind and Nature: A Necessary Unity*. New York: Dutton, 1979.

Bennett, M. J. "Toward Ethnorelativism: Developmental Model of Intercultural Sensitivity." In R. M. Paige (ed.), *Education for the Intercultural Experience*. Yarmouth, Me.: Intercultural Press, 1992.

Boyd, R. D. *Personal Transformations in Small Groups: A Jungian Perspective*. New York: Routledge, 1991.

Boyd, R. D., and Myers, J. G. "Transformative Education." *International Journal of Lifelong Education*, 1988, 7(4), 261–284.

Imel, S. "Summing Up: Themes and Issues Related to Learning in Groups." In S. Imel (ed.), *Learning in Groups: Exploring Fundamental Principles, New Uses, and Emerging Opportunities*. New Directions for Adult and Continuing Education, no. 71. San Francisco: Jossey-Bass, 1996.

Johnson, R. *Inner Work: Using Dreams & Active Imagination for Personal Growth*. San Francisco: HarperCollins, 1986.

Kasl, E., Marsick, V., and Dechant, K. "Teams as Learners." *Journal of Applied Behavioral Science*, 1997, 33(2), 227–246.

Kegan, R. *In Over Our Heads: The Mental Demands of Modern Life*. Cambridge, Mass.: Harvard University Press, 1994.

Kolb, D. *Experiential Learning*. Englewood Cliffs, N.J.: Prentice Hall, 1984.

Lewis, P. *Creative Transformation: The Healing Power of the Arts*. Wilmette, Ill.: Chiron, 1993.

Mezirow, J. D. *Transformative Dimensions of Adult Learning*. San Francisco: Jossey-Bass, 1991.

Raelin, J. (ed.). "Special Issue—The Action Dimension in Management: Diverse Approaches to Research, Teaching, and Development." *Management Learning*, 1999, 30(2).

Senge, P.M. *The Fifth Discipline: The Art & Practice of the Learning Organization*. New York: Doubleday, 1990.

Stromsted, T. "Re-Inhabiting the Female Body: Authentic Movement as a Gateway to Transformation." Unpublished dissertation. San Francisco: California Institute of Integral Studies, 2000.

von Bertalanffy, L. *General Systems Theory*. New York: Braziller, 1968.

10

Organizational Learning and Transformation

Lyle Yorks, Victoria J. Marsick

A dult education has traditionally taken the individual learner as its point of departure (for example, Brockett and Hiemstra, 1985; Brookfield, 1981, 1986; Candy, 1991; Cross, 1981; Knowles, 1984; Mezirow, 1981, 1991; and Tough, 1979). Recently a growing body of work has focused on group and team learning (ARL Inquiry, 1998; Brooks, 1994; Dechant, Marsick, and Kasl, 1993; Cranton, 1996; Group for Collaborative Inquiry, 1993; Group for Collabora-tive Inquiry and thINQ, 1994; Heimlich, 1996; Imel, 1996; Imel and Tisdell, 1996; Kasl, Marsick, and Dechant, 1997; thINQ, 1993). This emerging literature builds on the long-standing recognition that adult learning is often a socially interactive activity and that groups can provide an effective setting for facilitating learning (Rose, 1996).

The roots of the concept of group learning can be found in the literature on group dynamics, tracing back to the seminal work of Lewin (1958) and others such as Homans (1950), Rice (1965), and Trist and Sofer (1959). What is new in this literature is the idea that groups can learn as discrete entities in a way that transcends indi-vidual learning within the group. Kasl, Marsick, and Dechant (1997, p. 229) advance this idea very clearly by stating, "We define team learning as a process through which a group creates knowledge for its members, *for itself as a system*, and for others" (italics added). This interest in group learning has been stimulated by the popularity of the concept of the learning organization. Senge (1990, p. 10) describes teams, not individuals, "[as] the fundamental learning unit in modern organizations. . . . [U]nless teams can learn, [an] organization cannot learn." Watkins and Marsick (1993, p. 14) assert that "teams, groups, and networks can become the medium for moving new knowledge throughout the learning organization" and that such collaborative structures "enhance the organization's ability to learn because they offer avenues for exchange of new ways of working."

Organizational transformation is a theme that runs through the literature on learning organizations, typified by West (1996, p. 54), who writes, "The goal of organizational learning is to transform the organization, which is a somewhat different goal for transformative learning." This chapter takes as its starting point West's observation that transformational learning in organizations has different goals and implications than does transformative learning theory, as traditionally conceptualized in adult education. Consistent with adult education theory, transformative learning has focused on the individual. Defined as the transformation of a problematic frame of reference (see Chapter One), transformative learning emancipates individual learners through making them aware of how psychological-socioeconomic-cultural forces may have limited personal choice or have been the source for dysfunctionally constructed habits of mind. Mezirow (1991) does address collective transformations such as conciousness raising and social movements, although here the focus is on collective approaches for fostering transformative learning in individuals.

In contrast, the goal of organizational transformation is allowing the organization to more effectively realize its performance objectives. This goal may or may not be in conflict with transformative learning in terms of the impact on individual lives and choices. It does, however, involve substantial and fundamental change in how the organization functions, breaking with past patterns of organizational action and requiring entirely new behaviors on the part of organizational members (see Burke and Litwin, 1992). Transformational organizational change is often called discontinuous change to reflect the magnitude of the change being effected. In learning organizations, transformative learning on the part of individuals is desired for purposes of meeting organizational goals.

In this chapter we examine two strategies that, it is argued, can produce transformative learning for individuals, groups, and/or organizations: action learning and collaborative inquiry. Both strategies are concerned with learning around significant issues and have both a task and a learning dimension. The task dimension is more prominent in action learning, with collaborative inquiry focusing more on learning per se. Our discussion surfaces contradictions that implementation of these two approaches reveals between individual and organizational transformation.

Action Learning and Collaborative Inquiry

Both action learning (AL) and collaborative inquiry (CI) are highly participatory and designed to foster learning from experience through cycles of action and subsequent reflection on that action. Although not specifically developed for learning in organizations, each has been implemented in organizational contexts with the hope of enhancing organizational effectiveness. Action learning in particular has emerged as an intervention directed toward fostering learning organizations.

Action Learning

AL is "an approach to working with and developing people which uses work on a real project or problem as the way to learn. Participants work in small groups to take action to solve their project or problem, and learn how to learn from that action" (Yorks, O'Neil, and Marsick, 1999). Action learning is interpreted in many ways, but in all cases it involves learning in small groups through taking action on meaningful problems. Transformative learning as described in this volume is not necessarily the goal of AL. However, in the United States organizations that use AL do typically speak of it as a means to organizational transformation, though they may not explicitly pursue individual transformation (see, for example, Dotlich and Noel, 1998).

When an AL program is implemented in organizations, participants are often placed in project teams. Each team is presented with a challenge that is sponsored by a senior manager. These challenges are real, have significant performance implications, and are unstructured. Reasonable people may disagree about proper solutions. Project teams are intentionally composed of individuals with diverse areas of specialization and experience. Team members must learn to draw strength from these different frames of reference. Each project team is asked to make recommendations to the sponsor and a senior team of managers. Teams may take action to test or partially implement solutions along the way. If the recommendations are persuasive they will be implemented. Within this general structure, AL programs vary greatly in design (for examples, see Dennis, Cederholm, and Yorks, 1996; Dotlich and Noel, 1998; and O'Neil, Arnell, and Turner, 1996).

Based on an analysis of the various ways AL is practiced, O'Neil (1999) has identified four theoretical schools of action learning: the Tacit School, the Scientific School, the Experiential School, and the Critical Reflection School. Although schools share the basic elements of the definition just offered, they differ in their assumptions about learning—which in turn affects practice and learning outcomes.

Elsewhere (Yorks, O'Neil, and Marsick, 1999) we have postulated that these differences in outcomes can be conceptualized in the form of a pyramid (see Figure 8.1). We use the imagery of a pyramid to capture an inverse Guttman-type ordering of schools in terms of the kinds of learning that are most likely to be produced in an AL program.

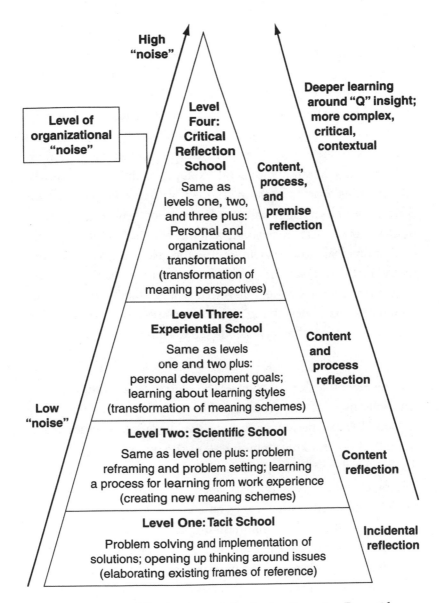

High "noise"

Deeper learning around "Q" insight; more complex, critical, contextual

Level of organizational "noise"

Level Four: Critical Reflection School

Same as levels one, two, and three plus: Personal and organizational transformation (transformation of meaning perspectives)

Content, process, and premise reflection

Level Three: Experiential School

Same as levels one and two plus: personal development goals; learning about learning styles (transformation of meaning schemes)

Content and process reflection

Low "noise"

Level Two: Scientific School

Same as level one plus: problem reframing and problem setting; learning a process for learning from work experience (creating new meaning schemes)

Content reflection

Level One: Tacit School

Problem solving and implementation of solutions; opening up thinking around issues (elaborating existing frames of reference)

Incidental reflection

Figure 8.1. Critical Reflection and the Action Learning Pyramid.

The Tacit School

At the base of the pyramid is the Tacit School, which seems to assume that significant learning will take place so long as participants are placed together, some team building is done, and information is provided by experts. Typically information and team building are provided up front before teams begin work on projects. Learning is closely tied to the project. The approach to action learning described by Noel and Charan (1988) is an example of this kind of design. Any learning apart from this is incidental. Accordingly, the Tacit School resembles a traditional executive development program linked to an action project. Reflection, when it occurs, is incidental and often individual rather than involving the group as a whole. Learning typically involves the elaboration of existing frames of reference—learning to further differentiate and elaborate previously acquired points of view that are taken for granted or learning within previously acquired habits of mind (see Chapter One).

The Scientific School

The Scientific School occupies the second level of the pyramid. This school of AL practice is rooted in the seminal theories of Reg Revans (1970), who is often described as the father of action learning and whose thinking permeates all of the other schools. Like the Tacit School, the Scientific School is essentially concerned with solving the problem facing participants. In addition, however, it infuses participants with a strong, rationalistic approach to problem solving coupled with an emphasis on problem resetting through periodic questioning insight into available data. This approach reflects Revans's background as a physicist, and in many ways his theories parallel other learning theories derived from applying the scientific model to learning through experience. Revans's theories emphasize the importance of asking questions and is expressed as $L = P + Q$, where L = learning, P = programmed instruction, and Q = questioning insight (1982). This emphasis on the interplay among received knowledge through learning and questioning insight raises problem setting as equal in importance to problem solving. Through striving for questioning insight, group reflection is emergent and tends to be on the content of the project.

In the Scientific School, learning coaches are used early in the process to help the group "develop an initial trustworthy cohesion through orderly debate" (Revans, 1978, p. 13). It should be noted that by "orderly debate" Revans refers to basic communication and discussion for exchanging experiences and understanding how the action learning process unfolds. Others in the group will be asking questions and members are expected to probe their experiences. This is different from Mezirow's concept of discourse that emphasizes highly empathic collaboration in a search for consensually construed meaning. The learning that is most likely to take place in the program involves both learning through existing points of view and learning new points of view—creating new meanings through questioning insight that are sufficiently consistent with existing ones to complement them by extending their scope.

The Experiential School

At the third level of the pyramid is the Experiential School. Practitioners in this tradition emphasize the role of explicit reflection throughout the process. Learning coaches help the group reflect on project work and various interpersonal and managerial competencies during structured periods of reflection on action. Goals encompass both problem solving around the project and the development of various interpersonal and managerial competencies. The primary foundation for their work lies in Kolb's (1984) familiar experiential learning cycle or variations of it (Mumford, 1995). This explicit intentionality around learning—using learning coaches to structure opportunities for reflection—increases the possibility of transformation of points of view. This occurs through frequent content and process reflection and dialogue.

The Critical Reflection School

The Critical Reflection School's place at the top of the pyramid reflects the accumulation of the learning goals of the earlier three levels along with a strong emphasis on reflecting on the premises that underlie the thinking of managers and provide the basis for their habits of mind. This difference in how learning coaches utilize reflection is the principal difference between this and the Experiential School (O'Neil, 1999).

Because of differences in program assumptions and design, we believe there is greater potential for personal learning through transformation of points of view and habits of mind in AL programs based on the Critical Reflection School. However, this kind of learning is by no means assured. Learning of this kind is neither predictable nor controllable by formula or technique. It depends in large part on the readiness of the learner to confront, rather than resist, the experience (a point to which we return later). It is also possible for some people to experience personally transformative learning in programs at all levels of the pyramid. In short, transformative learning in organizational settings is very unpredictable and one cannot easily plan for it, although some practices are more likely to foster it than others.

For similar reasons we also believe that transformational changes in an organization's culture are more likely to be triggered by programs toward the top of the pyramid, although this too is by no means assured. In short, as one moves from the bottom to the top of the pyramid, the kind of learning that is produced is more complex, critical, and contextual. This produces more "noise" in the organization and resistance to the process. For this reason most of the programs we are aware of in large corporate organizations are patterned most closely after the Tacit School. In these programs new solutions to complex and uncertain business problems often emerge from the AL process. The process itself is often characterized by behaviors valued by the existing organizational culture. Participants learn to think at a more strategic level, applying instrumental management skills and competencies to general management problems while learning more about the strength of their personalities when working with other "high-potential" executive candidates. In the process, existing organizational narratives are reinforced in the participants' experience rather than challenged. We think this is especially true of programs in companies marked by a strong, personal leadership culture, such as General Electric.

International Foods: A Critical Reflection Program

To illustrate the degree to which transformative learning can occur in organizations, we refer to a program that took place in a multinational foods company over a period of three years. The program was specifically aimed at organizational transformation because it was anticipated that, as a result of the project work, the company's structures and practices would be fundamentally transformed. The company was changing from a multinational organizational structure, comprising national brands with strong traditions and boundaries, to a functionally managed, integrated global network organization. Most managers and professional associates did not believe they had the competencies they needed for this transformation: global mindset, capacity for innovation and change, and what emerged as a synchronous cluster of competencies—interpersonal communication, teamwork, trust, conflict resolution, and leadership in a culturally diverse work environment. In learning, these individuals would most likely have to critically reassess their values, attitudes, and frames of reference.

Description of the Program

Three Action Reflection Learning programs* were conducted over a period of three years. Each program consisted of twenty upper-level managers drawn from different operating units around

*The terms Action Reflection Learning and ARL used periodically in this chapter are registered trademarks of Leadership in International Management (LIM) and used by permission.

the world. These participants organized themselves into four teams of five members, with each team working on a project sponsored by a member of the corporate executive team. The program met as a total community four times over approximately six months. These meetings were six days long, spaced approximately five to six weeks apart, and were held in different parts of the world. Additionally, teams worked on their projects during the periods between program meetings. The meetings were arranged by the team members even as they were doing their regular jobs. More detail on this program can be found in Yorks and others (1996, 1998).

What marks this as a critical reflection program is the emphasis placed on reflection and dialogue within teams and the larger community meetings. In addition to project work and periodic instruction around management topics, participants also engaged in cultural experiences as the program met in different locations around the world. Reflection and dialogue took place around these experiences as well. The senior executive team also approached the program with a recognized need to learn. The lead learning coach regularly worked with the senior executives, helping them reflect on their own practices as a management team and how they were reacting to the program.

Evidence of Transformative Learning

To what extent did transformative learning take place, if at all? Data from seventy-one interviews taken from throughout the organization, coupled with the field notes from a participant observer, demonstrate a pervasive pattern of transformative learning. Interview evidence and observation supported the existence of a perspective transformation around operating globally. Former participants interacted across existing organizational boundaries, effecting transactions without prompts from senior management and before any organizational restructuring to a global organization took place.

Interview comments reflect changes that transferred from the program to the organization and sustained themselves over time—changes that indicate a fundamental change in the participants' habits of mind. For example, in discussing a particular vice president several people independently commented on such a change. "[He] was just not approachable at all, he had the reputation of being a know-it-all. . . . [Now] He's coming and asking questions: 'can you confirm this?' or, 'do you know about this?' . . . to the point of even joking in the aisle. It's a 180 degree turnaround" (interview with a member of the North American Division). Another comment indicates the scope of such changes in parts of the organization and that such individual changes in habits of the mind were reinforcing among those who shared them and affecting the organization's culture: "[T]he whole reflection thing, where there's more of an attempt to draw people out as far as getting their opinions and information from them and letting it be a comment and accepting it for that and not necessarily needing a response or having to worry about criticism" (interview with an organizational member).

Even more pervasive were comments and actions representing changes in points of view. Interviewees reported noticing both individual changes as well as "some consensus about how to handle [situations], how to act." The range of changes reported reach from "significant changes" that we would code as indicative of changes of habits of the mind to "some change(s)," which we would code as representing changes in points of view. The most frequently reported changes were in the latter category. Interviews also suggest that sustaining changes in points of view in terms of behavior was most likely to occur with the continuing support of others. Participants who were isolated from other participants upon their completion of the program were less likely to exhibit changes in behavior. One participant, a woman from Asia, commented that one could not necessarily determine all that she had learned from how she acted in the organization. She may decide that acting on some insights was too risky. Her comment recalls findings by Brooks (1989) that whether critical reflection in organizations (as well as elsewhere) leads to changes in overt action depends on the political risk in the situation.

How Learning Occurred

How did the program trigger the learning? Confronted with an unfamiliar social situation (especially the early community-wide reflection and dialogue sessions), participants had to decipher this setting and make decisions about how they were going to present themselves to both their peers and the program staff. Early on, the program participants seemed to fall into one of three categories in terms of their adopted posture toward the program. Although it is possible to point to specific individuals as being prototypical of each category, in practice the boundaries among the groups are open to interpretation, with some participants blending characteristics of two of the categories.

The first category consists of participants who appear to embrace the program with *tentative trust and an openness toward experiencing the program on its own terms*. As the first week progressed these participants seemed to "absorb" the experience. They became more open and reflected easily on their own self-defined developmental needs.

A second, larger portion of the participants initially appeared to adopt a posture toward the program of what might be described as *constructive distancing*. Our attribution is that they began the experience prepared to be "good company soldiers" who would experience the program on their own terms. During the course of the week many of these participants seemed to connect with the process in ways that surprised them. Some of them seemed to move much more toward the first adaptive strategy, and in some cases crossed over to it.

A smaller number of other participants seemed to be "managing" the experience by adopting a *personal script* that permitted them to explain themselves to others in a way that was politically acceptable within the context of the program.

We considered these scripts to be consistent with, or identical to, the persona or masks presented by them in the organization out-side the program. These participants processed their experiences by integrating them into preexisting points of view. Any learning that took place while this adaptive strategy was in place was clearly non-transformative in nature.

As the program evolved some participants in the middle and third groups moved away from their initial adaptive strategy and toward the first grouping. This was itself evidence of transformative learning. For example, many experienced surprise during the sec-ond week when the effectiveness of their adaptive strategy began to break down. The intensity of work through cycles of reflection and dialogue made it difficult to maintain an unauthentic posture toward the community and in one's project team.

The program set in motion "streams of dissonance": among the adaptive strategies adopted by participants as they worked closely together; between experience within the program versus that of life in the larger organization between sessions; and between the design of the program versus preexisting expectations about corporate train-ing. The tributaries of these streams of dissonance became for many participants, through reflection and dialogue, streams of conscious-ness in unpredictable ways that were also, at times, combustible.

We make some additional observations about the learning pro-cess in this kind of program later. First we consider the second strat-egy, collaborative inquiry.

Collaborative Inquiry as an Adult Learning Strategy

Collaborative inquiry is a cousin of Action Learning. They stem, in part, from action research and are two of several participatory, action-based inquiry methods for improving practice and develop-ing new knowledge, especially in the fields of education, commu-nity development, and organizational studies (Brooks and Watkins, 1994). Collaborative inquiry takes its theoretical base from John Heron's (1981, 1985, 1988, 1996) seminal ideas about cooperative inquiry and Peter Reason and John Rowan's work (see Reason and

Rowan, 1981; Reason, 1994) on participatory human inquiry. Participation and democracy are seen as essential for meaningful inquiry into the human condition and the resolution of dilemmas, questions, and problems that are part of that condition. Collaborative inquiry also honors a holistic perspective on what constitutes valid knowledge. Effective collaborative inquiry treats research as a form of learning that should be accessible by those interested in gaining a better understanding of their world.

Collaborative inquiry is a process consisting of repeated episodes of reflection and action through which a group of peers strives to answer a question of importance to them. There are three parts to this definition: the repeated episodes of reflection and action, the notion of a group of inquirers who are truly peers, and the inquiry question (Bray, Gerdau-Lee, Smith, and Yorks, 2000). The notion of coinquiry—conducting inquiry *with* people rather than *on* them— is a defining principle (Reason and Rowan, 1981; Reason, 1994). Each participant is a coinquirer—shaping the question, designing the inquiry process, participating in the experience, making and communicating meaning.

This emphasis on participation, holistic understanding of experience, and democracy simultaneously makes collaborative inquiry more likely than Action Learning to foster transformative learning and less digestible for many organizational systems. In our experience it has been implemented in two school system settings, a university, a community college, and not-for-profit organizations with social service missions (see Bray, Gerdau-Lee, Smith, and Yorks, 2000; Zelman, 1995). Most of these interventions focused on the professional practice of individuals, and all demonstrated significant examples of transformative learning.

This brief description points to key differences between CI and AL. In CI, participation is always voluntary. Initiators seek out others who share their interest in a question. The final form of the question is framed by the group with no outside interference. Finally, the design and methods used are created by the coinquirers. The only boundaries are that all inquirers take action on the question and are willing to participate openly in reflection on their experience to build shared meaning.

The University Learning Organization Inquiry

Here we discuss one intervention that was specifically designed to foster learning at both the individual and organizational levels. The University Learning Organization Inquiry was part of a dissertation project into collaborative inquiry at Teachers College at Columbia University (Group for Collaborative Inquiry and thINQ, 1994; thINQ, 1993; Yorks, 1995). The site of the inquiry was a midsize state university that offered undergraduate and master degrees. To begin the inquiry, Yorks sought the interests and support of a colleague in the sociology department and a senior administrator who became coinitiators. The coinitiators approached several members of the college community about the possibility of participating in an inquiry into student learning. Participants in the inquiry included four faculty, representing education, fine arts, management, and sociology, plus two administrators, an associate dean, and the senior academic officer.

The group agreed to the inquiry question, How can we help students to take more responsibility for their own learning in a way that makes the university more of a learning organization? Universities are in the business of generating learning and it seemed valuable to explore the learning experience of students from a systemic view, examining how student culture, curriculum structure, and classroom methods coalesced.

There was tension in the early meetings in which members spent time discussing classroom experiences and student perspectives. On reflection it became clear that participants had brought their expectations from campus politics into the meeting room. The unspoken question was, Will this be just another faculty committee? As the inquiry progressed the group coalesced into a learning group (Yorks, 1995).

Evidence of Transformative Learning

There is considerable evidence that most of the members of the group experienced transformative learning in the form of changed habits of the mind. The following comment from a subsequent interview with one of the members of the group provides an example:

> One of my colleagues sat in to evaluate my teaching . . . and the comments, the things that he really valued or didn't value really were quite the opposite of what we're striving to do. And I spoke to him about that. . . and he really wonders about this. . . . [He] remembered the way I used to teach early on when I . . . [was] much more data-based. . . . When he wrote the evaluation he said that Roberta is going through a process of trying out different group situations, but that he really wishes [I] would get back to the lecture mode. . . . I knew he was coming and yet I refused to fall back into that [Yorks, 1995, p. 223].

During a group discussion this same faculty member commented, "I ended up this process questioning even more than I usually question things that I was doing. And so now I really need help to work out some of these situations because I'm opening up a whole can of worms" (Yorks, 1995, p. 228). Another member of the group commented during this same discussion:

> Maybe it's related to reflection, but I've been finding that I have been changing my views in so many areas, and I can't tell at times where it originated . . . but this group has been somewhat of an anchorage. . . . So I find that I've . . . looked at my classes differently, I've looked at other faculty differently, I've talked with colleagues differently because I have a different vision of what it should be [Yorks, 1995, p. 229].

Such examples of transformative learning regularly occur in CI groups (see Bray, 1995; Gerdau, 1995; Smith, 1995; and Zelman, 1995), in our experience more frequently than in AL programs. A frequently mentioned factor is the support for learning that the group provides.

Problematic Nature of Organizational Learning from CI

Conversely, transfer of learning at the organizational level is more problematic, in large part because, given the highly democratic nature of CI, many times there is less support from management. Part of the rationale for inviting the senior academic officer to participate was to begin building bridges to the larger organization in order to build support for action. In the spring the university CI group planned a learning community experiment for the upcoming fall semester. They created a cohort of freshman business majors who took four of their five courses together; their faculty met as a team to create learning links among the courses. The courses were Introduction to Sociology, Introduction to the Theatre, Introduction to Management, and College Writing. This experiment was reflected on, evaluated, and modified during the spring semester. Carrying out this effort required changes in scheduling of classrooms, registration processes, and other administrative systems. In turn there was potential for learning not only for the participating individuals but also for the larger organizational system.

For example, because the faculty teaching in the cluster met regularly to discuss their courses and student performance they became aware of decisions being made by the academic advisement center without consultation with faculty. There were several other instances where the fragmented nature of the university worked at cross-purposes to the needs of students. Eventually a similar design was expanded to include other faculty clusters on a voluntary basis. Through a circuitous route this design eventually became institutionalized in the form of a freshman semester design. This change is best characterized as learning and incorporating a new organizational point of view into preexisting organizational frames of reference, rather than as transformative changes in habits of the organizational mind set or culture.

In both the AL and CI examples just discussed, transformative learning occurred among several participants. Some learning of a transformative nature occurred in the organizations of which they were members as well. The organizational learning was more transformative in the AL example than in the CI one, although this could vary by program type.

Taken alone these two cases are illustrative but obviously limited in terms of making generalizations. What do they suggest, however, in terms of theoretical insight for future thinking about transformative learning in organizations, specifically for fostering transformative organizational learning?

AL and CI as Vehicles for Transformative Organizational Learning

Some scholars advocate that learning organizations, by definition, pursue the equivalent of transformative learning for individuals or organizations (Senge, 1990; Pedler, Burgoyne, and Boydell, 1991; Watkins and Marsick, 1993). Senge, for example, describes the learning organization as one in which "people continually expand their capacity to create the results they truly desire, where new and expansive patterns of thinking are nurtured, where collective aspiration is set free, and where people are continually learning how to learn together" (p. 3). Watkins and Marsick (1993, p. 8) define the learning organization as one that "learns continuously and transforms itself."

Creating Liberating Structures for Transformative Organizational Learning

We think that for transformative learning to occur in learning organizations, organizations must function effectively as a liberating structure that "involves a type of organizing that is productive and educates members toward self-correcting awareness" (Fisher and Torbert, 1995, p. 7). The question, then, is, How does one create spaces within organizations that function as liberating structures? We construe spaces that function as liberating structures as parallel structures, that is, alternative structures that coexist alongside those that currently are in place but that need to be reformed or transformed. Both action learning and collaborative inquiry open up spaces for learning in the organizational context through their ability to function as liberating structures (ARL Inquiry, 1998; Yorks, 1995).

Liberating Structures as Parallel Structures

The idea of a parallel structure was introduced by Lawler and Mohrman (1985) in describing the use of quality circles to create space for learning and change. Their research suggests the limitations of such structures; most quality circle efforts disappeared without having significant impact on their larger organizations. Those efforts that did have a significant impact eventually dissolved into the larger organization that adopted a more pervasive participative structure.

Extending this insight to AL and CI as parallel structures, one cannot expect such spaces to endure in organizations over extended periods of time. Rather, if they truly lead to transformation they will transition into other forms and open up space in the organization for transformative learning on a continuing basis. This happened in the international foods organization in several ways: incorporating stop-reflect discussions into meetings, redesigning regional management meetings around an AL format rather than the more traditional "show and tell"; team-building sessions that were mini-AL programs. All of these strategies seemed to normalize aspects of the learning process that had created conditions enabling organizational transformation and continued to open spaces for learning.

In the university CI example, members of the group had to learn how to act on the system to experiment with actions that grew out of their reflection. When certain changes appeared to have value for how the organization functioned, existing organizational entities absorbed them into the organization as formalized programs consistent with the preexisting structures (and points of view). Generating deeper transformative organizational learning would have required going beyond the scope of the group's initial inquiry question to have an impact on change in organizational strategy and on systems such as rewards.

Building Parallel Structures as Bridges to a Learning Organization: Reflections on the Two Cases

What are the implications of the two cases? AL and CI are parallel structures explicitly designed as structures for learning. One challenge is how lessons learned can be transferred back and institutionalized once the programs are completed. AL has organizational support, which provides potential for real organizational transformation because the leadership is committed. At the same time, because of the organizational sanctioning, limits may be placed on the design of the program and the degree to which individuals can truly engage in transformative learning without serious repercussions. CI has the freedom for individuals to be more solidly and critically reflective and, therefore, has greater potential for individual transformation. But because it does so at the expense of getting organizational support, it is more likely to be difficult to leverage the individual transformative learning into organizational transformative learning.

With CI it is more difficult to import the parallel structure into the organization because, though the learning may have been deeper, the individual is left to his or her own devices and sphere of influence to import it outside of the initiative. CI typically does not enjoy the same level of sanction from the organization as AL. However, AL programs may be more restricted in depth precisely because they can stir up waters that make the participants address multiple layers of the system, and therefore they go more slowly or challenge less deeply.

The AL program in the international foods company was initiated in the broader context of a wide consensus in the organization about the need for transformation. Prior learning events set the stage for the effort, including a search conference and a cultural survey that established the need for change. These efforts began the process of transformation in points of view. Search conferences involve representatives of an entire system in intensive questions and reflection around a challenge over several days. The search conference enabled a significant number of people to reflect on their premises regarding how the organization operated. In turn, the survey clarified the significant challenges in the way of transformation and the need for learning among all levels of the organization, including the senior executive team. However, these interventions could not accomplish the task of allowing the organization to act on these insights. AL was a bridge, opening up the space for changing the habits of mind that stood in the way of organizational transformation.

Dimensions of Transformation in Learning Organizations and Habits of Mind

Learning organizations seek to transform themselves along some combination of dimensions involving the changing nature of the organization's task environment; the organization's vision, mission and/or strategy; their products or services and/or how they produce or distribute them; the forms of organizational structure and processes through which the organization is managed (including management style); how members of the organization conceptualize their roles in the organization and the behaviors appropriate for carrying out these roles. (This includes learning new ways of interacting that will contribute to team, and consequently organizational, learning.) The particular combination of dimensions that are of concern to a given learning organization at any point in time is a function of the challenges (either immediate or anticipated) confronting the system in interaction with the interpretations its leaders hold regarding the nature of these challenges.

These dimensions correspond to or cut across several of the kinds of habits of mind described by Mezirow (see Chapter One)—in particular, sociolinguistic, epistemic, psychological, and philosophical.

Less typically will the organization seek transformative learning in moral-ethical habits of mind unless confronted with a public relations debacle.

The primary motivation to change these habits of mind is instrumental: the organization is intent on enhancing its performance. Accomplishing this usually requires communicative learning as well, as members of the organization come to new understandings of behavior. Hence they are encouraged to challenge their points of view by becoming critically reflective of the assumptions held in the organization about the content and processes of problem solving that are relevant to performance. At times people may be challenged to reflect critically on the premises they hold in defining the problem. This process of learning often requires transformative learning in the communicative domain as behaviors associated with effective team learning processes—framing, reframing, experimenting, crossing boundaries, and integrating perspectives (Kasl, Marsick, and Dechant, 1997)—are developed and exhibited.

Bounded Critical Reflection in Organizations

In virtually all instances, however, this learning is fostered by a kind of guided or even directed critical reflection on the organization's part. (If this seems like a contradiction in terms, it speaks to a conundrum facing the adult educator practicing in the workplace.) The focus of criticality is on the instrumental task performance issues at the individual, business unit, and organizational level: reframing of roles, rethinking assumptions about the larger business environment, and the like. At the level of the individual learner the organization may want to raise issues of what it means to be an employee and the need for taking charge of one's own career. However, for the most part the political dimension of how the organization functions is off limits, as are discussions of larger social consequences.

As practiced in most organization settings, the critical reflection is more of a critical thinking emphasis—a sort of bounded critical reflection. At first blush, its processes move the practice of adult education in the opposite direction of the intentions of critical theory—

namely in the service of further decoupling and colonizing the life-world by the system.

In the short term there appears little doubt this is the case. In the longer term the consequences are less clear. One of the problems of generative learning is that it is unpredictable and by definition not controlled. As consequences of actions become clearer organizations are often forced to embrace new sociolinguistic conventions that they initially resist or struggle with. Furthermore, while transformative learning occurs at the organizational level it also must occur at the individual level. Individual members of organizations may well find themselves more emancipated in their thinking, even in ways that they initially chose to keep private. At the end of the day, increasing people's awareness of the personal choices available to them is the important outcome of transformative learning. How this learning influences larger social discourse may go beyond what organizational leaders intend.

Transformations in learning organizations are directed toward making the organization more effective by changing those habits of mind that make the organization less than effective. As the organization chooses certain courses of action the larger social consequences of that action often create social and political forces for acts that mediate those actions. Faced with such pressures, organizations must further learn to adapt by changing their dominant narratives and the points of view and habits of mind that give them content. The long-term impact of organizational learning on society interacts with free avenues of information and democratic action in the society at large.

A Socially Critical Framework for Assessing Transformative Learning in Organizational Settings

Transformative learning theory is not synonymous with critical social theory, despite taking many of its seminal ideas from it. Nevertheless we can paraphrase Calhoun's description (1995) of critical theory as an interpreting body of work demanding critique. By substituting the term *learner* for *theorist* and integrating his thinking with transformative learning theory we arrive at a framework for assessing the viability of the practice of transformative learning theory in organizational contexts:

1. Do learners develop a critical engagement with their organizational and social world, increasingly recognizing that the existing state of affairs does not exhaust all possibilities and arriving at alternative courses of action?

2. Do learners develop an increasingly critical account of the cultural conditions on which their own habits of mind are based?

3. Do learners develop a commitment to a continuing critical reexamination of their points of view and habits of mind?

4. Does their critical examination make them more aware of how their historicity has influenced their existing habits of mind?

5. Are learners confronted with alternative interpretations of their experience in a way that makes visible both their good and bad points as well as the reasons behind their blind spots and misunderstandings? Is capacity enhanced for incorporating their insights into more inclusive and permeable habits of mind?

The applicability of transformative learning theory for the model of the learning organization is complex, in some degree bounded, and yet important. Our reflections on this issue are grounded in the belief that organizations are an important arena of practice for adult educators. Just as teams are a basic integrative building block of learning organizations, learning organizations are critical for the broader issue of learning societies. Representing the fundamental components of modern societies, organizational units in business, government, nonprofits, and schools are significant avenues for the transfer of learning from individuals and groups to the societal level of action and for the potential production of generative social learning. We are just learning how to use transformative theory to foster growth and development for both the organization and its members.

References

ARL Inquiry. "Cognitive Frame Phases in an Action Reflection Learning Program." In R. J. Torraco (ed.), *Academy of Human Resource Development Proceedings*. Baton Rouge, La.: Academy of Human Resource Development, 1998.

Bray, J. N. "The Noetic Experience of Learning in Collaborative Inquiry Groups: From Descriptive, Hermeneutic, and Eidetic Phenomenological Perspectives." *Dissertation Abstracts International*, 1995, 56(07), 2,524 (University Microfilms No. AAC95–39779).

Bray, J. N., Gerdau-Lee, J., Smith, L., and Yorks, L. *Collaborative Inquiry in Practice*. Thousand Oaks, Calif.: Sage, 2000.

Brockett, R., and Hiemstra, R. "Bridging the Theory-Practice Gap in Self-Directed Learning." In S. D. Brookfield (ed.), *Self-Directed Learning: From Theory to Practice*. New Directions for Adult and Continuing Education, no. 25. San Francisco: Jossey-Bass, 1985.

Brookfield, S. D. "Independent Adult learning." *Studies in Adult Education*, 1981, 13(1), 15–27.

Brookfield, S. D. *Understanding and Facilitating Adult Learning: A Comprehensive Analysis of Principles and Effective Practices*. San Francisco: Jossey-Bass, 1986.

Brooks, A. K. *Critically Reflective Learning Within a Corporate Context*. Unpublished doctoral dissertation. New York: Teachers College, Columbia University, 1989.

Brooks, A. "Power and the Production of Knowledge: Collective Team Learning in Work Organizations." *Human Resource Development Quarterly*, 1994, 5, 213–235.

Brooks, A., and Watkins, K. E. (eds.). *The Emerging Power of Action Inquiry Technologies*. New Directions for Adult and Continuing Education, no. 43. San Francisco: Jossey-Bass, 1994.

Burke, W. W., and Litwin, G. H. "A Causal Model of Organizational Performance and Change." *Journal of Management*, 1992, 18, 523–545.

Calhoun, C. *Critical Social Theory*. Cambridge, Mass.: Blackwell, 1995.

Candy, P. C. *Self-Direction for Lifelong Learning: A Comprehensive Guide to Theory and Practice*. San Francisco: Jossey-Bass, 1991.

Cranton, P. "Types of Group Learning." In S. Imel (ed.), *Learning in Groups: Exploring Fundamental Principles, New Uses, and Emerging Opportunities.* New Directions for Adult and Continuing Education, no. 71. San Francisco: Jossey-Bass, 1996.

Cross, K. P. "Adults as Learners: Characteristics, Needs, and Interests." In R. E. Peterson and Associates, *Lifelong Learning in America.* San Francisco: Jossey-Bass, 1981.

Dechant, K., Marsick, V. J., and Kasl, E. "Towards a Model of Team Learning." *Studies in Continuing Education,* 1993, *15*(1), 1–14.

Dennis, C. B., Cederholm, L., and Yorks, L. "Learning Your Way to a Global Organization." In K. E. Watkins and V. J. Marsick (eds.), *In Action: Creating the Learning Organization.* Alexandria, Va.: American Society for Training and Development, 1996.

Dotlich, D. L., and Noel, J. L. *Action Learning: How the World's Top Companies Are Re-creating their Leaders and Themselves.* San Francisco: Jossey-Bass, 1998.

Fisher, D., and Torbert, W. R. *Personal and Organizational Transformations: The True Challenge of Continual Quality Improvement.* London: McGraw-Hill, 1995.

Gerdau, J. A. "Learning in Adulthood Through Collaborative Inquiry." *Dissertation Abstracts International,* 1995, *56*(7), 25,247 (University Microfilms No. AAC95–39807).

Group for Collaborative Inquiry. "Democratizing Knowledge." *Adult Education Quarterly,* 1993, *44*, 43–51.

Group for Collaborative Inquiry and thINQ. "Collaborative Inquiry for the Public Arena." In A. Brooks and K. Watkins (eds.), *The Emerging Power of Action Inquiry Technologies.* New Directions for Adult and Continuing Education, no. 43. San Francisco: Jossey-Bass, 1994.

Heimlich, J. E. "Constructing Group Learning." In S. Imel (ed.), *Learning in Groups: Exploring Fundamental Principles, New Uses, and Emerging Opportunities.* New Directions for Adult and Continuing Education, no. 71. San Francisco: Jossey-Bass, 1996.

Heron, J. "Experiential Research Methodology." In R. Reason and J. Rowan (eds.), *Human Inquiry: A Sourcebook of New Paradigm Research.* New York: Wiley, 1981.

Heron, J. "The Role of Reflection in Co-operative Inquiry." In D. Boud, R. Keogh, and D. Walker (eds.), *Reflection: Turning Experience into Learning.* London: Kogan Page, 1985.

Heron, J. "Validity in Co-operative Inquiry." In P. Reason (ed.), *Human Inquiry in Action: Developments in New Paradigm Research.* London: Sage, 1988.

Heron, J. *Co-operative Inquiry: Research into the Human Condition.* London: Sage, 1996.

Homans, G. C. *The Human Group.* New York: Harcourt, 1950.

Imel, S. "Summing Up: Themes and Issues Related to Learning in Groups." In S. Imel (ed.), *Learning in Groups: Exploring Fundamental Principles, New Uses, and Emerging Opportunities.* New Directions for Adult and Continuing Education, no. 71. San Francisco: Jossey-Bass, 1996.

Imel, S., and Tisdell, E. J. "The Relationship Between Theories About Groups and Adult Learning Groups." In S. Imel (ed.), *Learning in Groups: Exploring Fundamental Principles, New Uses, and Emerging Opportunities.* New Directions for Adult and Continuing Education, no. 71. San Francisco: Jossey-Bass, 1996.

Kasl, E., Marsick, V. J., and Dechant, K. "Teams as Learners: A Research-Based Model of Team Learning." *Journal of Applied Behavioral Science,* 1997, *33,* 227–246.

Knowles, M. S. *The Adult Learner: A Neglected Species.* (3rd ed.) Houston, Tex.: Gulf, 1984.

Kolb, D. *Experiential Learning.* Englewood Cliffs, N.J.: Prentice Hall, 1984.

Lawler, E. E. III, and Morhman, S. A. "Quality Circles After the Fad." *Harvard Business Review,* 1985, *63*(1), 64–71.

Lewin, K. "Group Decision and Social Change." In E. E. Maccoby, T. M. Newcomb, and E. L. Hartley (eds.), *Readings in Social Psychology,* pp. 197–211. New York: Holt, Rinehart and Winston, 1958.

Mezirow, J. "A Critical Theory of Adult Learning and Education." *Adult Education,* 1981, *32*(1), 3–27.

Mezirow, J. *Transformative Dimensions of Adult Learning.* San Francisco: Jossey-Bass, 1991.

Mumford, A. *Learning at the Top.* Berkshire, U.K.: McGraw-Hill, 1995.

Noel, J. L., and Charan, R. "Leadership Development at GE's Crotonville." *Human Resource Management,* 1988, *27,* 433–447.

O'Neil, J. *The Role of the Learning Advisor in Action Learning.* Unpublished doctoral dissertation. New York: Teachers College, Columbia University, 1999.

O'Neil, J., Arnell, E., and Turner, E. "Earning While Learning." In K. E. Watkins and V. J. Marsick (eds.), *In Action: Creating the Learning Organization.* Alexandria, Va.: American Society for Training and Development, 1996.

Pedler, M., Burgoyne, J., and Boydell, T. *The Learning Company: A Strategy for Sustainable Development.* London: McGraw-Hill, 1991.

Reason, P. (ed.). *Participation in Human Inquiry.* Thousand Oaks, Calif.: Sage, 1994.

Reason, P., and Rowan, J. (eds.). *Human Inquiry: A Sourcebook of New Paradigm Research*. New York: Wiley, 1981.

Revans, R. W. "The Managerial Alphabet." In G. Heald (ed.), *Approaches to the Study of Organizational Behavior*. London: Tavistock, 1970.

Revans, R. W. *The A.B.C. of Action Learning: A Review of 25 Years of Experience*. Salford, U.K.: University of Salford, 1978.

Revans, R. W. *The Origin and Growth of Action Learning*. London: Chartwell Bratt, 1982.

Rice, A. K. *Learning for Leadership*. London: Tavistock, 1965.

Rose, A. D. "Group Learning in Adult Education: Its Historical Roots." In S. Imel (ed.), *Learning in Groups: Exploring Fundamental Principles, New Uses, and Emerging Opportunities*. New Directions for Adult and Continuing Education, no. 71. San Francisco: Jossey-Bass, 1996.

Senge, P. M. *The Fifth Discipline: The Art and Practice of the Learning Organization*. New York: Doubleday Currency, 1990.

Smith, L. L. "Collaborative Inquiry as an Adult Learning Strategy." *Dissertation Abstracts International*, 1995, 56(7), 2,533 (University Microfilms No. AAC95–39867).

thINQ. "Adult Learning Through Collaborative Inquiry." In D. Flannery (ed.), *Proceedings of the 34th Annual Adult Education Research Conference*. University Park: Pennsylvania State University, 1993.

Tough, A. M. *The Adult's Learning Projects: A Fresh Approach to Theory and Practice in Adult Learning*. Toronto: Ontario Institute for Studies in Education, 1979.

Trist, E. L., and Sofer, C. *Explorations in Group Relations*. Leicester U.K.: Leicester University Press, 1959.

Watkins, K., and Marsick, V. J. *Sculpting the Learning Organization: Lessons in the Art and Science of Systemic Change*. San Francisco: Jossey-Bass, 1993.

West, G. W. "Group Learning in the Workplace." In S. Imel (ed.), *Learning in Groups: Exploring Fundamental Principles, New Uses, and Emerging Opportunities*. New Directions for Adult and Continuing Education, no. 71. San Francisco: Jossey-Bass, 1996.

Yorks, L. "Understanding How Learning Is Experienced Through Collaborative Inquiry: A Phenomenological Study." *Dissertation Abstracts International*, 1995, 56(07), 2,534 (University Microfilms No. AAC95–39884).

Yorks, L., O'Neil, J., and Marsick, V. J. "Action Learning: Theoretical Bases and Varieties of Practice." In L. Yorks, J. O'Neil, and V. J. Marsick (eds.), *Action Learning: Effective Strategies for Individual, Team, and Organizational Development*, Vol. 1 (2): *Academy of Human Resource Development Mono-*

graph Series: Advances in Developing Human Resources. San Francisco: Berrett-Koehler, 1999.

Yorks, L., and others. "Boundary Management in Action Reflection Learning Research: Taking the Role of a Sophisticated Barbarian." *Human Resource Development Quarterly*, 1996, *7*, 313–329.

Yorks, L., and others. "Transfer of Learning from an Action Reflection Learning Program." *Performance Improvement Quarterly*, 1998, *11*(1), 59–73.

Zelman, A. W. "Answering the Question, 'How Is Learning Experienced in Collaborative Inquiry?' A Phenomenological/Hermeneutic Approach." *Dissertation Abstracts International*, 1995, *56*(7), 2,534 (University Microfilms No. AAC95–39885).

III

Moving Ahead from Practice to Theory

11

Analyzing Research on Transformative Learning Theory

Edward W. Taylor

In the twenty years since transformative learning emerged as an area of study in adult education it has received more attention than any other adult learning theory, and it continues to be of interest. This is particularly the case when it comes to the study of transformative learning as defined by Mezirow (1991a, 1995, 1997). For example, at the 1997 annual Adult Education Research Conference transformative learning was central to more than 10 percent of the presentations, more than any other topic. In looking back on what has been written about transformative learning, two general patterns emerge. One is published papers that have focused predominantly on theoretical critique on issues of social action, critical pedagogy, adult development, reflection, power, and context and rationality. The second pattern involves more than forty-five unpublished empirical studies completed mostly by graduate students for doctoral dissertations. These studies cover a wide range of areas, initially focusing on the relationship of transformative learning and adult lifestyle and career changes, followed by research of its essential components, such as critical reflection, context, and other ways of knowing, and with a present emphasis on how transformative learning can be fostered in an educational setting.

It would seem that this direction of published works, both theoretical and empirical, would promote a healthy debate among adult educators about the viability of transformative learning theory.

However, the discussion has resided predominantly in a theoretical domain, with little attention offered from an empirical perspective. This lack of empirical discussion is due to little research published in educational journals; instead most dissertations remain uncirculated in various university libraries. Only very recently has discussion of the related research on transformative learning started to emerge (Taylor, 1997, 1998). Without it there has been a redundancy of research, an insufficiency of in-depth exploration into the nature of particular components of a perspective transformation, and a reification of transformative learning as we presently know it, whereby its basic premises about learning have become accepted practice in adult education.

It is imperative, in this new millennium, that we set a new direction of research for transformative learning theory that focuses on understanding with greater depth its inherent complexities, that engages a wider range of research designs and methodologies, and that investigates most thoroughly transformative learning as a viable model for teaching adults. If this theory of adult learning is to remain of significance to adult educators it must continue to inform adult educators in ways they can improve their teaching practically and theoretically.

The purpose of this chapter, therefore, is to discuss the current research about the theory and practice of transformative learning as defined by Mezirow and to explore some of the questions about it that remain unanswered. To accomplish this we begin with a brief explanation of how the studies were selected for this review. This is followed by an extensive discussion of what is presently known from an empirical perspective about transformative learning. The chapter is organized around a series of themes that emerge naturally from the findings and others in response to unresolved and often debated issues about transformative learning. Each theme is discussed in concert with several studies that best bring the various issues to light and set a direction for future research. Examples of data are included from these studies, offering for the first time personal descriptions of various processes of transformative learning. The chapter concludes with a review of the various research methodologies generally employed and suggestions for future efforts.

Transformative Learning: An Update

To understand transformative learning from an empirical perspective it is important to return to the original study, where Mezirow (1978a) focused on the change in perspective, or frame of reference, experienced by women returning to school after a long hiatus. ("Meaning perspective" was the original term used for one's worldview and cluster of meaning schemes; it and "frame of reference" are used interchangeably here, depending on the study being reviewed.) Mezirow's is still by far the largest qualitative study on transformative learning. It reveals an emerging learning theory that begins to establish some fundamental assumptions about making meaning unique to adulthood. Learning was "understood as the process of using a prior interpretation to construe a new or revised interpretation of the meaning of one's experience in order to guide future action" (Mezirow, 1996, p. 162). Found essential to making meaning were understanding one's frame of reference, the role of a disorienting dilemma, critical reflection, dialogue with others, and conditions that foster transformative learning, to mention a few. It is these assumptions about transformative learning in concert with the purposes of the various research studies that become the themes that frame the preceding discussion about transformative learning. They reveal a picture of transformative learning theory that is much more complex and multifaceted than originally understood. The themes for this chapter are the following: adult learning theory, transforming a frame of reference, triggering a perspective transformation, the journey of a transformation, the role of critical reflection and affective learning, and the practice of fostering transformative learning. Also included are themes from various research studies that reveal assumptions about transformative learning that have been overlooked and need greater attention, such as a perspective of difference—the role of class, culture, and ethnicity in the process of change; the role of context in shaping the transformative experience; and transformation as "adult" learning theory.

One final comment before beginning this discussion: studies were selected for this review only if they refer to Mezirow's theory directly. This purposeful selection allows for a more consistent interpretation of Mezirow's transformative learning theory, because all the studies have a shared framework. Forty-six studies were reviewed, each involving Mezirow's model of perspective transformation or a related component in its purpose, conceptual framework, and/or design of the study. It is important to note that this chapter extends my earlier review (Taylor, 1997, 1998) in several ways. First, it includes seven additional studies that offer new insights, particularly in the area of fostering transformative learning. Second, it offers more discussion on the findings of different studies and less discussion on a critique and reconceptualization of transformative learning. Also, for the first time I am able to include actual data to illustrate particular findings, such as a meaning scheme, meaning perspective, and disorienting dilemma.

An Adult Learning Theory

The first theme is transformative learning as a learning theory that is uniquely adult. This is based on the assumption that "adults have acquired a coherent body of experience—assumptions, concepts, values, feelings, conditioned responses—frames of reference that define their world" (Mezirow, 1997, p. 5). Meaning perspectives are often acquired uncritically in the course of childhood through socialization and acculturation, most frequently during significant experiences with teachers, parents, and mentors. Only in adulthood are meaning structures clearly formed and developed and the revision of established meaning perspective takes place. However, there has been little research to support this claim, such that transformative learning has not been explored in relationship to learning and the age of the participants.

What we presently know about participants in the various studies is that they are mostly adults, usually between ages seventeen and seventy. But the age of many of the participants is not known because it was not seen as relevant to the intent of the research. The study that involved the youngest participants was by Whalley (1995), who investigated forms of reflection and the role they play in the transformation of meaning structures when learning a new culture. His study focused on Canadian and Japanese high school students (seventeen and nineteen years of age, respectively) who were engaged in a student exchange program. He found that these students did experience a revision of meaning schemes, though not a change in meaning perspective. Despite this finding, the age of the students was not explored in depth to see if it was a factor in the transformation process. As an area of research it would be helpful to understand when frames of reference become established in a young adult's life and whether they can be another indicator for becoming an adult. Also, transformative learning might inform meaning-making during childhood or adolescence, particularly understanding the impact and the processing of significant trauma (disorienting dilemma). This would likely be the case for older adults, but whether age is a factor in transformation is not known and needs to be better understood. Change, particularly significant change—such as the death of a loved one, ending a career, or moving into a retirement community—might be better informed through transformative learning. Questions are raised as to how transformative learning manifests itself with age. Does it take on a different face? What components and processes become most significant? Older adults have often been portrayed as resistant to change. How does transformative learning overcome this? Fostering transformative learning among older adults could offer insight into helping them deal with the challenge of change associated with the aging process.

The Recursive Journey
of a Perspective Transformation

The second theme is that of the recursive journey of a perspective transformation, originally defined by Mezirow (1978b, 1995) as a linear though not always step-wise process. This journey, or process of change, is one of the areas most researched about transformative learning and at the same time one of the least understood. As mentioned in Chapter One, the phases of perspective transformation have been confirmed in general by some studies (Dewane, 1993; Egan, 1985; Hunter, 1980; Lytle, 1989; Morgan, 1987; Williams, 1985). However, few of the studies provided actual data confirming each phase. Of the studies that were supportive, Lytle (1989), a study of nurses returning to school for a B.S.N. degree, was the most thorough in exploring the steps to a perspective transformation, although she found that only 30 percent of a sample of seven participants demonstrated all ten steps. (Lytle, like many who studied perspective transformation, refers to the phases as steps despite Mezirow's model.) Later studies find the process of perspective transformation to be more recursive, evolving, and spiraling in nature (Coffman, 1989; Elias, 1993; Holt, 1994; Laswell, 1994; Neuman, 1996; Saavedra, 1995; Taylor, 1994). Mezirow (1995) concurs in his later publications that the process does not always follow the exact sequence of phases but generally includes some variation of the identified phases.

One of the most in-depth studies that brought to light the less linear and more varied view of the transformative process was carried out by Coffman (1989), who sought to determine "what happens when a theological seminary enforces a policy of using inclusive language in all its endeavors" (p. 49). She conducted a phenomenological study by interviewing over a six-month period men and women in a master of divinity program during their first, second, and last year of school, as well as graduates and faculty of the program. By exploring the process of acceptance and feelings of resentment, she also attempted to see if a perspective transformation took place, such as how and if the participants came to recognize their culturally induced roles and took action to overcome them. She found that the earlier phases should be replaced with more inclusive feelings of intense surprise, not just limited to feelings of guilt or shame. Also, there should be an emphasis on the continued reassessment of one's disorienting dilemma in relationship to one's cultural norms and values and their unquestioning acceptance, indicative of a spiraling effect of learning that is continually repeated. Like Coffman's "intense feelings," Morgan (1987), whose research focused on the transformation of displaced homemakers, found that the most universal and profound stage was "anger" that had to be resolved before the participant could move on. Two significant findings emerge from these studies that set the direction for future research: first, without the expression and recognition of feelings participants will not engage their new reality, leave behind past resentment, and begin critical reflection; and second, the journey of transformation is less linear in nature than recursive, such that several phases are repeated as one is transformed.

More recent research is consistent with this. For example, Dewane (1993), who looked at the nature of adult learning in self-help groups, offers one of the few studies that provides data to support each phase of the original model of perspective transformation. In addition, she found "as the interviews unfolded that indeed the transformative process was not necessarily sequential nor was successful completion of one stage contingent upon the previous stages" (p. 167). Also, the factor of time is revealed by Pope (1996), who explored the transformation brought about in first-generation ethnically diverse working-class women through gaining higher education. She found that the phases "do not adequately explain the long-term processes of transformation. . . . Over a period of time that spans 2 or 3 decades in the lives of these women, 'steps' lose relevance and are forgotten" (p. 176). One possible explanation of this long process is the sometimes cumulative nature of transformative learning, whereby many meaning schemes change over time culminating in a perspective transformation.

Based on the present research it seems apparent that the journey of transformation is more individualistic, fluid, and recursive than originally thought. Also, certain phases or components, such as working through feelings, seem to be more significant to change than others. However, the surface has barely been scratched in understanding the process. More research is needed with particular emphasis on identifying the inherent components of the transformative process. This means not only identifying what learning strategies are essential but what conditions need to be present internally as well as externally for the process to unfold. It means asking, Are certain people predisposed to a transformation at a particular time in life? Is timing important? Are there transformative moments, in response to certain conditions, that come available and have to be seized lest they pass the individual by? Also, most studies on the individual change process have been conducted in retrospect, whereby individuals looked back on their transformative experience. The few longitudinal studies that have come out in the last few years offer some real insight into this process, but most have been bounded by a particular event, such as completing a training program or an educational course. The journey of transformation needs to be explored in everyday situations, looking at the process of change over a number of years. This long-term perspective could, for example, offer understanding about regression that might follow the transformative process. Also, it would provide a window into how the individual is acting on his or her life differently in response to the transformative experience.

The Illusive Nature of a Frame of Reference

Despite the abundance of studies looking at change in a frame of reference, it is still far from clear what warrants a perspective transformation. Part of the problem is defining what constitutes a frame of reference, how to put boundaries on it, and how it looks after it is transformed. According to Mezirow (1998), a frame of reference is the structure of assumptions and expectations (aesthetic, socio-linguistic, moral-ethical, epistemic, psychological) through which we filter and make sense of our world. It is indicative of a "habit of mind" that is expressed as a point of view. A point of view is made up of meaning schemes—"sets of immediate specific expectations, beliefs, feelings, attitudes, and judgments that tacitly direct and shape a specific interpretation and determine how we judge, typify objects, and attribute causality" (p. 5). This conceptual construction of a frame of reference, inclusive of meaning schemes though grounded theoretically, lacks a strong empirical foundation. At present only a few studies have confirmed this construction of a meaning structure. For example, Saavedra (1995) looked at the process of teacher transformation within a sustained long-term teacher study group and found meaning schemes early in the evolution of the group's development through the sharing of personal histories and biographies related to teaching. As the group developed over time these meaning schemes were revised, ultimately leading to a revision in meaning perspective for some of the group participants.

Another perspective is offered by Whalley (1995), who investigated forms of reflection and the role they play in the transformation of meaning structures in learning a new culture. His study of Canadian and Japanese high school students in a student exchange program showed that students in general found meaning schemes hard to identify because of their habitual nature, indicative of a kind of learning that often occurs outside the awareness of the learner. However, when his sojourners began to experience cultural difference the meaning scheme became more lucid. For example, the excerpt below from a journal of a young Japanese student visiting in Canada seems to indicate a meaning scheme revision:

Reviewing my journals, I found that I wrote repeatedly on the same topic: individuality. This may not be a very new discovery, but this what I was most impressed with. In Canada, individuality is more highly valued than in Japan. This is a big difference between the two countries, but it doesn't mean that I suffered from so-called culture shock. The general opinion that Japanese are not self-assertive is not always true. Even though we live in the same culture, everyone has their own culture. I found that I attempted to tie every difference to individualism. Having such preconception—difference is derived from individualism—is not good, I thought. Still it's true that I felt strong individualism in this society [p. 153].

Vogelsang (1993) explored the types of educational activities that are helpful in promoting transformative learning in higher education. Twenty adult women were interviewed during their senior year while completing an undergraduate degree. She found that during their time in college some students only experienced a revision of meaning schemes, whereas others experienced a revision of meaning perspectives (a perspective transformation). She determined that this difference was based on the types of reflection the students employed, such that "some students may reflect on context and process only (transformation of meaning schemes) or on content, process and premises (transformation of meaning perspectives)" (p. 99). Also, some changes in meaning schemes were found not to be as important to the identity of some individuals as others. An example of a meaning scheme revision that did not contribute to a perspective transformation was offered by Kristen, who prior to entering college saw all teachers and professors as more valuable and important than other people. She stated that, due to her educational experience, she had come to believe that "professors and stuff are just people, and I don't necessarily think of them as highly as I used to. I used to think they were way above the rest of us, and they are just people" (p. 103).

When it comes to identifying a change in meaning perspective, most studies were carried out in retrospect, as mentioned earlier, and do not clearly show the participants' perspective prior to a transformative learning experience that might give them a new perspective. Also, many studies offer little actual data to support their findings (for example, participant descriptions, field notes of individuals acting in different ways in response to a change in perspective). A good example of a changed frame of reference is revealed in a study by Schlesinger (1983), who explored the process of change among twenty-two Jewish women returning to the workforce. Each woman had been working for at least a year and prior to reentry into the workforce had spent at least five years as a full-time homemaker. She found that traditional Orthodox Jewish women experienced the most significant change when returning to work. For example, Marcie, who went through many changes in her marital and family life, realized that her religious role was most profoundly affected by her return to work:

> I am only realizing now that we all are wearing our own handcuffs. We don't realize, though, that we also have the keys. . . . We impose our own prison walls. I only realized this recently, as I was preparing for Passover. I was fed up. To celebrate the holiday of freedom, I was really put in bondage. There had to be a better way. I looked for it, and only then did I find it. One day I just said I couldn't take it any more. Boy was that a revelation. First of all that I could say it, and then that others listened. Why did I wait so long? I forgot that there were options. Now I exercise them [p. 167].

Another example is revealed by Taylor (1993), who looked at transformative learning as a model for the learning process of intercultural competency. He interviewed twelve interculturally competent individuals who had become competent in a second culture outside the United States. A participant in the study, Lobo, an American, described his perspective transformation in response to living in Honduras for two years as a Peace Corps volunteer:

> I definitely see the world in a whole different light than how I looked at the world before I left. Before I left the States there was another world out there. I knew it existed, but I didn't see what my connection to it was at all. You hear news reports going on in other countries, but I didn't understand how and what we did here in the States impacted on these people in Honduras, in South America, Africa, and Asia. Since I did not have a feeling for how our lives impacted their lives it was as if the U.S. were almost a self-contained little world. After going to Honduras I realized how much things we did in the States affected Hondurans, Costa Ricans. How we affected everyone else in the world. I no longer had this feeling the U.S. was here and everybody else was outside. I felt that the world definitely got much smaller. It got smaller in the sense [that] throwing a rock in the water creates ripples. I am that rock and the things I do here in the States affect people everywhere. I feel much more a part of the world than I do of the U.S. I criticize the U.S. much more now than I would have in the past [Taylor, 1993, p. 175].

Looking back over the two examples of a meaning scheme and a meaning perspective, differences start to emerge, providing insight into how to delineate between the two. Consistent with their definition, meaning schemes seem to be more specific and less global, and refer to a particular belief. Also, they seem to operate often on an unconscious level, revealing themselves when individuals experience difference or through sharing personal habits or narratives. And meaning perspectives seem to be more global and metaphorical in nature, reflecting a more inclusive worldview. These initial findings seem to be consistent with the description given by Mezirow (1991b) concerning meaning schemes and meaning perspectives. Furthermore, research is beginning to show that a change in perspective is indicative of not only developing a revised frame of reference but a willingness to act on the new perspective. Several recent studies reveal that action is inherent in a perspective transformation (Pope, 1996; Saavedra, 1995). Saavedra states that "action, acting upon redefinition's of our perspectives, is the clearest indication of a transformation" (p. 373).

Even though most studies concur with the present definition of a perspective transformation, others have found it too narrow and too rationally based. It seems to imply that as a result of a perspective transformation an individual becomes more in touch with his or her logical-rational side, again discounting other ways of knowing. Clark (1991), however, identified three dimensions to a perspective transformation: psychological (changes in understanding of the self), convictional (revision of belief systems), and behavioral (changes in lifestyle). In Van Nostrand's (1992) synthesized model of lifestyle changes of female ex-smokers, she operationalized a perspective transformation as a revelation that included new concepts of knowledge, mystical experience, personal power, and a redefined perspective followed by a sustained change over time. Additional characteristics of a transformation emerge from other studies as well, such as an increase in personal power (Hunter, 1980; Pierce, 1986; Pope, 1996; Schlesinger, 1983; Scott, 1991; Sveinunggaard, 1993; Turner, 1986; Van Nostrand, 1992), spirituality, a transpersonal realm of development (Cochrane, 1981; Hunter, 1980; Lucas, 1994; Scott, 1991; Sveinunggaard, 1993; Van Nostrand, 1992), compassion for others (Courtenay, Merriam, and Reeves, 1998; First and Way, 1995; Gehrels, 1984), creativity (Scott, 1991), a shift in discourse (Saavedra, 1995), courage (Lucas, 1994; Neuman, 1996), a sense of liberation (Bailey, 1996), and a new connectedness with others (Gehrels, 1984; Laswell, 1994; Weisberger, 1995).

Making sense of meaning schemes and meaning perspectives is quite challenging, and the research reveals very individual responses to a change in perspective. One overarching characteristic seems to be that most transformation deals with subjective reframing (critical reflection of one's assumptions) as opposed to objective reframing (critical reflection of others' assumptions). However, considering the relational nature of transformative learning it is difficult to determine the different types of reframing. Needed is a more in-depth synthesis of these characteristics, hopefully finding areas of commonality. Also needed is to move the focus to a behavioral level, beyond the verbal descriptions of a perspective transformation. In other words, How does a perspective transformation manifest itself such that participants act on their lives differently? How are people behaving differently in response to a change in a frame of reference? What does a perspective transformation look like behaviorally? Research studies need to be initiated that allow the research to observe the change in behavior in response to a perspective transformation.

Triggering a Transformative Experience

Perspective transformation is most often explained as being triggered by a significant personal event. This event was identified in Mezirow's original study as a disorienting dilemma, an acute internal and personal crisis. Most of the studies that explore the complete process of perspective transformation concur with this. An example of a disorienting dilemma is given by Morgan (1987), who studied displaced (divorced or separated) homemakers and their transition to independence. One woman described her husband's leaving as initiating a perspective transformation: "My husband came home at 5:30 in the morning and said that he was leaving. He needed some space. 'I need to find myself. I am not a happy man and I can't make my family happy.' By noon that day he was gone. . . .

Yes, the shock of him saying, and it was all of a sudden, that he was going to leave, he did want a divorce" (p. 112).

Later studies reveal the process of triggering a transformation as being much more complex. In addition to a disorienting dilemma, Clark (1991, 1993), who explored the impact of context on the process of perspective transformation, found that not only is a disorienting dilemma a trigger to transformative learning but so are "integrating circumstances." These are "indefinite periods in which the persons consciously or unconsciously search for something which is missing in their life; when they find this missing piece, the transformation process is catalyzed" (pp. 117–118). Generally they do not appear as a sudden, life-threatening event; instead they are more subtle and less profound, providing an opportunity for exploration and clarification of past experiences. An example is illustrated by Rosa, a participant in Clark's study. Rosa's transformation centered on her becoming a feminist. Prior to that she had an negative view of feminists, who she identified as angry women who would not work or relate to men and other women. Three events occurred that created an integrated frame that had been missing from her life. One was the birth of her daughter, connecting her deeply to other mothers. Second was developing a close relationship with a highly intellectual and nurturing feminist. Third was participating in a women's studies class while in graduate school. Rosa describes this integrating structure: "All these experiences . . . were floating sort of aimlessly around. . . . Talking to Felicity was like building a toothpick scaffold [because] then these pieces had someplace to go. And then taking the course fleshed this toothpick structure out into a more complex, sturdy building or structure. And then all these things that had been floating had someplace to live" (p. 120).

Another characteristic of a triggering event is its internal and external orientation (Lytle, 1989; Scott, 1991). Scott, in a study on the nature of transformation resulting from a leader's participation in a community organization, identified two types of disequilibrium (disorienting dilemma) that were necessary for initiating change in beliefs. One was an external event (neighborhood crime) that provokes an internal dilemma (a sense of helplessness), and the second was an internal disillusionment (faith in local government) whereby the participants recognized that previous approaches and solutions were no longer adequate. A recent characteristic discovered of a triggering event is that it is less a singular significant experience and more a long cumulative process. Pope (1996), who explored the impact of ethnically diverse working-class women attending higher education, found triggering events to be "a gradual accumulation of energy . . . like an unfolding evolution rather than a response to a crisis" (p. 176). This seems to fit with Courtenay, Merriam, and Reeves' study (1998) of the meaning-making process among those diagnosed as HIV positive. They found an "initial reaction" at diagnosis that lasted from six months to five years. This was followed by a "catalytic experience" that helped HIV patients view their diagnosis in a new and more productive way.

Despite this more in-depth research into the catalysts of transformative learning, there is little understanding of why some disorienting dilemmas lead to a perspective transformation and others do not. What factors contribute to or inhibit this triggering process? Why do some significant events, such as death of a loved one or personal injury, not always lead to a perspective transformation whereas seemingly minor events, such as a brief encounter or a lecture, sometimes do? Two studies provide some insight into factors that can influence or act as a precursor for the triggering process. Elias (1993), in a study about the development of socially transformative leaders, identified eight categories of common learning experiences that lead to a new perspective. These experiences supported the values and capacities necessary to become a leader for social transformation, such as developing multiple intelligences, cultivating critical thinking, and expressing one's voice. The baseline experience in his study for women was successfully confronting authority; for men it was developing a greater awareness of their feelings. In a second study, Clevinger (1993), who explored the transformative experience of kidney transplant patients, found sociocultural distortions to be a precursor of transformative learning and "if identified before the fact, perhaps they could qualify as predictors of transformative learning" (p. 99). These sociocultural distortions are revealed in other studies as contextual factors inclusive of historical, geographical, and life histories that predispose the individual to respond to a triggering event in a transformative manner. This contextual perspective of transformative learning is discussed in greater depth later.

The Interdependency of Critical Reflection and Affective Learning

Another major theme has been the emphasis on rationality in transformative learning theory, manifested as critical reflection as the means to effecting a perspective transformation. "[B]y far the most significant learning experiences in adulthood involve critical reflection—reassessing the way we have posed problems and reassessing our own orientation to perceiving, knowing, believing, feeling, and acting" (Mezirow and Associates, 1990, p. 13).

Most research that focuses on reflection in relationship to transformative learning seems to do so at the level of critical reflection (premise reflection). Of those studies, most concur with Mezirow on one level: critical reflection is significant to transformative learning. Examples include two quantitative studies: Williams's investigation of spouse abuse therapy (1985), which found that men who demonstrate the greatest increase in the use of reasoning tactics (reflection) also had the greatest decrease in physically abusive behavior; and Van Nostrand's study (1992) of perspective transformation among female smokers and nonsmokers, which found a significant correlation between the variables of critical analysis, life dissatisfaction, and social support. Taylor (1994), who investigated the learning process of intercultural competency, offers a good example of premise reflection by an American who shares a reflective moment that occurred during a particular intercultural experience while meeting with locals in Indonesia:

> The first half hour is all these speeches that they give at every single meeting. It's just a formality welcome, welcome, thank you, thank you, thank you by everybody 800 times and all this. All of these speeches start with the same, let's call it a paragraph, maybe it's two. It's like . . . peace be on to you in the Arabic way. . . . You can do it in Arabic if the audience is known to be almost all Moslem. Then you go into the English stuff for the Christians in the crowd. It's always the same and . . . I just refused to do that. I thought I am not copping out. These guys need to learn how to have a meeting where they don't waste all this time. . . . But you know what clicked for me in a meeting where it really pissed me off at first and then I thought "What an adolescent! I thought you had finally learned this." You know in those adolescent days when you just refuse to do something because you're refusing to do it not because there is anything intelligent or mature going on, you're just going to refuse to do it, because it's the principle of the thing. And that's what I was doing. An American guy came in who was working with our university on a different project. I watched him at one of these meetings. This guy couldn't say hello to you walking down the street in Indonesian to save his life, but someone somewhere had helped him memorize that opening of a speech in a meeting. So the first time he went to one of these meetings he stands up and he gives that speech. They [the Indonesian hosts] didn't care what he said the rest of the day. He said the right speech. He was in like Flynn. This guy is wonderful. I just thought, "Shit, I've been spend-

ing all my life trying to speak Indonesian and deal in substance, all I've got to do is get the form right and these
guys will appreciate what I am doing." Some of those
lessons came hard. I was really stubborn. The American
culture was my personal style that I wouldn't let go of.

However, several studies concluded that critical reflection is
granted too much importance and does not give enough attention
to the significance of affective learning—the role of emotions and
feelings in the process of transformation. For example, Brooks (1989),
in a study focusing on critical reflection and organizational change,
found that "critically reflective learning processes consist of more
than just the critical thought strategies generally thought to comprise them" (p. 175). In other words, transformative learning is more
than rationally based; it relies on the affective dimension of knowing, such as developing an empathic viewing of other perspectives
and trusting intuition. Morgan (1987), Coffman (1989), and Sveinunggaard (1993) found that critical reflection can only begin once
emotions have been validated and worked through. Gehrels (1984),
in his study exploring how school principals made meaning from experience, found feelings to be the trigger for reflection. Egan (1985)
found, while exploring the learning process in family therapy, that
a "more complex learning occurred when an affective change occurred" (p. 216).

Based on the research it seems quite clear that both critical reflection and affective learning play a significant role in the transformative process. In Mezirow's original study (1978b) teachers
seem to be very aware of the feelings women returning to school are
experiencing. They see it as their goal "to take the fear about coming back to school" (p. 18). However, Mezirow as well as most other
studies looked at these two concepts (affective learning and critical
reflection) separately and did not give enough attention to their in-
terrelationship in the transformative process. It is this interdependent relationship that Neuman (1996) sheds significant light on.

He offers the most extensive study to date and one of the few carried out in an ongoing research design (as opposed to a retrospective design). He observed critical reflection developmentally and its relationship to transformative learning among participants in the National Extension Leadership Development Program. The program curriculum attempted to foster reflection framed within the basic principles of practicing transformative learning. He conducted a qualitative case study of nine participants utilizing in-depth interviews, reflective writing, reflective questionnaires, dialogues, and participant observations throughout the entire program experience over twenty-four months. As a result of his research he identified several essential aspects of fostering critical reflection that reveal its interdependent relationship with affective learning:

1. A prerequisite to the initial development of a Critical Reflective capacity (critical reflection and critical self-reflection) was "acquiring the ability to recognize, acknowledge and process feelings and emotions as integral aspects of learning from experience" (p. 460).

2. The role of affect demonstrated both provocative and evocative characteristics. Provocatively, feelings were often the trigger for reflective learning. An unwillingness to respond to these feelings often resulted in a barrier to learning. Evocatively, exploring one's feelings in depth led to greater self-awareness and the initiation of changes in meaning structures.

3. Affect played a multifaceted role in learning from experience. Affect was part of both the reflective learning and the content process, and "when current affect was incorporated into reflective processing, it often produced clues and insights for directing reflection's focus toward the more fundamental or assumptive basis underlying meaning structures and perspectives" (p. 462).

4. The processing of feelings and emotions related to experience was both enabling (expanded the power and scope of critical reflection) and therapeutic (appreciation of working through negative feelings as essential for personal development).

5. The outcome of affective learning resulted in a greater sense of self-confidence and self-worth. "Perspective transformations included affective outcomes such as greater appreciation for differences, tolerance for ambiguity and feelings for courage, self-trust and inner strength" (p. 463).

6. Episodes of transformative learning and critical self-reflection often involve intensive emotional experiences, particularly grieving the loss of old meaning structures and the acquiring of new ones.

Based on the present research concerning both the latter discussion and those studies mentioned earlier in this chapter, it is quite clear that affective learning plays a primary role in the fostering of critical reflection. Furthermore, it is our very emotions and feelings that not only provide the impetus for us to critically reflect, but often provide the gist of which to reflect deeply.

Therefore, research in this area needs to move beyond the debate about the significance of feelings in transformative learning to one, as Neuman (1996) mentions, that reveals more insight into its relationship to critical reflection. Research should begin focusing on particular feelings, such as anger, fear, shame, happiness, and the like, and explore how they individually inform the reflective process. It would also be helpful to identify specific strategies similar to what has already been developed for fostering and encouraging critical reflection (Brookfield, 1996) that would help educators maximize the use of feelings in the reflective process. Furthermore, Neuman talks about the importance of looking at critical reflection in relation to adult development, exploring how each informs the other, particularly in the area of learner readiness. "Further research is needed to discover what types of prior learning and development experiences may contribute to initial learning readiness especially for developing Critical Reflective Capacity and engaging in transformative learning" (1996, p. 496).

The Relational Nature of Rational Discourse

Rational discourse is seen as the essential medium through which transformation is promoted and developed. In contrast to everyday discussion, it is used "when we have reason to question the comprehensibility, truth, appropriateness (in relation to norms), or authenticity (in relation to feelings) of what is being asserted or to question the credibility of the person making [the assertion]" (Mezirow, 1991, p. 77). Identified are a series of assumptions that rational discourse rests upon, such as the goal of achieving greater understanding; conditions that promote understanding; objectivity; actions and statements that are open to question and discussion; and understanding derived by weighing evidence and measuring the insight and strength of supporting arguments. It is within the arena of rational discourse that experience and critical reflection are played out. Research, however, is revealing a picture of discourse that is not only rationally driven but equally dependent on relational ways of knowing.

Relational knowing of transformative learning refers to the role that relationship with others plays in the transformative process. As previously mentioned, the original model gave only minor attention to the role of relationships generally in association with rational discourse and the final phases of a perspective with the intent of maximizing understanding between participants (Mezirow, 1995). This lack of attention is particularly manifested in the more subjective elements of relationships (trust, friendship, support) and their impact on transformative learning. These more subjective elements seem to provide the conditions essential for effective rational discourse. Relationships, connected ways of knowing, were conceptualized in a variety of ways in different studies, such as modeling (Bailey, 1996;

Brooks, 1989; Hunter, 1980), interpersonal support (Morgan, 1987), social support (Van Nostrand, 1992), family connections (Pope, 1996), networking (Elias, 1993; Schlesinger, 1983), learning-in-relationship (Group for Collaborative Inquiry, 1994), friendships (First and Way, 1995; Holt, 1994; Taylor, 1993, 1994), and developing trust (Egan, 1985; Gehrels, 1984; Saavedra, 1995). In essence, it is through establishing trustful relationships that individuals can have questioning discussions wherein information can be shared openly and mutual and consensual understanding be achieved.

A good example of this is described in a study by Hunter (1980), who explored the learning process of people who radically changed their nutritional beliefs and practices. Very often her participants were ostracized by significant others in response to their change in lifestyle: "Social loss was overcome by replacing that which had been lost with new relationships and a new identification with a minority group of those who share a common belief in the toxin theory" (p. 123). Therefore developing relationships with like-minded individuals became essential for the transformative process. She goes on to say: "Moving to a new perspective and sustaining the actions it requires is dependent upon an association with others who share the new perspective. Not only do you take their way of seeing for your own, but you must have their support and reinforcement to enable you to take action the new viewpoint reveals is in your interest" (p. 126).

Gehrels (1984), who explored the learning process of creating meaning from experiences as an elementary school principal, found that helping others was essential to the transformative process. He states that "the helping process is one of helping others recognize perspectives, of trusting them to accept their own values and beliefs, so that the other person then can engage on a personal journey of self-transformation and integration" (p. 156).

The importance of relationships was found to be the most common finding among all the studies reviewed. This contradicts the autonomous and formal nature of transformative learning as we presently understand it, and instead reveals a learning process that is much more dependent on the creation of support, trust, and friendship with others. There is a lack of attention given to the role that relationships play in transformative learning. This omission is demonstrated most directly in the ideal conditions for fostering transformative learning. It is through building trusting relationships that learners develop the necessary openness and confidence to deal with learning on an affective level, which is essential for managing the threatening and emotionally charged experience of transformation. Without the medium of healthy relationships, critical reflection would seem to be impotent and hollow, lacking the genuine discourse necessary for thoughtful and in-depth reflection. And it would seem that through relationships emotions and feelings could be safely explored in the process of transformative learning.

Notwithstanding all this research supporting the significance of relationships in transformative learning, there is much not known about how relationships and related elements (trust, honesty, friendship) play a role in transformative learning. They have been discovered more as outcome of transformative learning, with little understanding of how they can be initiated safely in the classroom setting. One effort that begins to address this area was by the Group for Collaborative Inquiry (1994), which attempted to reconceptualize transformative learning and social action, recognizing learning-in-relationships and whole person learning. Despite these initial efforts many questions remain unanswered: When during the transformative process are supportive relationships most helpful? What do helpful relationships look like? What kind of discourse takes place in these significant relationships that might offer more insight into the transformative process? How can relationships be safely manifested and managed in the context of the classroom?

Robertson (1996) reminds us that there is little guidance and support for adult educators in the area of student-teacher relationships, particularly about fostering transformative learning; these are often fraught with professional challenges "such as transference, counter transference, confidentiality, sexual attraction, supervision, and burnout, each with attendant ethical, legal, and efficacy considerations" (p. 44). His recommendations for addressing this problem are to affirm adult education models that encourage helping relationships in transformative learning; encourage a teacher-learner–centered theoretical focus; promote research on helping relationships; revise preparatory curriculum for adult educators to address the dynamics of relationship building; develop a code of ethics; and provide confidential consultative support.

Difference and Context in Transformative Learning

The original research of transformative learning of women returning to school was criticized, for the women's experiences "were studied as if they stood apart from their historical and sociocultural context" (Clark and Wilson, 1991, p. 78). This concern brings to light two areas of transformative learning, context and culture, that have been only marginally looked at in how they influence transformative learning. Of the two, the role of context is better understood. Research has identified both personal and sociocultural contextual factors as significant in transformative learning. The influence of personal contextual factors on a perspective transformation is found in what is referred to by other studies as a readiness for change (Bailey, 1996; Hunter, 1980; Pierce, 1986; Van Nostrand, 1992), the role of experience (Coffman, 1989), prior stressful life events (Vogelsang, 1993), and a predisposition for a transformative experience (Turner, 1986). Taylor (1994), in his study on the transformative nature of intercultural competency, found that the participants "were ready for change due to former critical events, personal goals, or prior intercultural experiences" (p. 169).

There is also sociocultural context and background factors inclusive of related historical and geographical influences, revealed in research by Scott (1991) as life histories; by Weisberger (1995) as historical factors; by Edwards (1997) as decontextualization; by Elias

(1993) as traditions and a legacy from childhood; and by Schlesinger (1983) as the pretransition stage. A good example of the sociocultural nature of context is demonstrated by Olson and Kleine (1993), who found that prior high school experience of rural midlife college students influenced the nature of trigger events leading to college entry. Schlesinger (1983), in a study of the transition process of Jewish women entering the workforce, found that women "felt that their changes had to be understood within the context of what their lives had been like before they began the entry process. . . . Their early married years provide clues as to why they approached the transition bridge" (p. 85). Most importantly, this return to the workforce was not a random event experienced by a few individuals but was indicative of a national trend in response to larger and more complex historical events.

Because context seems to play such a significant role in shaping transformative learning, it would seem just as obvious that a participant's culture would have an impact as well. However, despite the focus on context there has yet to be a study that its primary focus is exploring transformative learning in relationship to difference. This lack of diverse perspective is most evident in the minimal inclusion of research participants along the lines of race, class, ethnicity, and sexual orientation. Of the studies that did attempt to offer a cultural balance among participants (Bailey, 1996; Herber, 1998; Elias, 1993; Pope, 1996; Whalley, 1995), even fewer investigated the relationship of cultural difference in depth in relation to transformative learning theory. For example, Pope's study explored the impact of higher education among ethnically diverse working-class women who were first in their family to graduate from college. Her study involved fifteen participants—five Alaskan Natives, five African Americans, and five Caucasians. Even though the findings were not analyzed along lines of ethnicity her study reveals some insight into the differences experienced by working-class women. She found transformative learning inadequate at explaining the "sometimes gradual, often erratic fluctuations of energy and power leading to many of the transformations in the lives of these women" (p. 190). The process of transformation for these working-class women was best explained from an evolutionary systems perspective, that of being in a continual state of change, a recursive process such that they repeatedly returned to issues until they had enough power to make significant change, and the importance of learning through relationships.

Another study by Herber (1998) also begins to crack the door to understanding cultural difference and transformative learning theory. She explored whether transformative learning of preservice teachers could be precipitated by direct contact with historical records and artifacts of the African American civil rights movement. Eighteen preservice teachers (six black, nine white, and three self-described as mixed) participated in a five-week summer foundation course in urban education involving a series of experiential activities: a tour of the National Civil Rights Museum, observation of a religious service, and a reading of the novel *Roll of Thunder, Hear My Cry* by Mildred Taylor (1976). The study revealed gender differences in the focus group setting where the men quickly moved beyond Mezirow's phase of self-examination of guilt and shame and focused their discussion of racism on a societal level. But women spent much more time discussing the affective nature and personal encounters with racism. Race seemed to be a factor as well, such that an African American student found his learning experience consistent with Clark's (1991) description of an integrative experience: "In contrast to the disorienting dilemma, this opens a person to further development or clarifies their past experiences, and invites rather than demands further action" (Clark, cited in Herber, 1998, p. 130).

These former studies begin to provide insight into the cultural and contextual variations that exist within transformative learning theory. Differences begin to emerge in how certain groups respond to and make meaning of significant experiences in life. However, they barely scratch the surface of understanding the complexity associated with difference. Much more research is still needed with a primary focus on the role of culture and transformative learning. Most helpful would be a longitudinal comparative study of two groups responding to a similar significant life event.

Fostering Transformative Learning

In the last decade there has been an increase of interest in understanding how transformative learning can be fostered in an educational setting. At least twelve studies (Bailey, 1996; Cusack, 1990; Dewane, 1993; Gallagher, 1997; Herber, 1998; Kaminsky, 1997; Ludwig, 1994; Matusicky, 1982; Neuman, 1996; Pierce, 1986; Saavedra, 1995; Vogelsang, 1993) looked at promoting transformative learning in a variety of settings, such as teacher study groups, self-help groups, teaching for racial understanding in a teacher education program, promoting collaborative inquiry among doctoral students, and the use of drama in education as a means to facilitate change, just to mention a few. It is important to note that many of these studies looked at how personal change was facilitated from a variety of theoretical perspectives (Freire, Vygotsky, Boyd), not exclusively Mezirow's, and in a variety of settings (not just classrooms). Also, none of these studies involved the actual application and testing of the ideal learning conditions outlined by transformative learning theory and, like most of the research conducted on transformative learning, few of the later studies had reviewed any of the earlier studies in an effort to build upon previous work. Regardless, they reveal a number of interesting findings that support the ideal conditions outlined by Mezirow as being essential for fostering transformative learning. Some, for example, cite the need to promote a sense of safety, openness, and trust; the importance of instructional methods that support a learner-centered approach and encourage student autonomy, participation, and collaboration; and the importance of activities that encourage the exploration of alternative personal perspectives via problem posing and critical reflection. A good example of the importance of these conditions is revealed in a study by Gallagher (1997), who explored how drama in education contributed to changes in understanding. One participant says the success of the experience was due to group support. Pat, one of the participants, describes the nature of that support:

> I think part of the reason that what happened did happen was that everybody supported each other and it was clear that when I was through what I was going through, it was as if the rest of the group were a pod of dolphins supporting me in the water . . . at least that's what it felt like . . . they were supporting me—they were supporting the whole process, they were supporting the development of the story and the drama. They were involved like I was involved . . . in the story part [p. 235].

However, the findings also revealed an array of other conditions equally important to establishing a learning situation that is democratic, open, rational, and has access to all available information. These include the need for teachers to be trusting, empathetic, caring, authentic, sincere, and demonstrative of high integrity; emphasis on personal self-disclosure; the need to discuss and work through emotions and feelings before critical reflection; the importance of feedback and self-assessment; the need for experiential hands-on learning activities; and the importance of solitude and self-dialogue. A good example of the importance of authenticity by facilitators is offered by Pierce (1986), who focused on high learners in a management training program. She interviewed such individuals, managers of a Fortune 500 company who had experienced the greatest degree of change in perspective as determined by a self-administered survey, about their learning experience and the related educational practices used in an intensive one-week residential management training workshop. The participants said that the authenticity of the instructors was a significant factor in facilitating learning. Two descriptions of instructors were offered by participants: "I got the impression you were emotionally involved in the course, which I'd never seen before"; "The difference came at the point in time where you gained my confidence that you weren't playing with us, that I realized you weren't dishonest, that you believed what were you were saying, that it was valuable" (p. 252).

Other studies reveal some additional conditions that are worth mentioning in more depth. One is a longitudinal study of the Davis Teachers' Study group involving six teachers meeting on a weekly basis for over two years with the general intent to analyze issues and strategies related to the teaching in each participant's classroom, student learning, and the learning and knowledge development of each participant (Saavedra, 1995). Through the use of video and audiotape, reflective journals, and field notes Saavedra was able to bring to light previously unmentioned essential factors of transformative learning within a group setting. One is the members' cultural background, such that it was necessary for all participants to have an opportunity to situate themselves historically, politically, and culturally within the context of the group. In order to create an open and democratic environment in the group, issues of positionality (race, class, gender, ethnicity) need to be discussed in relationship to the overall objective of the group. A second group factor was the importance of dissonance and conflict, such that embracing conflict among group members, as opposed to avoiding it, was necessary for transformative learning. She found that the conflicts within and between group members offered real learning opportunities and provided an excellent medium for exploring differences. A third group factor was the need to act on new ideas; it isn't enough just to experience rational discourse, conduct critical reflection, or even make a decision to act. Instead it is important that group members have opportunities to validate and explore newly acquired assumptions and beliefs. It was the critical interaction between the study group and other interdependent settings that teachers worked in that helped them reconstruct their teaching practice.

Another factor in fostering transformative learning is time, something that many regular adult education classrooms have little of

(Gallagher, 1997). Kaminsky, in her study of a transformative learning group in a higher education setting (1997), found that adhering to the conditions outlined by Mezirow for promoting rational discourse resulted in a significant challenge. "[Inclusiveness] in terms of stakeholder membership practically guarantees that groups will have different agendas about what needs to be done, making coming to a consensus an onerous, time-consuming task" (pp. 274–275). Furthermore, it seems that the very conditions that foster transformative learning—a democratic process, inclusiveness of agendas, striving for consensus, critical reflection, dialogue—create such a necessity for time.

These studies suggest that to foster transformative learning much time, intensity of experience, risk, and personal exploration are required of both student and teacher. Much more research is needed to understand how adult educators establish these conditions within classes that meet a few hours each week. Other questions are raised as well: How do we accomplish our course objectives, teach essential skills, and still allow for in-depth personal exploration? How many of us feel comfortable and capable as adult educators in dealing with emotionally laden issues in our classrooms? How ethical is it for adult educators to create conditions that put their students in such emotionally challenging classroom experiences? Whose interests are we serving by fostering transformative learning?

The Future Direction of Research

Let us step back and get a sense of what has been emphasized so far. For starters, not all the studies discussed in this chapter exclusively investigated Mezirow's transformative learning theory; other theoretical models were often included. Some were the work of Freire (1970), Boyd (1991), and Vygotsky (1978), who conceptualized how adults make meaning of change experienced in their life. Of the studies that explored the model of a perspective transformation, most did so in the context of shared learning events (change in lifestyle, a cross-cultural experience, therapy, personal illness, and the like). As a design issue, this involved identifying participants for a study based on their participation in the particular event, such as having a kidney transplant or participating in a self-help group.

Other researchers explored how transformative learning is fostered in various settings. Until recently this was poorly understood, but in the last few years there has been a significant increase in studies focusing on the realities of practicing transformative learning.

Another area of interest has been the few studies that identified participants based on criteria indicative of a particular component or outcome of transformative learning, such as having experienced a perspective transformation. Also, most studies on transformative learning have been carried out in retrospect, where participants were asked to reflect back on their transformative experience as opposed to observing and recording the learning experience as it was actually happening. However, this has begun to change, with a number of recent studies taking a longitudinal perspective (Gallagher, 1997; Kaminsky, 1997; Neuman, 1996) of the transformative process.

Concerning the various methodological designs, all of the studies employed naturalistic research designs (qualitative, phenomenological), most of which involved semistructured interviews of participants who reflected on their previous transformative learning experiences. Several studies included quantitative as well as qualitative methods (Herber, 1998; Kennedy, 1994; Lytle, 1989; Matusicky, 1982; Morgan, 1987), with only three studies using the quantitative approach as its primary method (King, 1997; Van Nostrand, 1992; Williams, 1985). Overall, few significant findings were found among the studies using quantitative methods (particularly correlations among demographic variables), though they do provide insight into inherent characteristics of the process and the outcome of a perspective transformation. From this brief summation of the research on transformative learning, four general foci emerge that help inform the direction of future research. They include theoretical comparisons, in-depth component analysis, strategies for fostering transformative learning, and the use of alternative methodological designs. Each of these areas is discussed here in conjunction with studies that have made forays in this direction of research of transformative learning.

In some ways many of the questions and concerns raised about transformative learning cannot be answered by the present model proposed by Mezirow (1995). Possibly, by conducting theoretical comparisons, insight might be gained in the areas that are poorly understood. As mentioned earlier some of the studies reviewed for this chapter looked at several different models of change in relation to transformative learning. One example is Gallagher (1997), who looked at drama in education and how it contributed to changes in understanding. She suggested that Vygotsky (1978) "lends insight to the discussions on the social contextual and experiential aspects of change in understanding" (p. 107). She identified three concepts essential to the discussion of change in understanding: the zone of proximal development (interdependent process of development), using a holistic approach to analysis, and the importance of studying phenomena in process as opposed to performance. The most in-depth example of a theoretical comparative study was completed by Scott (1991), who explored the nature of transformation from a leader's experience in a community organization. She analyzed this particular context of leadership from two different perspectives on transformative learning, that of Mezirow and Boyd. Boyd's 1991 model of transformative learning is grounded in the analytical (depth) psychology work of Carl Jung. It focuses on the process of individuation, that lifelong process of discovering new talents, developing confidence and a sense of empowerment, a deeper understanding of the inner self, and a greater sense of self-responsibility. For example, due to this theoretical comparison a change in frame of reference (perspective transformation) was found to have less to do with personal autonomony and more to do with social interdependence and compassion. It is through comparisons of different theoretical models that major insight can be gained into the complexities of transformative learning.

The second direction that research on transformative learning should take is that of in-depth component analysis. This refers to conducting studies with a microscopic orientation on particular components that are known to be essential to transformative learning. A number of studies have taken this direction, focusing on such as things as courage, critical reflection, context, and affective and whole person learning in relationship to transformative learning (Brooks, 1989; Clark, 1991, 1992; D'Andrea, 1986; Group for Collaborative Inquiry, 1994; Lucas, 1994; Neuman, 1996; Sveinunggaard, 1993). Lucas's 1994 study, which explored the role of courage and transformative learning, brought into relief the significance of a little-discussed phenomenon that proves to be essential to successful transformative learning. She identified four types of courage: to be, to believe, to feel, and to do. This micro-orientation to transformative learning helps bring to light related complexities that have been often overlooked in the general trend of studies that focus on perspective transformation in relation to different life events. Other examples that need to be looked at in depth include the role of specific feelings, such as anger, happiness, shame, and the management of emotions during transformative learning. Also, what does acting on a new perspective look like? What is the planning process taken by individuals when beginning to act on new perspectives?

A third direction for research on transformative learning should be in the area of strategies for fostering transformative learning. As mentioned earlier, there has been a resurgence of interest in fostering transformative learning, with several studies revealing much insight in this area. But how transformative learning is promoted and facilitated in a typical classroom is still poorly understood. A study that begins to shed light on topic is that of Herber (1998), who attempted to determine if direct contact with the struggles of African

Americans for civil rights could precipitate a transformative learning process among preservice teachers in a foundation urban education course. She found that transformative learning can be initiated in a college course. In her case, having the students attend the National Civil Rights Museum and read related material initiated a disorienting dilemma for some. The identification of specific strategies like the former can help teachers begin to better manage the challenges associated with fostering transformative learning. More studies are needed that identify other strategies, as well as help guide one through the "land mines" often associated with transformative learning in the classroom.

A fourth direction involves exploring new and varied research designs and methods of data collection. As mentioned earlier, the predominant approach has been qualitative designs conducted in retrospect of the transformative learning experience. This has serious limitations, especially in the area of recall by the participant in remembering particular events, kinds of learning, and reflection. The more recent longitudinal studies have made great headway in addressing these concerns. By following participants with regular interviews and varied assessment tools throughout the learning experience, recall of the events is less difficult. A good example of a longitudinal study is offered by Neuman (1996), who followed a group of nine individuals for two years as they went through the National Extension Leadership Development Program at the University of Wisconsin at Madison. However, these longitudinal studies have disadvantages as well; they still put the burden of recall exclusively on the participant. Interviewing participants on a regular basis relies on the idea that all significant learning was conscious to the learner and does not account for the learning that happens outside the learner's awareness. To help address this concern the researcher needs to be present during the transformative experience so he or she can observe and record in addition to interviewing the learner. Several studies have taken this research design; one is that of Kaminsky (1997), who looked at how the collaborative process of community building and related practices affect conceptualizations of voice, action, and empowerment and what the implications were for legitimate knowledge among a cohort of thirteen doctoral students in a transformative learning program. Over a ten-month period data was collected via participant observation of intensive weekends, document analysis of reflective papers, and informal interviews. The use of ongoing data collection methods from both the perspective of the participant and the researcher makes this study significant.

Another area of qualitative research on transformative learning that shows promise is that of collaborative inquiry—"the systematic examination through dialogue of a body of data and lived experience by researchers whose intentions include the construction of formal knowledge that contribute to the theory" (Group for Collaborative Inquiry and thINQ, 1994, p. 58). In collaborative inquiry the participants are both the researchers and the researched. A good example is offered by Edwards (1997), who explored the learning process by which women constructed and reconstructed their sexual identities in relationship to current sexual codes. The six women formed a group and drew on their life experiences as the primary source of data. This allowed the members to tell their life histories through the use of narratives. Sharing stories of transformative experiences helps individuals within the group recognize the unstoried experiences in their lives. "Collaborative inquiry as a form of research dignifies newly narrated experience as formal knowledge and moves it out of the position of subjugated knowledge and into the position of one of multiple possible narratives in which others can find their own unstoried experience expressed" (Brooks and Edwards, 1997, p. 42).

An area of qualitative research similar to collaborative inquiry that has been generally overlooked as a research method is that of action research. "[Action research] is any systematic inquiry, large or small, conducted by professionals and focusing on some aspects of their practice in order to find out more about it, and eventually to act in ways they see as better or more effective" (McCutcheon, cited in McCutcheon and Jung, 1987, p. 148). By having adult educators explore the use of transformative learning in their classroom, it moves the theory into the realm of the practical and the everyday. Much of the present research is obtuse, overly academic, difficult to access, and only now and then has direct implications for classroom teaching. Encouraging practitioners to explore how they can improve their teaching through implementing strategies essential to transformative learning, such as promoting critical reflection and establishing trusting and authentic relationships with students, has the potential to not only improve their teaching but to offer tremendous insight into the everyday practicalities of fostering transformative learning.

Many find quantitative research impractical because of the amorphous nature of transformative learning. In many ways positivism seems to contradict the constructivist orientation that is so indicative of transformative learning theory. Despite these challenges two studies have made an extensive effort to confront the related challenges. Williams (1985) explored transformative learning as an explanation of change in abusive behavior among male spouse abusers in group therapy. Through the use of pre- and post- multiple self-report instruments and interviews (analyzed by multiple raters) he was able to demonstrate a significant relationship between an increase in reasoning tactics and lessening of abusive behavior. It was the first attempt by a researcher to operationalize the process of a perspective transformation. Since this study, the predominant quantitative emphasis has been to explore the demographics of the participants and their relationship to perspective transformation. None of the related studies have found any real significance, mostly due to small samples. One other quantitative study that seems to offer some real potential is that by King (1997). Through the use of a survey she attempted to delineate learning activities that contribute to a perspective transformation. More than four hundred adult learners from four higher education institutions reported that, 25 percent of the time, class discussions, critical thinking skills activities, and the teacher in a facilitator role were seen as contributing to a perspective transformation. Conducting research in this vein offers the potential for greater generalizability and the opportunity to see the relationship of transformative learning and other important variables (learning styles, personality types) that have an impact on learning. Also, using assessment and surveys in conjunction with traditional qualitative methods offers an easy way for practitioners to evaluate their practice.

In conclusion, this chapter has attempted to update the reader about what is presently known about transformative learning theory from an empirical perspective. It is quite apparent that much has been learned over the last twenty years. Research has revealed an adult learning process consistent in a variety of situations and experiences, from changing nutritional habits to moving up the career ladder, returning to school, and giving up smoking, just to mention a few. In conjunction with understanding how an individual makes meaning of new experiences, we have also gained much insight into the conditions, processes, and strategies that inform and promote a more inclusive frame of reference. Furthermore, the present research has revealed a picture of transformative learning that is much more complex that what was originally understood. There is much support for Mezirow's theory, but at the same time there is a need to reconceptualize the process of a perspective transformation. The research reveals a learning process that needs to recognize to a greater degree the significant influence of context, the varying nature of the catalyst of the process, the interdependent relationship of critical reflection and affective ways of knowing, the relational nature of rational discourse, and an overall broadening of the definitional outcome of a perspective transformation. Research needs to continue particularly in the areas of cultural diversity and fostering of transformative learning in the classroom.

Future research needs to take on a multifaceted approach. It should encourage more investigation into theoretical comparisons with other models of learning, develop a microfocus on the variety of variables that affect the process of transformative learning, and explore the challenges and practicalties of fostering of transformative learning in the everyday classroom. Designs of research need to be more innovative as well, looking beyond a basic phenomenological approach. They should include ongoing longitudinal collaborative studies utilizing multiple methods of collecting data. Action research should be used to explore transformative learning as a practical form of classroom intervention. Lastly, quantitative research should be continued, seeking to operationalize the various components of transformative learning and increasing its opportunities for greater generalizability.

As transformative learning moves into this new millineum it offers a theory of learning that has great potential to continually inform the process of adult learning. With the encouragement and support of the adult education academy, future researchers can publish their work and much can still be learned about this illusive but informative theory of adult learning.

References

Bailey, L. D. "Meaningful Learning and Perspective Transformation in Adult Theological Students." Unpublished doctoral dissertation. Deerfield, Ill.: Trinity Evangelical Divinity School, 1996.

Boyd, R. D. (ed.). *Personal Transformations in Small Groups*. New York: Routledge, 1991.

Brookfield, S. D. *Understanding and Facilitating Adult Learning*. San Francisco: Jossey-Bass, 1996.

Brooks, A. K. "Critically Reflective Learning Within a Corporate Context." Unpublished doctoral dissertation. New York: Teachers College, Columbia University, 1989.

Brooks, A. K., and Edwards, K. A. "Narratives of Women's Sexual Identity Development: A Collaborative Inquiry with Implications for Writing Transformative Learning Theory." Paper presented at the 38th Annual Adult Education Research Conference Proceedings (pp. 37–42), Stillwater, Okla., 1997.

Clark, C. M. "The Restructuring of Meaning: An Analysis of the Impact of Context on Transformational Learning." Unpublished doctoral dissertation. Athens: University of Georgia, 1991.

Clark, C. M. "The Restructuring of Meaning: An Analysis of the Impact of Context on Transformational Learning." Paper presented at the 33rd Annual Adult Education Research Conference Proceedings. Saskatoon: University of Saskatchewan, 1992, pp. 31–36.

Clark, C. M. "Changing Course: Initiating the Transformational Learning Process." Paper presented at the 34th Annual Adult Education Research Conference. State College: Pennsylvania State University, 1993.

Clark, C. M., and Wilson, A. "Context and Rationality in Mezirow's Theory of Transformational Learning." *Adult Education Quarterly*, 1991, *41*, 75–91.

Clevinger, J. E. "Exploring Transformative Learning: The Identification and Description of Multiple Cases Among Kidney Transplant Recipients." Unpublished doctoral dissertation, Knoxville: University of Tennessee, 1993.

Cochrane, N. J. "The Meanings That Some Adults Derive from Their Personal Withdrawal Experiences: A Dialogical Inquiry." Unpublished doctoral dissertation. Toronto: University of Toronto, 1981.

Coffman, P. M. "Inclusive Language as a Means of Resisting Hegemony in Theological Education: A Phenomenology of Transformation and Empowerment of Persons in Adult Higher Education." Unpublished doctoral dissertation. Dekalb: Northern Illinois University, 1989.

Courtenay, B., Merriam, S. B., and Reeves, P. M. "The Centrality of Meaning-Making in Transformational Learning: How HIV-Positive Adults Make Sense of Their Lives." *Adult Education Quarterly*, 1998, *48*, 65–84.

Cusack, P. J. "Preaching the Passion of the Earth and Perspective Transformation." Unpublished doctoral dissertation. Toronto: University of St. Michael's College, 1990.

D'Andrea, A. M. "Teachers and Reflection: A Description and Analysis of the Reflective Process Which Teachers Use in Their Experiential Learning." Unpublished doctoral dissertation. Toronto: University of Toronto, 1986.

Dewane, C. M. "Self-Help Groups and Adult Learning." Unpublished doctoral dissertation. State College: Pennsylvania State University, 1993.

Edwards, K. A. "Troubling Transformations: A Collaborative Inquiry into Women's Learning Experiences in the Construction and Reconstruction of Identities." Unpublished doctoral dissertation. Austin: University of Texas, 1997.

Egan, S. J. "Learning Process in Family Therapy: An Experiential Perspective." Unpublished doctoral dissertation. Toronto: University of Toronto, 1985.

Elias, D. G. "Educating Leaders for Social Transformation." Unpublished doctoral dissertation. New York: Teachers College at Columbia University, 1993.

First, J. A., and Way, W. L. "Parent Education Outcomes: Insights into Transformative Learning." *Family Relations*, 1995, *44*, 104–109.

Freire, P. *Pedagogy of the Oppressed*. (M. Ramos, trans.). New York: Herter and Herter, 1970.

Gallagher, C. J. "Drama-in-Education: Adult Teaching and Learning for Change in Understanding and Practice." Unpublished doctoral dissertation. Madison: University of Wisconsin, 1997.

Gehrels, C. "The School Principal as Adult Learner." Unpublished doctoral dissertation. Toronto: University of Toronto, 1984.

Group for Collaborative Inquiry. "A Model For Transformative Learning: Individual Development and Social Action." Paper presented at the 35th Annual Adult Education Research Conference Proceedings. Knoxville: University of Tennessee, 1994, pp. 169–174.

Group for Collaborative Inquiry and thINQ. "Collaborative Inquiry for the Public Arena." In A. K. Brooks and K. E. Watkins (eds.), *The Emerging Power of Action Inquiry Technologies*. San Francisco: Jossey-Bass, 1994, pp. 57–67.

Herber, M. S. "Perspective Transformation in Preservice Teachers." Unpublished doctoral dissertation. Memphis, Tenn.: University of Memphis, 1998.

Holt, M. E. "Retesting a Learning Theory to Explain Intercultural Competency." In K. Obloj (ed.), *High Speed Competition in New Europe*. Paper presented at the 20th Annual Conference of the European International Business Association. Warsaw, Poland: University of Warsaw International Management Center, 1994, pp. 53–78.

Hunter, E. K. "Perspective Transformation in Health Practices: A Study in Adult Learning and Fundamental Life Change." Unpublished doctoral dissertation. Los Angeles: University of California, 1980.

Kaminsky, A. L. "Individual-Community Tensions in Collaborative Inquiry: Voice, Action, and Empowerment in Context." Unpublished doctoral dissertation. Ithaca, N.Y.: Cornell University, 1997.

Kennedy, J. G. "The Individual's Transformational Learning Experience as a Cross-Cultural Sojourner: Descriptive Models." Unpublished doctoral dissertation. Los Angeles: Fielding Institute, 1994.

King, K. P. "Examining Activities That Promote Perspective Transformation Among Adult Learners in Higher Education." Unpublished doctoral dissertation. Philadelphia: Widner University, 1997.

Laswell, T. D. "Adult Learning in the Aftermath of Job Loss: Exploring the Transformative Potential." Paper presented at the 35th Annual Adult Education Research Conference Proceedings. Knoxville: University of Tennessee, 1994, pp. 229–234.

Lucas, L. L. "The Role of Courage in Transformative Learning." Unpublished doctoral dissertation. Madison: University of Wisconsin, 1994.

Ludwig, G. D. "Using Adult Education Perspective Transformation Principles in the Evaluation of Training Program Proposals for the Economically Disadvantaged." Unpublished doctoral dissertation. New York: Teachers College at Columbia University, 1994.

Lytle, J. E. "The Process of Perspective Transformation Experienced by the Registered Nurse Returning for Baccalaureate Study." Unpublished doctoral dissertation. Dekalb: Northern Illinois University, 1989.

Matusicky, C. A. "In-Service Training for Family Life Educators: An Instructional Model." Unpublished doctoral dissertation. Toronto: University of Toronto, 1982.

McCutcheon, G., and Jung, B. "Alternative Perspective on Action Research." *Theory into Practice*, 1987, *24*, 144–150.

Mezirow, J. *Education for Perspective Transformation: Women's Re-Entry Programs in Community Colleges.* New York: Teachers College at Columbia University, 1978a.

Mezirow, J. "Perspective Transformation." *Adult Education Quarterly*, 1978b, *28*, 100–110.

Mezirow, J., and Associates (eds.). *Fostering Critical Reflection in Adulthood.* San Francisco: Jossey-Bass, 1990.

Mezirow, J. *Transformative Dimensions of Adult Learning.* San Francisco: Jossey-Bass, 1991a.

Mezirow, J. "Transformation Theory and Cultural Context: A Reply to Clark and Wilson." *Adult Education Quarterly*, 1991b, *41*, 188–192.

Mezirow, J. "Transformation Theory of Adult Learning." In M. R. Welton (ed.), *In Defense of the Lifeworld.* New York: SUNY, 1995.

Mezirow, J. "Contemporary Paradigms of Learning." *Adult Education Quarterly*, 1996, *46*, 158–172.

Mezirow, J. "Transformative Learning: Theory to Practice." In P. Cranton (ed.), *Transformative Learning in Action: Insights from Practice.* New Directions for Adult and Continuing Education, no. 74. San Francisco: Jossey-Bass, 1997.

Mezirow, J. "On Critical Reflection." *Adult Education Quarterly*, 1998, *48*, 185–198.

Morgan, J. H. "Displaced Homemaker Programs: The Transition from Homemaker to Independent Person." Unpublished doctoral dissertation. New York: Teachers College at Columbia University, 1987.

Neuman, T. P. "Critically Reflective Learning in a Leadership Development Context." Unpublished doctoral dissertation. Madison: University of Wisconsin, 1996.

Olson, G., and Kleine, P. "Perspective Transformation Themes Among Rural Mid-Life College Students: Subtle Vs. Dramatic Changes." In D. Flannery (ed.), *35th Annual Adult Education Research Conference Proceedings*. University Park: Pennsylvania State University, 1993.

Pierce, G. "Management Education for an Emergent Paradigm." Unpublished doctoral dissertation. New York: Teachers College at Columbia University, 1986.

Pope, S. M. "Wanting to Be Something More: Transformations in Ethnically Diverse Working Class Women Through the Process of Education." Unpublished doctoral dissertation. Los Angeles: Fielding Institute, 1996.

Robertson, D. L. "Facilitating Transformative Learning: Attending to the Dynamics of the Educational Helping Relationship." *Adult Education Quarterly*, 1996, *47*(1), 41–53.

Saavedra, E. R. "Teacher Transformation: Creating Text and Contexts in Study Groups." Unpublished doctoral dissertation. Tucson: University of Arizona, 1995.

Schlesinger, R. C. "Jewish Women in Transition: Delayed Entry into the Workforce." Unpublished doctoral dissertation. Toronto: University of Toronto, 1983.

Scott, S. M. "Personal Transformation Through Participation in Social Action: A Case Study of the Leaders in the Lincoln Alliance." Unpublished doctoral dissertation. Lincoln: University of Nebraska, 1991.

Sveinunggaard, K. "Transformative Learning in Adulthood: A Socio-Contextual Perspective." In D. Flannery (ed.), *35th Annual Adult Education Research Conference Proceedings*. University Park: Pennsylvania State University, 1993.

Taylor, E. W. "A Learning Model of Becoming Interculturally Competent: A Transformative Process." Unpublished doctoral dissertation. Athens: University of Georgia, 1993.

Taylor, E. W. "Intercultural Competency: A Transformative Learning Process." *Adult Education Quarterly*, 1994, *44*, 154–174.

Taylor, E. W. "Building upon the Theoretical Debate: A Critical Review of the Empirical Studies of Mezirow's Transformative Learning Theory." *Adult Education Quarterly*, 1997, *48*, 32–57.

Taylor, E. W. "The Theory and Practice of Transformative Learning: A Critical Review." Columbus, Ohio: HERIC Clearinghouse on Adult, Career, & Vocational Education (Information Series No. 374), 1998.

Taylor, M. D. *Roll of Thunder, Hear My Cry.* New York: Dial Press, 1976.

Turner, T. T. "An Ethnography of Physicians for Social Responsibility: Non-Formal Adult Education for Social Change." Unpublished doctoral dissertation. Madison: University of Wisconsin, 1986.

Van Nostrand, J. A. "The Process of Perspective Transformation: Instrument Development and Testing in Smokers and Ex-Smokers." Unpublished doctoral dissertation. Denton: Texas Women's University, 1992.

Vogelsang, M. R. "Transformative Experiences of Female Adult Students." Unpublished doctoral dissertation. Ames: Iowa State University, 1993.

Vygotsky, L. *Mind in Society: The Development of Higher Psychological Processes.* Cambridge, Mass.: Harvard University Press, 1978.

Weisberger, R. D. "Adult Male Learners in a Community College Setting: Possibilities of Transformation." Unpublished doctoral dissertation. Amherst: University of Massachusetts, 1995.

Whalley, T. "Toward a Theory of Culture Learning: A Qualitative Study of Japanese and Canadian Students in Study-Abroad Programs." Unpublished manuscript. Burnaby, B.C.: Simon Fraser University, 1995.

Williams, G. H. "Perspective Transformation as an Adult Learning Theory to Explain and Facilitate Change in Male Spouse Abusers." Unpublished doctoral dissertation. Dekalb: Northern Illinois University, 1985.

12

Theory Building and the Search for Common Ground

Colleen Aalsburg Wiessner, Jack Mezirow
with the contribution of Cheryl A. Smith

When piecing together a puzzle, individuals may work together collaboratively to create a picture. Often beginning with the border, the frame is constructed to hold the inner pieces. Next, pieces that clearly fit together are sorted and used to connect a section of the puzzle that is distinctive. Finally, the larger sections are connected using more obscure pieces whose place in the puzzle have eluded participants in the process. Many adult educators have studied and applied Transformation Theory since its introduction by Mezirow some twenty years ago. Other scholars have independently developed parallel but related research. Many questions about theory and practice of transformative learning are still unanswered. Most of the puzzling over transformative learning has been done by individuals working alone. Educators often do not benefit from the work they do because there has been no forum for sharing it; their pieces of the puzzle have not been connected to those of others. How to connect the pieces of the puzzle in order to create a picture of transformative learning is a challenge facing scholars and practitioners. Efforts at building theory and searching for common ground are presently being pursued in a number of ways.

The First National Conference on Transformative Learning

The First National Conference on Transformative Learning was designed to address the puzzle of how adults learn. It was one attempt to build the puzzle, or create a picture, by connecting previously separate pieces of both theory and practice. The conference, *Changing Adult Frames of Reference*, took place at Teachers College, Columbia University in April 1998. One hundred fifty scholars and scholar-practitioners gathered to participate in research and discourse on the theory and practice of transformative learning.

The conference filled a void by providing a place for discourse among scholars and practitioners interested in transformative learning. An additional goal was to explore the need for a consortium to provide a continuing forum for professional discourse on this topic. The conference was designed as a research event, and participants were invited to become coresearchers in a process of collaborative inquiry.

Program Design

The goal of the conference was to bring together interested professionals to further develop the theory, research approaches, and educational practice of transformative learning. One day of the conference was devoted to each of these three areas.

The following research questions were framed:

- What can we validate in Transformation Theory?

- How does the theory need to be changed or expanded?

- What does transformative learning look like in practice?

- What research is presently being done?

- What further research is needed?

Cheryl Smith and Colleen Aalsburg Wiessner coordinated the event. A values-driven model for program planning (Breitbart and others, 1996) guided the design in keeping with the tenets of transformative learning.

The Preconference

Research was the focus of the preconference day. Presentations and discussions included recently conducted, ongoing, and needed research. How to effectively research transformative learning was also addressed. We planned the day originally to assist doctoral students writing dissertations on transformative learning. The number of registrants for the day indicated a wider interest in and concern about research, however, resulting in an expansion of the program.

Mezirow began the day, summarizing research conducted by Taylor (1997), Elias (1997), and Courtenay, Merriam, and Reeves (1996). Taylor's research reviewed thirty-nine studies of transformative learning. Following Mezirow's framing of the status of research on transformative learning, several people who had conducted research projects reported on their work. Judith Cohen and Deborah Piper presented "Re-Writing Our Lives: Stories of Transformation in an Adult Learning Community," based on their research on adult students at Lesley College. Elizabeth Kasl presented "The Epistemology of Group Learning," based on her research with four groups of collaborators. "Studying Transformation Learning—It Can Be Done!" was the presentation given by Sharon Lamm. Kathleen Taylor reported on and invited participants into her research, "Developing Adult Learners: Teaching for Transformation." Later in the day doctoral students were given the opportunity to present their research topics briefly, which facilitated making connections with other researchers with common interests.

Focus groups were divided into practice areas where research is conducted: Theory and Research Methods, Community and Social Action, Workplace and Organizations, Classroom and Professional

Development, and Personal and Family Development. The day ended with a faculty panel that discussed issues recorded in the focus groups.

The Conference

The theory of transformative learning was the focus of the first day of the conference. Jack Mezirow began the day by presenting a paper prepared on the "Core Concepts of Transformative Learning." This paper framed the puzzle, clarifying Mezirow's understanding of the status of transformative learning. Later, Robert Kegan invited participants into an interactive process designed to learn about "Transformation and Development." Stephen Brookfield's presentation was titled "The Critical Reflection Dimension." The day ended with a celebration of the life and work of Paulo Freire.

The practice of transformative learning was the focus of the final day of the collaborative inquiry. Patricia Cranton guided participants through a process focused on "Fostering Transformative Learning." Mary Belenky and Ann Stanton talked about "Women and Transformative Learning: Connected Ways of Knowing and Development of a Public Voice." "Transformative Learning in Organizations" was the focus of Victoria Marsick's presentation. "Insights from Off-Site" were shared by Laurent Parks Daloz. The day ended with a final plenary with Jack Mezirow focused on "Considering a Consortium."

As important as the presentations at the conference were, encouraging and creating discourse was a significant goal of the conference. That discourse took place within the plenary sessions and during the focus and discourse groups. Discourse groups followed each major presentation to assess the evidence and arguments supporting the presentations. Focus groups were designed to share common experience around areas of practice. The final day, discourse groups centered on four areas of practice: community and social action, workplace and organizations, classroom and professional development, and personal and family development. This process aided in looking for missing puzzle pieces. Focus groups addressed the following topics:

1. Culture and social context; power and influence; class; race; gender learning differences
2. Emotion, intuition, spirituality, narrative
3. Taking action: psychological, cultural, social, political
4. Discourse; critical reflection; rationality; learning, situated or universal; metanarratives; learning theory

What We Learned Through Collaborative Inquiry

Throughout the conference we discovered, in several ways, new pieces to the puzzle of transformative learning. Our findings related to the three areas: Transformation Theory, practice of transformative learning, and processes for building theory or finding common and uncommon ground.

Nature of Transformative Learning

An expanded view of the nature of transformative learning resulted from the conference. According to Mezirow, transformative learning involves ten phases. Six of the ten phases characterizing a transformation were confirmed by Taylor's study (1997). However, researchers studied by Taylor found the process to be more recursive, evolving, and spiraling in nature than described by Mezirow. Transformative learning is often prompted by a disorienting dilemma, an experience that causes a person to question what he or she has previously believed to be unquestionable. Taylor affirmed the existence of these dilemmas but questioned their nature, offering further ways they might take place. Mezirow and others talked about the possibility of both epochal transformations (occurring suddenly) and cumulative transformations (unfolding over time).

Nature and Practice of Critical Reflection

Critical reflection is a key element in transformative learning and a theme that would be expected to emerge in a conference on Transformation Theory. The amount of focus it received in the conference was not anticipated, however. A new or clearer picture emerged as puzzle pieces related to critical reflection were combined with each other. Brookfield critiqued the entire practice of critical reflection. As previously stated, several presenters talked about or demonstrated use of questioning as a way of reflecting. Action and critical reflection were closely linked by several presenters.

How reflection is done was another aspect of this conference theme. Mezirow reported that the Taylor study (1997) found agreement that critical reflection is central to transformation processes, but that it must "centrally include elements beyond cognition: intuition, feelings, empathy, spirituality and other factors outside of focal awareness." Marsick clarified that most reflection in workplaces is simple reflection, rather than critical. Stanton reported that reflection is related to developmental stage, as defined in *Women's Ways of Knowing* (Belenky, Clinchy, Goldberger, and Tarule, 1986). Cranton demonstrated varying ways reflection is done by different people. Brookfield emphasized that power and hegemony should be the central focus for critical reflection.

Emotion and Intuition

A common critique of Transformation Theory relates to its not addressing emotion adequately. The presence of the affective emerged as a significant theme during the conference. During his presentation Mezirow gave examples of learning based in feeling and emotion. Kasl reported that a collaborative learning group found that love, compassion, and commitment resulted from working together. Cranton pointed out the humor in the room during her presentation. "Exciting, energizing, and a little enervating," were the words Daloz used to describe the final day of the conference. The centrality of emotions was clearly emphasized in both focus and discourse groups.

The role of intuition in transformative learning was referred to at a number of points during the conference. The most attention given to it was during Cranton's presentation, recognizing that intuitive people reflect in their own way and that intuition is one way of learning transformatively. Kasl's presentation also supported the role of intuition in learning transformatively as a group.

Social Action

Social action became the primary focus of conference references to taking action. As one conference participant said, "Talk about social action permeated everything." Another participant reported being "surprised by the pull towards social action." The importance of taking action was emphasized by Mezirow, Kegan, Cranton, Marsick, and Belenky. According to Mezirow, "A new way of seeing has to lead to some kind of action." However, the type of action "depends on the nature of the insight." Kegan talked about testing the edge of the cliff. When trying to put a change into action, he said, it is important to "take small steps, testing if there is actually ground there." He suggested that participants "design a modest, safe, small test of the big assumption." Marsick's remarks about action were framed in the practice of Action Reflection Learning. People learn through projects that are real and meaningful; they take action by working on real challenges in the organization. For Belenky, learning happens through engagement in action projects. Social action is both a goal and a means of learning in preparation for further action.

Concern about social action was raised throughout the conference. Many different focus groups on research, aside from the social action group, found themselves talking about social action and social responsibility. When this fact was reported to the whole audience it prompted Mezirow to ask, "What does it mean that talk about social action permeated everything?"

Creating Space

In addition to insights about Transformation Theory, learnings about the practice of transformative learning also emerged. Careful attention was paid to creating ideal conditions for discourse at the conference. Interestingly, one of the ways practice was extended around the issues of making a space for transformative learning and ways of talking within that space. For some, the space they want to create is a literal space apart. Belenky talked about creating public home spaces where people can share in full-circle conversations. Daloz talked about the Whidbey Institute, an attempt to establish an institutional base for doing the work of cultural transformation. Piper talked about the old mansion where her Lesley College program takes place as a physical setting that invites exploration, encourages imagination and wonder, and allows people to leave their day-to-day life settings and roles behind for a time. For others, creating a space means making a figurative space, within an actual space, where transformative learning can be fostered.

A Different Way of Talking

Once space is created for transformative learning, ways of listening and speaking within that space become important. The need to discover or create new ways for talking was often expressed by participants during discourse in focus groups. After the pieces of the presentations were connected it became clear that presenters shared a common concern for this theme. Belenky referred to full-circle conversations as a way of involving everyone and "bringing a voice into the community that had not been heard." "Discourse of inner contradictions" and "developmental discourses" are two phrases used by Kegan. He said, in "discourse communities certain forms of speaking are encouraged or allowed and other forms are discouraged or not allowed." Mezirow and Belenky spoke most about ideal conditions for talking. Belenky emphasized understanding those who are different. "Dialogue depends on the skills of the connected knowing; deep listening to people who are so different from one's self." She found being listened to was mind-opening for people she worked with and "gave them vitality." Mezirow emphasized the importance of empathic listening in discourse. Listening is one way of bringing people into voice, a prerequisite for being involved in ways of talking that lead to transformative learning.

Using Questions and Narrative

Questions and narrative, two special ways of talking, became a focus of the conference. Use of questions is effective in establishing an environment for participants to figure things out for themselves and to apply those insights to their own practices. Questioning is an important way of talking in a constructive process such as transformative learning. Marsick used questioning in her presentation, demonstrating its value, talking about its importance, and identifying what makes questions helpful in learning. She said questioning frequently opens up new avenues for understanding, helping people see things they have not seen before. A learning community is often formed out of this process focused on a common problem or on individual challenges people bring to the table.

Kegan and Cranton both designed their presentations using a series of questions that led participants to new insights. Working with Kegan, answering one question at a time about their commitment and problems of realizing it, moved participants slowly to the point of identifying a previously unrecognized "big" assumption guiding their lives. Rather than present information on different ways of reflecting and experiencing transformative learning, Cranton helped participants discover these insights, thereby helping them own outcomes and become committed to using insights about differences for their own learning and in their practices with others.

Another specific way of talking during the conference was use of narrative. Stories were a common part of many conference presentations, serving a variety of purposes. Cranton used a narrative activity at the beginning of her presentation to help people focus on a metaphor of their own, and then used it in developing the next learning activity. Kegan used a humorous story to set up a metaphor he then wove throughout his presentation. Stanton used concrete examples and stories from students involved in her study to help listeners understand more clearly what she was describing. This use, the most common use of narrative in teaching, was a part of other presentations as well.

The usefulness of narrative in transformative learning was referred to briefly at four points in the conference. Three of these were related to learner biographies or autobiographies and ways they shape assumptions (Kegan), affect learning (Edward Taylor), and play a role in helping to make learning happen (Brookfield). Yorks pointed to narrative approaches to inquiry as potentially more effective in studying transformative learning than other more linear and quantitative approaches.

The greatest overlap in use of story was between Belenky and Marsick. Belenky studied women who used stories as a mirror, holding them up to help women working on projects realize their success, what they had accomplished, and how capable they had become. Marsick said success stories are helpful when change is attempted because they travel around organizations very quickly. Stories that capture the history of a group are also valuable. Stories of changes occurring help facilitate learning as they are made part of public discourse. Belenky pointed to the empowering potential of stories. She also talked about listening to each other's stories as an important aspect of work done together. She said, "Careful dialogue is where people listen to each other's stories." Marsick stated her belief that people make meaning best through stories.

Cohen and Piper emphasized two additional aspects of narrative. Curiosity and wonder help people unpack their stories and begin to imagine and integrate their lives in different ways. Disorienting dilemmas that result in interrupted life narratives and compromise adult learning can be addressed through use of story, which also has potential to awaken critical faculties and reflexivity.

Roles, Responsibilities, and Ethics

Three related but somewhat surprising foci of learning were roles, responsibilities, and ethics of adult educators. They were mentioned by several presenters and were frequently discussed in focus groups. Presenters advanced a number of clear statements about values and ethics. For example, Mezirow said, "Adult educators are never neutral. Adult educators are activists committed to supporting and extending those features of the culture, social practices, and institutions that foster freer, fuller participation in reflective discourse." Kegan stated that adult educators have both opportunity and responsibility to influence how people talk with one another.

Topics related to ethics also emerged. Ethics in research was an issue in several research focus groups, spanning practice areas, and was addressed to the faculty panel at the end of the research day. The ethics of use of knowledge created or gathered was raised. Building in ways for participants to give voice to knowledge they create was encouraged. Related questions were also asked: To what degree can the participant lead the research? Whose voice will be heard? How can a participant become a designer of his or her research? How do we assure that voices are included, not coded out, in our research? Mezirow also reported on Elias's concern about the "urgency of developing a framework of values that will provide directions and boundaries for our experiments" (1997).

Marsick warned about the responsibility of change agents to not put people at risk in the process of fostering transformative learning in workplaces. Yorks expressed hesitancy about ethics of organizations, citing the fact that transformative learning takes time even though most corporations want things to happen overnight. He was also concerned about organizations appropriating vocabularies, such as the language of transformative learning. Related to the issue of ethics and values is the question, Whose agenda does the adult educator focus on? His or her own? The learner's? The organization's?

Several images of adult educators emerged. Partnership was one image presented for the work of adult educators. Mezirow emphasized the role of the adult educator as colearner, saying that getting people to participate as "coequals in the learning experience" is fundamental to what adult education is about. Belenky talked about raising up, not ruling over. She described the need to stand in the background and find people to push forward. This includes bringing grassroots women's leaders to meetings where their voices can be heard. Adult educators, according to Belenky, are supposed to be bridge makers who are always reaching out. She also referred to the role of being listening partners. Marsick named a similar role, "learning coach," saying, "A lot depends on the relationship you can build as a learning coach." Brookfield reminded participants that development of trust between the educator and the learners is a crucial element in the relationship.

Connection and Collaboration

Many participants expressed surprise at validation of aspects of their learning and practice, diverse uses of transformative learning, and commonalties found, in spite of differences in perspectives and practice areas. We also learned that attending the conference helped many practitioners and scholars realize they were no longer alone in fostering transformative learning.

We learned that what appeared to be disagreements with the theory among scholars may not be contradictions but rather "pieces of a whole" brought about by approaching transformative learning from different perspectives and applying it in different settings and contexts. For example, both Brookfield and Cranton focused on critical reflection in their presentations. However, Brookfield focused on the role of critical reflection in the theory, its philosophy, and its epistemology, whereas Cranton's hands-on, interactive presentation illustrated the use of critical reflection as it relates to individual learning styles. Marsick used critical reflection in a questioning process, and Kegan walked participants through a process he uses with learners to identify assumptions and core commitments. Similarly, Marsick and Belenky, although working in very different forums—organization and workplace learning, and community and women's development and learning, respectively—continually pointed to connections in their work. Each follows a constructivist approach, even though applied in very different contexts, and both emphasize critical reflection on action.

It was suggested that Euro-American values may not always pertain and, in fact, the theory might be enhanced by introduction and integration of non-Western values and models. For example, Belenky spoke of fostering connected knowing by using models from cultures with "deep knowledge" of community building. Kasl talked about the role of the unconscious. Brookfield presented a critique of critical reflection as both male and Western European in nature. Daloz talked about the "transformative power of the other" and the need to create a "sacred space" for transformation, a place for "pause, space, solitude, and silence" as well as connection. He called the conference a "gathering of the clan" of committed, ethical, and activist adult educators coming together to become better at what they do.

Creating a Conference Model for Collaborative Inquiry

The program design resulted in a model that may be replicated in other areas of adult education. Designing a conference as a collaborative inquiry may, in fact, enable learning to be advanced more quickly, facilitate making connections between theories and scholars, and expand theories and practice both within and across disciplines. It is a way for scholars and practitioners, who normally work in isolation, to connect ideas and practices. Returning to the imagery of a puzzle, a picture is created. Instead of each person holding onto his or her separate pieces, they are combined and an overview can be achieved. That overview comes from meeting face to face with the goal of learning collaboratively.

Innovation: Electronic Conference Proceedings

The Conference Proceedings were published in an electronic format (Smith and Wiessner, 1999). The process of creating the proceedings was a source of additional incidental learning that resulted from the conference (Wiessner, 1999a; 1999b). The presentation summaries included in the proceedings were created using audio recordings of presentations. Although it meant the conference proceedings were not immediately available, a traditional conference practice, this process had several advantages. We were able to capture and report the learning that took place at the conference. Presentation summaries included statements made by presenters about their own insights and observations. Many presenters reported connections they identified, in the course of the conference, between their work and that of others, adding to the learning that took place.

Additionally, a summary of each focus/discourse group was included on the disk, highlighting questions and issues, suggested solutions, and suggested readings and activities. Summaries of each focus group enable all participants to gain a sense of the concerns raised, helpful in providing an overview of contents of all small group discussions, in addition to those participants attended. The summaries created for the proceedings disk captured both the content and the process of presentations. Although important to adult educators, reflection on process is often not a part of traditional proceedings. At this conference learnings were created through both content and process, and both were captured in the proceedings.

Conclusion

In keeping with one of the missions of the conference, establishment of an ongoing collaborative inquiry and learning community in the area of transformative learning in adults, suggestions were elicited from participants about ways to continue the dialogue that was begun. Use of technology was a subject raised continually throughout the conference and many suggestions involved its use as a vehicle for provision of on-going connections and discourse. Specific methods suggested included establishment of an on-line Journal of Transformative Learning and creation of a Website, ListServ, or electronic bulletin board. Inclusion of scholars and practitioners from various parts of the country and world could be enabled through use of teleconferences. Finally, establishment of the conference as an annual event was highly recommended. A second conference was held in San Raphael, California, in August 1999 and a third conference is planned for October 2000 at Teachers College, Columbia University.

Important questions about transformative learning, raised in the conference, remain unanswered: Why do some significant events not always lead to a transformation, when some seemingly minor ones sometimes do? If one does come to an understanding of transformative learning, how do you get other people to understand what transformative learning is all about so that they are open to it in schools and other settings? The confusion between learning and development is still not clearly resolved for many people. The intersection between postmodern critique and transformative learning calls for further exploration. Each part of the transformative learning puzzle that is clarified opens the door to new areas of exploration and further expansion of the theory. The puzzling over transformative learning goes forward in new ways.

Issues and Insights

Transformation Theory has been developed by initial research that identified a significant pattern of adult learning and by two decades of increasing our understanding of its components, significance, limitations, conditions, and consequences—collectively fitting pieces of a puzzle to create a full picture is an apt metaphor. Professionals coming together in conferences to share reservations and ideas and experiences, writing articles and critiques, engaging in research, and sharing insights and differences on the subject by writing a book together are the dynamics of collaborative inquiry.

Jurgen Habermas names the mode of inquiry by which Transformation Theory has been developed "constructive science." As distinct from empirical-analytical science, this constructivist approach to research analyzes symbolically structured reality and seeks to isolate, identify, and clarify conditions required for communication and learning. Examples include Chomsky's generative grammar, Piaget's theory of cognitive development, Kohlberg's theory of moral development, and Habermas's theory of communicative action.

Because many facets of Transformation Theory are not amenable to traditional hypothesis testing and measurement modes of empirical-analytical research, the theory has been primarily validated through qualitative studies and professional discourse—an assessment of the reasons advanced in support of the theory—leading to a tentative best reflective judgment by those most informed and interested. This is a judgment that has been and will continue to be modified by assessing new arguments or evidence as they appear in subsequent discourse (see Chapter One).

Research

Chapter Eleven updates Edward Taylor's 1997 review of thirty-nine studies of transformative learning, including thirty doctoral dissertations. He found much support for the theory but cites the need for a more holistic conceptualization of transformative learning with greater emphasis on the central role of feelings, learning that takes place out of one's focal awareness, the importance of relationships, and the role of the collective unconscious in looking beyond the self and recognizing others. Greater emphasis is also needed on the significance of context, such as "situated learning," the context of disorienting dilemmas, and a recognition of the social and political forces acting on one's learning experiences. There is need for examining the practical implications of implementing conditions conducive to the ideas of discourse and the practical implications associated with facilitating and encouraging learners to revise their meaning perspectives.

Discourse

Over the past two decades the original findings regarding trans-formative learning have been assessed and reassessed by colleagues in professional journals, through correspondence, in national con-ferences, and through the participation of Jack Mezirow and others in scores of conferences and seminars dealing with transformative learning organized by universities and professional associations throughout North America and in fifteen countries in Europe, Asia, and Latin America.

Theory Development

Among changes in the theory that have resulted from the many studies and this extended discourse is an acknowledgment that there may be variations in the phases of transformative learning in con-texts different from that identified in the original study of women returning to college. Another, resulting from comments by Sue Col-lard, led to changing the identification of what was initially identified as three major domains of learning—instrumental, communicative, and emancipatory (as adapted from Habermas)—to recognize the last as a *process* that pertains in different ways to both instrumental and communicative learning domains.

More emphasis has been placed on the crucial importance of the unconscious, affect, and intuition in transformative learning, al-though we have only scratched the surface of elaborating their roles. Key terms, such as *meaning perspective*, have been replaced by *frame of reference*, which refers to "habits of mind" and resulting "points of view." "Meaning schemes" have been recast as elements consti-tuting a point of view. These changes occurred in response to col-legial advice to avoid the use of unfamiliar jargon. Colleagues have pointed out that the original list of frames of reference—socio-linguistic, epistemic and psychological—was only suggestive, and others have been added in Chapter One. In response to others, the Western rational cultural context of the theory has been explicitly acknowledged.

Professional discourse has clarified the different uses of critical reflection, as reported in the typology described in Chapter One. Thanks to Dorothy Ettling, her colleagues, and Laurence Robert Cohen, a new recognition of the role and power of critical self-reflection in helping disadvantaged learners regain a new sense of identity with which to meet life's serious challenges has greatly enriched the promise of transformative learning for adult education. These insights have yet to be fully elaborated within the context of the theory.

A related promising area of study that has been highlighted by professional discourse pertains to understanding the nature of frames of reference and how to help learners identify their own. Kegan's constructive-developmental perspective provides new insight here. Some of the work done in "phenomenal patterning" in psychology is also suggestive as to how to inductively understand frames of reference and to transform them from subjects to objects (Koziey, 1990).

Recognition by colleagues of the importance of socioeconomic conditions and educational qualifications in the development of personal autonomy has resulted in a more limited focus by the theory—on autonomous *thought*—as a cognitive capacity of judgment and a major outcome of transformative learning. Several colleagues have correctly stressed the importance of greater recognition of the ubiquity of power and influence in transformative learning and adult education. This somewhat neglected dimension needs to be incorporated more prominently in the theory.

Chapter One reflects the influence of professional discourse in the theory's current emphasis on differentiating situated learning from the generic capabilities of adult learners.

How can we make a claim that one frame of reference is more dependable than another? The original claim of the theory was limited to movement toward greater inclusivity, differentiation, permeability, critical reflection, and integration of ideas. Affective insight is a recent addition.

This claim became elaborated through professional discourse that supported the contention that the criteria should be more practical. In response, the theory has been modified by adding an additional pragmatic test of functionality: whether a frame of reference is more likely to produce interpretations, opinions, and judgments that will prove to be more true (is as purported to be) or justified (through discourse) than would those produced by other frames or beliefs.

Critiques that have challenged the theory as neglecting social action have resulted in a clarification of this relationship in Chapter One and here in differentiating different ways of interpreting transformative learning.

All of these ideas and many more have resulted from an extended professional discourse pointing out strengths and shortcomings of earlier iterations of Transformation Theory. There has been a decade of collegial exchanges in *Adult Education Quarterly*. Selected postmodern issues are summarized and discussed in a recent *Proceedings* of the Adult Education Research Conference (Mezirow, 1999).

This process of validating, amending, appending, or invalidating elements of this theory can only be a continuous one. The current formulation in Chapter One is a tentative best judgment; continuing dialectical assessment is inevitable and essential to more fully develop our understanding of significant adult learning.

Collaborators' Theoretical Insights

Kegan recognizes the validity of Brookfield's concern that the term *transformative learning* has become used by many others for their own purposes. A major reason is that many of the authors of this book and other adult educators and developmental psychologists writing about this concept focus on understanding the learning (or epistemological) *process* involved in adults living through a transformation in varying contexts.

Others tend to focus instead on a social goal, such as greater respect and understanding of the planet (O'Sullivan, 1999), social action, or organizational change. From this point of view transformative learning becomes a means of changing frames of reference as required to initiate and support the prescribed personal, social, or organizational change.

This important distinction has to do with whether transformative learning is fostered within the context of an organization, social movement, labor organization, community development program, higher education, or elsewhere. Transformation Theory contends that the attainment of more dependable knowledge and justified belief depends on the use of more effective cognitive-affective-conative processes of critical reflection and discourse. But the resulting ways of knowing may address social, community, group, organizational, or personal objectives. The difference has to do with the distinction between the goals of adult education and the learner's objectives.

The *goal* of adult education is to help the learner develop the requisite learning processes to think and choose with more reliable insight, to become a more autonomous thinker. Of course, the adult educator attempts to help the learner assess and achieve his or her learning *objective* whether it is personal, social, or organizational. This distinction between learner's objective and adult educator's goal is important for understanding how educators with different orientations use the term *transformative learning* and how these differences are part of a larger reality. It also clarifies the contested relationship of transformative learning to adult education for social action.

Still another variation of transformative learning, as conceptualized in Chapter One, is captured by the concept of epistemological development, advanced by Kegan and by Belenky and her colleagues in *Women's Ways of Knowing* (1986). Each posit passage through a sequence of increasingly complex epistemological forms or perspectives. Their theories are mutually reinforcing. Their "constructive-developmental psychology" is a most promising approach for understanding movement of and toward transformative learning through the lens of developmental psychology.

We can anticipate that these challenging formulations will continue to generate much study, discourse, and empirical evidence to support them. Kegan holds that there are five transformations of form throughout the life span but reserves self-transformation as a function of his final and most complex epistemology. Transformation would refer to movement to the next more complex epistemological perspective until attaining the final one. The writings of Basseches (1984) and King and Kitchener (1994) complement this general orientation of movement through epistemological forms.

Transformation Theory identifies frames of reference more functionally, as sets of assumptions and expectations that pertain to sociolinguistic, psychological, epistemic, moral-ethical, philosophical, aesthetic, and instrumental beliefs, paradigms, and mind-sets. Before we can fully reconcile these differences in definition between constructive-developmental concepts and Transformation Theory, we must look to constructive-developmental psychology to provide us with more information about the major qualitative differences in transformative learning involved in moving from childhood to youth and through adulthood, within and between each epistemological perspective, the structure and process of transforming epistemological perspectives, and the movement of transformation from outside of awareness to full awareness. There are also questions regarding invariance within hierarchies and the role of experience in hierarchical development (Phillips and Kelly, 1975). In addition, we need clarification of how the term *consciousness* is being used.

Transformation Theory, as reported in Chapter One, has been formulated through the lens of adult education—without reference to movement through epistemological categories or to the development of consciousness per se—but has focused instead on the process of *meaning becoming clarified,* a focus on the potential for greater control over thinking, feeling, and will as the organizing concept.

From this vantage point, our task is to delineate the conditions, understandings, skills, and dispositions involved in adulthood. Although adult learners understand and learn with different degrees of awareness and insight, meaning becomes clarified when adults have greater motivation to learn, more experience and self-confidence as learners, access to other learners coping with similar problems, and earlier socioeconomic experiences more favorable to learning.

Meaning becomes clarified when learners become more critically reflective of their assumptions and those of others in assessing contested meaning; when they are able to validate beliefs empirically or participate more fully and freely in discourse to arrive at tentative best reflective judgment; and when they gain insight on how to more effectively take action and do so reflectively. This is a transformative learning process.

Meaning becomes clarified when one's beliefs and frames of reference are more likely to produce judgments and opinions that prove true or justified than those based on other frames and beliefs. Meaning becomes clarified when learners become more autonomous as thinkers and learners—that is, negotiate their own purposes, values, judgments, and feelings rather than act on those of others. Meaning becomes clarified by making a decision to act when this is feasible, to learn what one needs to know, to have the emotional stamina to take action effectively, and to learn from the results of taking action when one does so.

When a learner is unable to become critically reflective of his or her own assumptions and those of others, unable to freely and fully participate in discourse to validate a belief and to make a decision whether and when to act on a reflective insight, he or she will become stalled in the movement toward clarifying meaning.

Transformation Theory focuses on deliberate efforts by adults to learn that involves critical reflection—often critical self-reflection—on assumptions, determining whether what has been asserted is as it is purported to be through empirical measurement or by determining its justification through discourse. An especially cogent challenge to adult educators is Kegan's cautionary note concerning the importance of fully understanding that "when the socialized mind dominates our meaning-making, what we *should* feel is what we *do* feel, what we *should* value is what we *do* value, and what we *should* want is what we *do* want. Their goal therefore may not be a matter of getting students merely to identify and value a distinction between two parts that already exist, but a matter of fostering a qualitative evolution of mind that actually creates the distinction."

Kathleen Taylor discusses relationships between Transformation Theory and constructive-developmental theory and explores a new dimension of professional discourse by detailing how adult educators may teach with "developmental intentions."

Belenky and Stanton raise valuable questions and present many insights regarding how adult educators can work with immature and marginalized learners who have not yet moved from a socialized mind-set to be able to transform their frame of reference. They correctly point out that Transformation Theory has not detailed this crucial description. In illustrating how movement toward Connected Knowing may be facilitated, these authors begin the needed job of filling a crucial gap.

Daloz identifies another undeveloped and crucially important concern in transformational learning—the relationship of the self and society. The example of the extraordinary Nelson Mandela admirably grounds this inquiry in a fascinating and relevant case study. Daloz's four conditions of transformation by which engagement with otherness may lead to greater social responsibility—the presence of the other, reflective discourse, a mentoring community, and opportunities for committed action—will undoubtedly guide future research on transformations in social activists.

Brookfield contends that all knowledge is so shaped by ideology—ideas implicated in the very constitution of knowledge in society that hide or legitimate arbitrary power—that our use of critical reflection and transformative learning should be confined to ideology critique. Transformation Theory posits that discourse and becoming critically reflective of assumptions are generic human capabilities, the ways human beings come to more fully understand what is communicated to them and the result of a deliberate effort to mindfully cope with the plethora of contested meanings arising in this process. It is the same common learning process that underlies paradigm critique in science, significant change through psychotherapy, the creation of new schools of art and new theories of philosophy, education, and social science as well as the critique of ideology.

Bookfield implies that critical reflection and transformative learning are equivalent processes, but most transformations of frames of reference do not involve critical reflection at all; they occur outside of awareness. Learning is assimilative, as when we fall in love, leave home to marry or to go to college, learn to think like a doctor, policeman, or teacher, or spend a couple of years in a village in Asia or Africa as a Peace Corps volunteer. When critical reflection on assumptions results in a change in point of view, it may or may not lead to a cumulative transformation in habit of mind.

Transformation Theory views critical reflection on assumptions and making an action decision as processes by which we become able to *mindfully* transform *all* problematic frames of reference. Beyond critical reflection, the process of transformation involves discursively testing new insights against the experience of others, that is, applying "reflective judgment" (King and Kitchener, 1994) to make an action decision, planning the action and coping with the emotional and social consequences. This process may also include task-oriented, instrumental problem solving (solving a medical, math, design, architectural, physics, engineering, or accounting problem). It may include learning (epistemic) preference for seeing new things by focusing on parts or wholes, sensory preferences, frequency of events needed to identify patterns, scope of awareness, concrete or abstract thinking, and others. These concepts are not insightfully subsumed under ideological critique.

For Brookfield, these—and even art, spirituality, sexual conduct, and music—are all "structured by and entail power relationships, dominant and contending discourses and unequal access to resources" and hence he concludes that ideology critique is what critical reflection and transformative learning are all about. Power relationships, like concepts of class, race, and gender, clearly do pertain to some degree in most human affairs, but an unequal power relationship is not the only problem with which adults must cope. From a Transformation Theory perspective, critical reflection of assumptions is an element of the transformative learning process by which we may challenge problematic frames of reference in every field of inquiry and in relation to every problematic value, belief, feeling, narrative, or understanding.

It would be self-defeating to arbitrarily limit our definition of every problematic frame of reference to a study of ideology or any other solely privileged dimension of learning. The more comprehensive view of critical reflection and the discursive practice of reflective judgment by Transformation Theory includes ideology critique (pertaining to "sociolinguistic" frames of reference) but sees critical reflection and discourse as human capabilities that may pertain to dealing with every contested belief in communicative learning. This orientation offers a much wider range of relevance and more useful insights than that proposed by arrogating either critical reflection or transformative learning to ideology critique alone.

Cranton highlights the importance of recognizing personality differences in transformative learning. She has identified Jungian personality types as frames of reference that shape our preferences for learning. When their limitations become problematic, they may require transformative learning. Knowledge of these personality types may enhance the ability of educators to relate learners to learning tasks that make different demands on them and to understand dispositional learning preferences. Transformation Theory was originally interpreted in Freudian terms but, clearly, transformative learning may be insightfully interpreted from several different psychological theories (see Cranton, 1997).

Cohen and Piper suggest that a major challenge of undertaking research on transformative learning "is to get behind language and be able to spot transformation in action rather than thorough verbal or written responses." Do subsequent changes in learners' lives reflect transformative learning?

Here it is important to differentiate between transformations that occur outside of awareness and those involving mindful and deliberate efforts to understand. An adult learner may gain insight into prior transformations occurring outside of awareness. This process of self-reflection by which one acquires insight into one's own tacit process of transformative learning can be, and often is, of great value to the learner. It renders experience coherent and meaningful and provides insight into how one learns more effectively.

Cumulative transformations involve a series of related reflective insights resulting in changes in frame of reference that culminate in a change in habit of mind. So Cohen and Piper suggest that awareness in transformative learning, in addition to being epochal or cumulative, may also be retroactive. This was also an unreported finding in our early study of women returning to college and is an obviously important contribution to the theory. Their perceptive analysis of transformative learning in the context of a residential adult learning community is also groundbreaking.

Yorks and Marsick extend the concept of transformative learning to organizational development with the assertion that groups learn in ways that transcend individual learning within the group, an issue requiring further discourse. These authors review the relevance of Action Learning and Collaborative Inquiry as ways of fostering transformative learning within profit and nonprofit organizations respectively to more effectively realize their performance objectives.

Bridging the gap between transformative theory's educational goal of enhancing autonomous learning and that of organizational development as an educational objective, Yorks and Marsick conclude that, although organizational focus is usually on objective reframing, "at the end of the day it is increasingly people's awareness of the personal choices available to them that is the important outcome of transformative learning. How this learning influences larger social discourse may go beyond what organizational leaders intend."

Kasl and Elias draw upon Transformation Theory, Kegan's theory, and Jungian concepts to study the evolution of transformative consciousness within a collegial group of educators. These authors redefine transformative learning as "the expansion of consciousness *in any human system*" (my italics). This, they write, "is facilitated when two processes are consciously engaged interactively: the process of critically analyzing underlying premises and the process of appreciatively accessing and receiving the symbolic contents of the unconscious."

As one reviews these colleagues' insights and those pertaining to constructive-developmental psychology, the potentialities inherent for understanding transformative learning in the concept of altered states of consciousness is fascinating. But our anticipation must be tempered with great trepidation; the concept of consciousness is a formidably sticky wicket.

The Latin term *conscire* means "to know" or "to be aware of." Consciousness has been regarded as a focal point of awareness, feeling, perception, and knowledge. The term may refer to a relation between an object being known and a knowing subject or to a relation among three dimensions: an activity of knowing, the content being known, and the awareness of them both. It may mean the constituents and operation of awareness at any given moment or the actual mental states as they occur, such as a concept, an image, or an emotion. It may also refer to the ability to symbolically identify mental states. It may refer to the totality of actual and previous experiences that are at the disposition of an individual or only that which is experienced here and now. The contents of consciousness may be present in greater or lesser quantities, as in the preconscious, subconscious, or unconscious.

Kasl and Elias posit consciousness as a function of any human system. Colleagues who use this construct to explain transformative learning must pick their way cautiously through a precarious field of mind mines and clearly specify the meaning of consciousness to which they ascribe.

We have learned a lot about transformative learning over the past two decades and yet have only begun to more fully understand the theoretical and practice implications of what we know. There is growing interest in aesthetic, spiritual, moral, psychic, poetic, mythic, and somatic learning dimensions. This inquiry and discourse will continue for many of us. A third annual international conference on transformative learning will be conducted at Columbia University in October 2000. There is considerable interest in the development of a journal devoted to transformative learning to encourage scholars and scholar-practitioners to publish in this area.

There is still much to learn about transformative learning. But the greater challenge is to work toward finding common ground among our many diverse but related theories of learning—self-directed learning, learning how to learn, situated learning, social learning, postmodern dimensions of learning, experiential learning, logical learning, mindful learning, dialectical thinking, everyday understanding, action learning, women's ways of knowing, critical reflection, implicit learning, narrative learning, emotional learning, conditioned response learning, learning reflective judgment, learning in cognitive and other forms of psychotherapy, intuitive learning, informal and incidental learning, transformative learning, and others. Books have been published in each of these areas. We need to collaborate across disciplines, theories, and paradigms to build a comprehensive theory of adult learning to guide educators of adults. At this writing, to begin this bridge building an International Adult Learning Collaborative is in the planning phase.

References

Basseches, M. *Dialectical Thinking and Adult Development*. Norwood, N.J.: Ablex, 1984.

Belenky, M., Clinchy, B., Goldberger, N., and Tarule, J. *Women's Ways of Knowing*. New York: Basic Books, 1986.

Breitbart, V., "Women as Change Agents: A Values-Driven Model." Unpublished paper. New York: Teachers College, Columbia University, 1996.

Courtenay, B., Merriam, S., and Reeves, P. "The Centrality of Meaning-Making in Tranformational Learning: How HIV-Positive Adults Make Sense of Their Lives." *Proceedings of the 37th Annual Adult Education Research Conference*. Tampa: University of South Florida, 1996, pp. 73–78.

Cranton, P. (ed.). *Transformative Learning in Action: Insights from Practice*. New Directions for Adult and Continuing Education, no. 74. San Francisco: Jossey-Bass, 1997.

Elias, D. "It's Time to Change Our Minds: An Introduction to Transformative Learning." *ReVision*, 1997, *20*(1), 2–6.

King, P., and Kitchener, K. *Developing Reflective Judgment*. San Francisco: Jossey-Bass, 1994.

Koziey, P. "Patterning Language Usage and Themes of Problem Formation/ Resolution." *Canadian Journal of Counseling*, 1990, *24*(4), 230–239.

Mezirow, J. "Transformation Theory: Postmodern Issues." *Proceedings*, 40th Annual Adult Education Research Conference. DeKalb: Northern Illinois University, 1999, pp. 223–228.

O'Sullivan, E. *Transformative Learning; Educational Vision for the 21st Century*. London: Zed Books, 1999.

Phillips, D., and Kelly, M. "Hierarchical Theories of Development in Education and Psychology." *Harvard Educational Review*, Aug. 1975, *45*(3), 351–375.

Smith, C., and Wiessner, C. (eds.). *Proceedings*, First National Conference on Transformative Learning. New York: Teachers College, Columbia University, 1999.

Taylor, E. "Building upon the Theoretical Debate: A Critical Review of the Empirical Studies of Mezirow's Transformative Learning Theory." *Adult Education Quarterly*, Fall 1997, *48*(1), 32–57.

Wiessner, C. "Women as Change Agents: A Values-Driven Model." Unpublished paper. New York: Teachers College, Columbia University, 1996.

Wiessner, C. "Reflections on a Happening: Themes of the First National Conference on Transformative Learning." Unpublished masters thesis. New York: Teachers College, Columbia University, 1999a.

Wiessner, C. "Reflections on an Innovation." *Proceedings*, First National Conference on Transformative Learning. New York: Teachers College, Columbia University, 1999b.

Name Index

Subject Index

A

Action learning, 255–265; critical reflection school in, 260–261; explicit reflection and dialogue in, 259; individual transformation and, 272; organizational learning from, 270; as parallel organizational structure, 271–272; theoretical schools of, 256–261

Action Reflection Learning programs, 261–265

Action research, 320–321

Adult development, as learning process, 24–26

Adult education practice: classroom strategies in, 318–319; connected knowing in, 95–96; developmental goals and intentions in, 26–31, 159–167, 348; experience-based activities in, 164–165; hegemonic assumptions about, 138–139, 145; power dynamics in, 92, 136–137, 145; psychological predispositions and, 201–202; radical pessimism and, 145–146; role in, 340

Affective learning, critical reflection and, 301–306

Age, and transformative learning, 288–289

Agency, sense of, 25–26, 162

Argument culture, 11–12

Asymmetrical relationships: discourse participation and, 73–74; feminine-masculine, 75–76; polarized thinking and, 74–77

Autonomy: fostering of, 26–27, 28–29, transformative learning and, 25–26

B

Best judgment: consensus and, 12, 15; in meaning–making framework, 87, 89, 90

C

Collaborative inquiry, 255, 265–270; individual transformation and, 272; organizational learning from, 269–270; as parallel organizational structure, 271–272; theoretical base of, 265–266

Collaborative learning, 8–10, 15; of adult educators, 31; reflectivity in, 21. See also Group learning

Common Fire study, 105, 113, 115, 120

Common good, social justice and, 105. See also Social responsibility

Communicative learning theory, 86–87